For my dad.
Thank you for instilling in me the drive and determination
to follow my dreams, no matter what

CONTENTS

AUTHOR'S NOTE

This book was written using a combination of memories, blog posts, photographs and conversations with travellers I met on the road. At times, I have changed the names and identifying details of certain characters in order to protect the innocent and not-so innocent. The overall timeline has been compressed and, in a few instances, slightly altered to improve narrative pace and spare the reader from unnecessary details. Two very minor characters have been combined into one composite to streamline the story, and several destinations have been excluded in order to condense my trip around the world into a succinct read. Finally, conversations throughout the book have been recalled to the best of my ability, but are not verbatim.

PROLOGUE

There was no doubt about it: I was going to die.

The air erupted with screams and I gaped as a stream of frantic people overtook me in their sprint to safety. A pick-up truck came careering around the corner and screeched to a halt outside the airport. I made to run towards it, but a woman elbowed me in the neck and leapt up on to the back, pulling her children up to join her. The crowd surged towards this chance for safety, cramming on after her until the truck was full. As it drove off into the distance, I began to chase after it. The first thing you're told to do in a natural disaster is to leave your belongings and run, but I was pushing 30 kg of luggage up a hill and a tsunami was on its way.

The stitch in my side caused me to bend over double and I felt like I was being torn in half. As I battled to catch my breath, I caught a glimpse of the scenes of panic behind me and forced myself to continue. In the still air, exhaust fumes from overloaded motorbikes and pick-up trucks were suffocating my every breath.

I heard a loud bang and let out a whimper. This was it. The end. I twisted my neck, expecting to see an enormous black wave, but the ocean was calmly twinkling behind the airport. Several metres behind me, a middle-aged woman sat bawling on the ground, her suitcase wide open and her clothes strewn across the road. I hesitated for a second, deliberating whether to help, but shook my head and turned away. Guilt flooded my stomach and I broke down in tears. Nobody even glanced at me. When faced with the prospect of our own mortality, we were all fighting for ourselves.

This past month had been one of the best of my life, spent island-hopping in Thailand while learning how to relax after yet another traumatising travel incident. Right now, I was supposed to be on a plane to the north of the country but instead, I was running away from the airport with a thousand terrified strangers. It had all happened so quickly: the earthquake; the tsunami; the evacuation.

When I'd announced I was going to travel the world, the initial support from friends had lasted only until they'd realised I was serious. Then it had transformed into snide jokes and comments about how I'd be home within weeks. 'You can't go,' my mum had told me. 'You'll never last. Travel is too dangerous, especially for someone like you.'

Especially for someone like me. I'd decided I wanted to travel when I was 18 years old, several years after I experienced my first panic attack. I'd always been a nervous child, shy and timid, I'd struggled to make friends and was terrified of everything, but travel had always calmed my mind. I'd been miserable at home, too afraid to leave the house, so desperate for control that I'd developed an eating disorder and was always convinced that living life would result in my death. Despite these barriers, I'd been hopeful that seeing the world could help put my fears into perspective. I'd wanted to visit the places I'd spent years obsessing over and had wondered if spending some time away would help me gain control of my life.

For the first few months of my trip, I'd been convinced my friends and family were right. Travel was supposed to have been the best thing I'd ever done, but my lack of life experience had thrown me from one traumatising incident to another: I'd been scammed by Chinese teenagers, fainted on my first day in Hong Kong, had the brakes of my motorbike fail in Thailand and fallen into a rice paddy in Indonesia.

It felt like a cruel kind of irony for this to be happening to me now, then, just as I was starting to gain control of my anxiety; just as I had stopped panicking that everything I did would result in my death. I was 23 years old and had spent my entire life trying to melt into the background. Now that I was finally learning how to live, it was all going to be taken away from me.

A deafening roar brought me back to the moment and I spun around to face the sea. The Thai teenagers who had been sunbathing on a nearby patch of grass rose to their feet. Out of the corner of my eye, I saw desperate parents pushing their children up palm trees and on top of walls.

I stood frozen to the spot, 100 m from the glistening turquoise ocean, and waited to die.

CHAPTER 1

I should have been at the airport.

Instead, I was sprawled face down on my bedroom floor with what felt like a broken ankle. I turned to look at my phone and gaped at the screen in a slack-jawed stupor.

The night before, I'd sat with a notepad and pen and carefully planned out my morning: wake at 3.30 a.m., finish packing, research how airports work, say goodbye to my family, leap headfirst into my new life with a one-way ticket in hand.

It was supposed to be simple. Stress-free, even. But when it came to me, life was rarely either of those two things. Somehow, I'd managed to set my alarm for an hour too late and, upon waking, had flung myself out of bed and twisted my ankle in the process. I hoped this wasn't a sign of things to come.

'Shit,' I muttered.

I struggled on to all fours and began to drag myself through my bombsite of a bedroom. Khaki pants with 17 pockets, an anorak squashable to the size of an apple, mosquito repellent containing

100 per cent DEET, pickpocket-proof underwear: they all lay strewn around me, threatening to sabotage what was supposed to be the best day of my life. My flight to Croatia was leaving at 6.30 a.m., and I was terrified I was going to miss it.

I gulped hard and with a sudden burst of determination, power-crawled to my backpack. Pawing at my clothes, I tried to shove them all inside at once.

'Dad!' I roared into the darkness, not realising I was attempting to drag my swollen ankle through the sleeve of my jumper. 'Dad! Where are you? We need to go!'

I'd imagined how this day would pan out countless times over the past five years. In my fantasy, I'd leapt out of bed, freshly scrubbed, like a mountaineer whose backpack is always full of granola bars and maps. Since I had never once climbed a mountain, this fantasy had been quite a stretch, but it had also seemed more likely than oversleeping, twisting my ankle and missing my flight.

My dad came crashing into my room, interrupting the start of my breakdown. He switched on the light and I blinked rapidly, like a baby mole-rat waking from its slumber. A baby mole-rat that was woefully behind in packing for its trip around the world.

'What's going on?' he yawned. When he noticed my pitiful face, sobbing amidst the rolling hills of things I should have packed the night before, his sleepy expression turned to one of concern.

'It's four thirty!' I cried. 'We need to be leaving for the airport but I haven't even started packing. I overslept – I think I set my alarm wrong. Dad, I'm going to miss my flight. I can't...'

He backed out of my room in a hurry. 'Just pack your bags. I'll get your mother.' He never did like displays of emotion.

With my arms flailing, I started to hurl everything on the floor into my backpack. After having spent days carefully perfecting my packing technique, I was now possessed by urgency. I crumpled clothes into balls and threw them inside, slamming toiletries in behind them.

The house descended into chaos while Victoria, my younger sister, continued to sleep. The mayhem was a welcome distraction from the inevitable goodbyes. To calm myself down, I recalled the moment when I'd decided to travel.

Being British, this decision had naturally come to me in a pub. I was 18 years old, fresh out of college, and surrounded by people whose only plan was to get drunk. I had always been the odd one out when it came to my circle of friends. I didn't drink, I was painfully shy and I was obsessed with reading about countries I didn't have any real plans to visit.

With a cold pint of orange juice in hand, I pretended to listen to the latest gossip while dreaming of a beach in Cambodia. I shivered; it had been one of those dreary spring days in London where the sun forgets to shine and the clouds show no sign of shifting, no matter how much you glare at them. I peered out of the window at a grey sky emptying itself on to a street of miserable-looking shoppers and sighed. This country's infamous weather had got to have been the catalyst for all great English explorers. Pretending I was seventeenth-century nobility, I began to plan my own Grand Tour. Outside, the rain spat at me defiantly. *Sunny*, I thought. *I need to go somewhere sunny.*

'What's up, Lauren?' my friend Gisela had asked, pulling me from my daydreams. She shook out her black curls and shot me a quizzical look. Born in Sri Lanka, Gisela was a typical South Asian beauty, all dark skin and chocolate eyes. Not so typical was her obsession with rock music and wearing anything with skulls on it. We'd become friends in college almost immediately after discovering we had the same taste in music.

'Nothing,' I said, feeling everyone's eyes on me.

'Liar,' she said with a giggle. 'You were totally deep in thought.'

I hesitated for a second before sharing my idea. Surely no British person before me had decided to go somewhere warm and foreign. 'I was just thinking about this beach in Cambodia. I was reading today that...' I trailed off when I noticed everyone was smirking at me. 'What?'

'We were wondering how long it would be before you started talking about travel,' Gisela said with a laugh. 'You're always wishing you were somewhere else.'

I waved my hands dismissively. 'Hey, you know that's not true.'

She nodded. 'Totally true. I reckon you should really think about going travelling after you graduate from uni. You're obsessed.'

How could I admit that I was already considering doing exactly that? Just that morning, everyone had witnessed me walking into a lamppost while trying to the cross the road. I pictured the woeful understanding that would flash across Gisela's face when she'd heard I'd been run over by an oven-wielding man on a scooter in Vietnam.

'Seriously,' she said, interrupting my train of self-loathing. 'I think you should do it.'

My eyes met hers and I could tell she meant it. As the table began to buzz with the possibility of adventure, I ran through my list of dream destinations in my head. Though I refused to say it out loud, I was exhilarated by the idea of buying a one-way ticket out of England. I turned back to my drink, deep in thought.

Travel the world? I gave a slight nod. *I could do that. How hard could it be?*

As it turned out, it was harder than I'd expected.

'Do you need this money belt, Lauren?' my mum called from downstairs.

'Yes, please!' I shouted back. I'd devoured dozens of packing lists over the past month and made sure to buy everything mentioned as a necessity.

'What about this?' she asked, rushing into my room. I looked up and saw her holding out a small bag. 'It says it's a silk sleeping bag liner?'

'Yes, please,' I said. 'It'll protect me from bed bugs in dodgy hostels.' I grabbed the small pile of gear from her hands and forced it inside my backpack. When I realised my room was clear of clutter, I looked up at her in surprise.

'I think I'm finished,' I said, and I was filled with the urge to vomit. I pretended not to see her gaping as I struggled to lift my backpack from the floor.

'Are you sure you need all that?'

'It's fine! I'm okay,' I squeaked, hoisting it on to my shoulders. 'I'm just getting used to the weight.' It wasn't even that heavy. I'd opted for a 45-litre backpack in an attempt to limit what I could take with me and it had ended up weighing just over 10 kg. When combined with my daypack – a 20-litre carry-on bag stuffed full of technology, I had close to 20 kg hanging from my shoulders. For someone as tiny and feeble as me, it felt like my spine was seconds away from crumbling to dust.

I was hoping that travel would improve my fitness and build up my muscles. I'd always been slim but never toned, thanks to a minuscule appetite and the fear that any kind of exercise would lead to a heart attack. People described me as petite and fragile – a stereotypical English rose. I was 5 ft 1 in, with pale skin and wavy brown hair, often mistaken for being 13 years old.

I waddled to the stairs and began my descent, as I struggled to stay upright. My parents stood and watched, no doubt wondering if this would be the last time they'd see me alive.

They weren't the only ones. Though my friends had offered encouragement on that rainy day in the pub, they seemed to change their minds when I announced I was actually going to do it.

'You're going to die,' they insisted. 'You won't last longer than a week.' Bets were placed on how long it would be before I gave up and went home, and the odds were depressingly short.

As unsupportive as it sounded, I understood why they thought I'd fail. To say I'd lived a sheltered life was a vast understatement. I'd grown up in a small, close-knit family, who were sensible and careful. My parents went to bed at 9 p.m., had never been drunk in front of me and liked the house to be kept in silence. I grew up reading quietly in my room with the television playing at an acceptable volume.

My parents were generous, kind-hearted and desperate for me to succeed. They lovingly built a snug-fitting comfort zone around me and kept me safe inside, cozy and warm, and never challenged.

At school, I was the person to ace every test but never say a word. As I immersed myself in my books, my friends began to grow up around me and left me far behind. During my first week at secondary school, we'd had a class on the dangers of drinking, smoking and harder drugs, and I'd taken every word to heart. *Just say no* became my mantra. Hey Lauren, fancy going to a party tonight? *Just say no!* Want a drag of my cigarette? *Just say no!* When my best friend told me she'd tried smoking, I'd stared at her as if she'd told me she'd killed someone.

Suddenly, I was 18 years old and nervously heading off to study physics at university. While everyone else around me threw wild parties and experimented with all manner of vices, I spent my evenings entertaining myself with a textbook on quantum mechanics and a jumbo pack of Haribo. Eventually, even my most sheltered friends began to gain life experience while I remained about as functional as a nine year old. My mum would drive me to the supermarket once a week so I could stock up on food; I was too embarrassed to admit I'd never been on a bus before so would regularly cancel on friends if I had no other way of getting there; and I was so intimidated by food that I'd never eaten rice or eggs.

My lack of life experience meant I didn't have much common sense, which led to near-death experiences on a seemingly daily basis. I regularly fell down stairs, I once temporarily blinded myself when I tried to spray perfume on to my eyelids and had even managed to drive into the wall of my parents' home when I'd first passed my test. I was the definition of a walking disaster.

My dad carried my backpack out to the car and I turned to face my mum. Victoria waved a drowsy greeting from behind her, having recently emerged from bed. I took a deep breath and walked towards them with my arms outstretched. We were on the brink of a display of raw sentimentality when—

'My boarding pass!' I cried out, throwing my arms in the air. 'I forgot to print my boarding pass. Damn it! *Damn it!*'

I untangled myself from their grasps and hobbled to the office. After fumbling with the printer and ripping my laptop from my daypack, I stood helplessly, waiting for both to turn on.

'I'm going to miss my flight,' I moaned. 'I can't believe I'm going to miss my flight.' I had fallen at the first hurdle. I hated the voice in my head that was telling me it was for the best and I hated myself more for agreeing with it. I hadn't even been able to nail the logistics of packing a bag, setting an alarm and getting out of bed without injury. What hope did I have for surfing in Bali or skydiving in New Zealand?

The printer beeped into life as I limped back and forth in front of it. 'Why is this happening to me? Why does this *always* happen to me?'

'Lauren, calm down,' my mum sighed, reaching out to grab my arm. 'Gatwick's only forty-five minutes away and you've got an hour before check-in closes. It'll be tight but you can make it.'

I snatched my boarding pass when it emerged and hopped back towards the front door. There was no time for heartfelt goodbyes or speeches I'd been practising for weeks. Like ripping off a plaster, our goodbye would be painful but quick. It was best not to prolong it.

I hugged Victoria first, shocked to feel her shoulders trembling as she gripped on to me. I couldn't remember the last time I'd seen her cry and it set me off sobbing all over again. My mum broke down at this point and the three of us stood in the hallway clutching at each other and quivering. We looked like a rugby scrum in the midst of an epileptic fit.

'I've got to go,' I whispered to them. 'I'm sorry.'

My dad was waiting in the car when I clambered inside.

'Ready?'

I took a deep breath. 'Ready.'

It was 5 a.m. on a Tuesday morning and the roads were full of cars being driven to work or home to sleep. I was surrounded by hundreds of people who knew exactly what they were going to be doing that day and it was giving me unexpected pangs of jealousy. I longed for that certainty. I didn't even know if I would make my flight, let alone survive my first night in a hostel. I didn't cope well with not knowing.

I felt a sudden urge to tell everyone – perfect strangers – that I was leaving the country on a one-way ticket and I was scared. I wanted someone to tell me it was going to be okay. Anyone who knew about my propensity for disaster was convinced I was making a huge mistake – I could count the number of people who believed in me on one hand.

I watched the sun rise over the M25, illuminating a scene I'd passed through a thousand times before. As I squinted out at the familiar details I usually ignored, I was struck by the urge to memorise how it felt to be in England. Every detail, from the sheep on the slopes of the reservoir to the graffiti-ridden signs: I wanted to remember it all. A sudden downpour broke my focus. Its presence was soothing, like an old friend who never changed their ways.

My dad leaned over and gave me a nudge. 'I've got a surprise for you.'

I watched him fiddle with his iPod, as he plugged it into the stereo and scrolled through the menu. 'I've made a playlist of all of our favourite songs,' he told me, smiling at the screen.

I squeezed my eyes to keep the tears inside and began to sing along to 'California Dreamin'' in a trembling voice. It was the song I associated most with him – he'd always pressured me into duetting with him for as long as I could remember; always to this song. I'd been irritated by it at the time, but now I couldn't stop thinking about when we'd get to sing together next.

'Are you going to go to California?' he asked, as we pulled up outside the airport.

'Maybe,' I said. 'I don't really have any plans after the first few months. I actually have no idea where I'll end up.' I found the idea of such freedom both empowering and terrifying.

I'd been changing my mind about where I wanted to visit ever since I first decided I was going to do this. From a three-month volunteering stint in Uganda to riding the Trans-Siberian Railway from Moscow to Beijing, I'd considered everything. My current plan wasn't as adventurous: a month travelling overland through Eastern Europe, a couple of months in Eastern Asia, six months in Southeast Asia, a campervan trip around Australia and New Zealand, and a tentative plan to move on to South America if I hadn't run out of money.

I dragged my overstuffed backpack from the car and together we hurried inside against horizontal rain and gale-force winds. It was a typical summer's morning in London and the perfect weather for leaving.

My brand new hiking boots squeaked against the polished floor as we searched for the check-in desks. I'd been fighting off the beginnings of a panic attack all morning but it was at this point I started to feel queasy. *Why on earth had I thought I was ready for travel? I'd never even checked in for a flight before by myself.* I had no idea what I was doing.

'Do you have any checked luggage?' droned the heavy-lidded woman behind the counter.

Confused, I glanced at my backpack. 'Checked? No. I don't own anything that's checked. My backpack has stripes.'

She didn't return my nervous smile. 'Ma'am, do you have any checked bags? I don't have time for games.'

'What? What games? I just showed you. Nothing I have is checked. My backpack is striped and my daypack is plain blue.' I held them up for her to see.

'Oh,' she said. 'You're not joking. Ma'am, are you taking both bags on the plane with you or is your big backpack going in the hold?'

'My big backpack is going in the hold,' I repeated back to her.

'I see you didn't pay for any,' she paused, '*checked luggage* when you booked your flight. You'll need to pay for that here.'

'Oh, really?' I said. 'That seems strange. Are you sure?'

'Yes, I'm sure.'

I rummaged through my pockets despite knowing they were empty, then gritted my teeth and motioned my dad over.

'Hey, Dad? Would you maybe, possibly, please be able to lend me some money? I forgot to pay to put my backpack on the plane! Can you believe that?'

'What? You *forgot* to pay for your luggage?' He looked incredulous as he pulled out his wallet. 'I just don't know how you're going to travel the world, Lauren, I really don't.'

After a surprisingly calm goodbye, I was swallowed up by security and spat out into the other side of the airport, the one full of duty-free gin and cheap crime novels. I wandered into a bookstore and thumbed through a Tom Clancy Cold War-era novel with shaky hands. *Isn't Tom Clancy also a cocktail?* I wondered. *No, wait – that's a Tom Collins. I could definitely use a Tom Collins right now.* I'd been teetotal up until a few months ago, but had just started to experiment with alcohol once my departure date was looming. I wanted the full travel experience and I wanted to feel like a normal 23 year old as I did it. *Did normal 23 year olds partake in daytime drinking?* A booming announcement interrupted my navel-gazing.

This is the final call for passenger Lauren Juliff for Flight EZY5425 to Dubrovnik.

It echoed through the terminal before I could process what was happening.

'Eeeeeeeeep!' I turned around and shrieked at the guy stood behind the register. 'Eeeeeeeep! Eeeeeeeeep!'

'Are you okay?'

'That was me! *I'm* Lauren Juliff! I'm going to miss my flight! They're final-calling me! Eeeeeeeeeep! What should I do?'

'I... would probably suggest running?' he said with an astounded look on his face.

'Running. Right. Okay. Thank you! I'll try running.'

I turned on my sore ankle with a yelp and began sprint-hobbling towards the gate. I looked like a hysterical goblin, limping and weaving around the obstacle course of suitcases, backpacks and excited families who *would not stand to one side* on the moving walkways. When I caught a glimpse of my gate up ahead, I began to shout.

'LAUREN JULIFF! LAUREN JULIFF!' I bellowed, attracting stares from everyone around. I staggered up to the two gate attendants, neither of them looking overly thrilled with me. 'I'm Lauren Juliff! That's me! I'm so sorry I'm late! I didn't realise the flight was boarding and I was just wandering around some shops and I thought I might buy myself a book because I dropped mine under a train last week and I had to—'

'Your passport and boarding pass, please?'

I handed them over and stepped on the plane.

Two hours later, I arrived in Dubrovnik, greeted by a new language, currency and climate to get used to. I took a taxi to my hostel, too nervous to try to figure out how public transport worked just yet.

'Welcome to Dubrovnik!' a voice called out, as I dawdled outside the hostel, trying to work up the courage to head inside. A plump middle-aged lady with rosy cheeks rushed out of the building and greeted me with a warm hug. 'Hello, hello,' she said. 'Welcome to our hostel. Are you Lauren?'

'I am,' I said, hugging her back.

'We've been expecting you, Lauren. Let me show you to your room – we've just finished making your bed. My name is Anna, by the way. You can come and see me if you have any problems.' My fears faded away as I walked alongside her. I felt more welcomed than at any hotel I'd stayed.

A dorm room looked just how I'd imagined it to – there were eight bunk beds arranged around the edges of the room, and an explosion of backpacks and clothes were strewn across the floor.

'I'm afraid all we have is the top bunk left so you will have to climb the ladder,' she said, pointing up at the only pristine bed in the room. 'I'll let you move in now but remember, come and find me if you need anything.'

'I will. Thank you so much.'

I looked around. There was one other girl in the room. She was pretty and tanned with long blonde hair, typing on her laptop. She looked up at me standing by my backpack and I began to worry about what I was supposed to do next.

'Hey ya,' she called out in an Australian accent. 'Where're ya from?'

I had read about how travellers always ask each other the same questions and I knew this was one I'd be coming up against frequently. I felt like I'd just been going through the motions up until now, but being asked where I was from had finally made me feel like I was travelling. 'London,' I said, trying not to let on how happy I was to be having my first conversation with a backpacker. 'You?'

'Sydney.'

'Nice,' I exclaimed. 'I'm actually hoping to go to Australia in a few months. I'll probably be visiting Sydney first.'

'Sweet. You'll love it there – *such* a great city. I miss it a lot. How long are you travelling for?'

I pulled a face, not sure how to answer. 'I don't know at the moment. Maybe a year. Maybe two.' I shrugged. 'I'm sort of winging it.'

'Oh, me too,' she laughed. 'In fact, I'm *totally* winging it. I've been travelling through the Balkans for the past three months but I think I'll head to Southeast Asia soon. I'm running low on money.' She stood up and slipped on a pair of flip-flops, and I stared in awe at the tan lines that criss-crossed her feet like roads on a map. 'You been travelling long?' she asked.

I hesitated before answering. 'This is actually the first day of my trip.'

'No way! That's wild. We'll have to celebrate tonight.' She picked up a navy blue beach bag and swung it over her shoulder. 'Hey, a group of us are actually just about to go down to the beach if you want to come too?'

I nodded. 'Yes, please. Give me a minute to grab my things.' I dove into my backpack and pulled out a towel and some money. With an enormous grin on my face, I threw them into my daypack and rushed outside.

As we walked down the cobblestone steps I asked her name.

'Chloe,' she replied. 'I always forget to ask people's names! You'll find that as you travel you'll always be asking and answering the same questions. "Where are you from?" "Where have you been?" "Where are you going?" "How long are you travelling for?" Nobody ever seems to ask what your name is or what you do back home.'

After introducing me to her friends – an eclectic mix of guys from Austria, New Zealand and Israel – we wandered down to the beach. I was astounded at how my luck had turned around over the space of a few hours.

In that moment, surrounded by newfound friends, I allowed myself to relax – properly relax – for the first time in a year. I allowed myself to forget about my unsupportive friends, to forget about my life back home and to forget about how I'd just jumped head first into the deep end of my new life. Today, I was determined to push aside my worries to make room for happiness.

As the sun began to set, Luke – the backpacker from New Zealand – produced a bottle of *rakija*, a local Croatian spirit, from his bag and poured some into five plastic cups.

'A sundowner, Lauren?' he asked, holding it out to me.

I nodded, my stomach filled with nervous anticipation. At any other point in my life, I would have turned it down, but I wanted the new version of me to say yes to just about everything.

I raised the cup to my mouth and took a big gulp, shuddering seconds later as the unfamiliar burning sensation worked its way down my throat and into my stomach. I buried my face in my hands and coughed. In that moment, I felt like just another traveller, making friends from around the world, napping on the beach, grinning as the cold Adriatic Sea tickled my toes and wondering why I'd ever been so scared. I felt *normal*.

I looked around at our group and smiled. Under ordinary circumstances our paths would have never crossed, but after spending an entire day together they already felt like some of my closest friends.

Luke was on the final few days of his round-the-world trip – he'd been travelling for 18 months, had visited 50 countries and was dreading going home. Mark was from Israel and travelling around the Balkans for six months after finishing a stint in the military. Simon, from Austria, had just been fired from his job as an engineer and was using his savings to see the world before heading back to job-hunt. And Chloe – like me – had just graduated and had always dreamed of travel.

When the sky grew dark, we returned to the hostel, where Anna was cooking an enormous feast for us all.

'Sit down, sit down,' she gushed, as we wandered into the common room. Without waiting for a response, she wrapped her arms around us, gathered us up and took us outside. On the balcony stretched a long wooden picnic table with a dozen or so people sat around it. I smiled and took a seat beside Chloe.

'Hey guys, welcome,' said a guy with jet-black hair and freckles. 'We were all just discussing what made us want to travel. You guys are all travelling solo, right?'

'Yeah,' the five of us said in unison.

'So what made you want to do it?'

Psychosomatically drunk from the *rakija* on the beach, I spoke up first.

'I've always been obsessed with travelling the world,' I told the group. 'For as long as I can remember, I've spent an unhealthy amount of time reading about countries and staring at maps. And as for doing it solo, I was actually supposed to be travelling with my boyfriend. I'd been planning this big round-the-world trip with him, but then he broke up with me. I guess I was just like, "Screw you then, Jeremy! I'll just go alone."'

'Amen,' Chloe said, raising an imaginary glass in the air.

'Wait!' Anna called from the kitchen. She emerged a few seconds later with a stack of glasses and a bottle of dark-purple liquid. 'Grape brandy,' she told us. 'For you to cheers.'

'To not needing a man,' Chloe announced.

'To not needing a man,' I repeated, tapping my glass against hers.

As everyone else began to share their stories, my mind drifted. I'd somehow managed to come across like I was confident and self-assured, but the truth was far more painful. Jeremy had been my soul mate, my best friend, my support network, my everything. After that rainy day in the pub when I'd decided I wanted to give travel a go, he was the first person I told.

'Do you want to go travelling with me?' I'd asked him. 'We can save up over the next five years and as soon as I graduate we can just pack our bags and leave. We can travel the world together.'

He'd hadn't taken much convincing, blurting out that he loved the idea and he'd always wanted to go to India.

'India,' I'd gasped, widening my eyes as I imagined catching dysentery and being run over by a cow. 'I'm not sure I want to go to India,' I'd confessed. 'India seems too scary. I'm not sure I'd survive.'

After receiving the green light from Jeremy, I threw myself into planning. I'd imagined the two of us hiking across glaciers, climbing volcanoes and bungee jumping off bridges. We'd learn to surf, drive across deserts and climb crumbling ruins enveloped in jungle.

I took on several retail jobs that I could fit around studying and resolved to not buy anything I didn't need. Travel was my priority now and reminding myself that every £15 I saved would give me an extra night in Southeast Asia was all the motivation I needed. It worked: after five years of working as many hours as I could, I had £20,000 in my bank account – more than enough to travel for a year.

What I hadn't counted on was Jeremy changing his mind less than a year before we were due to leave.

It took just 2 hours. Two hours to receive the phone call from Jeremy telling me that he no longer loved me. So I packed up my life and carried it in boxes to my parents' home. I was 22, had been in love and didn't have the coping skills to deal with the end of what had been a defining relationship. From there, my life fell apart.

I was suspended from my job for being too wrapped up in heartbreak to realise I was being scammed out of a cash drawer-worth of money. I stopped paying attention at university, and watched my grades drop from an average of 95 to 40 per cent.

I commuted to university when I felt like it, but mostly spent my time hiding under my bedcovers and sobbing inconsolably. I lost friends when I disappeared for months at a time, crawling into my shell and out of their lives, too wrapped up in my sorrow to care. I even begged my doctor for antidepressants, convinced I was on the verge of a breakdown.

It was hitting rock bottom that convinced me I should leave anyway. When I looked at my life, I felt like a failure. I was living with my parents, my relationship was over, I was failing my classes and all but a few of my friends had moved on without me. I was miserable, broken and confused. *What did I have to lose by leaving?*

I knew I'd never be able to shake the worry that I was making the biggest mistake of my life – just the thought of getting on a plane had been enough to fill me with dread – but I also didn't want to live my life with regrets. *How would I know if I was making a mistake unless I forced myself to try?*

And now I was here; alone in Dubrovnik, but surviving. As I sat and listened to Chloe telling a story about the time she'd left her passport behind, I realised I was more than surviving. It may have only been 12 hours, but I'd already fallen in love with travel.

I awoke the following morning and peered out from my bunk, trying to work out where I was. I blinked a couple of times and wondered why two large eyeballs were dancing in front of my face.

'*Dude!*' the eyes exclaimed. I frowned, trying to place the voice. I blinked until the guy came into focus. 'Are you sleeping with your backpack on?'

I tried to sit up but my arms seemed to be pinned behind my back.

'Oh!' I gasped, horrified. 'I *am* sleeping with my backpack on. Isn't that what you're supposed to do on the top bunks?'

An explosion of giggles erupted around me as the guy pulled on his backpack and mimed getting in and out of bed with it.

Eager to escape the teasing of what felt like the entire hostel, I set off alone and ashamed on my first full day of travel. Anna had handed me a bus timetable as I'd left, letting me know it would be an hour's walk to the Old Town otherwise. I'd thanked her and pocketed it, and walked straight past the bus stop. I'd told myself it wasn't because I didn't know how buses worked, but because I needed to improve my fitness.

It took roughly 5 minutes for me to start reconsidering my plan to follow summer around the world. A heatwave was surging through Dubrovnik, and temperatures were reaching as high as 35°C. The heat was making me delirious and, after 10 minutes of walking, I was already convinced I was lost.

I rummaged through my daypack and immediately realised I was doing this all wrong – I should have packed a bottle of water instead of a pocket knife, should have got my phone unlocked so

I could navigate using GPS rather than assuming I'd magically develop a sense of direction and I should have packed some sun cream instead of my DSLR and three heavy lenses.

No matter how much I'd researched, I had no idea if I was travelling with the right things. I'd been devouring packing lists in the months leading up to my departure date to try to make sure I'd have everything I would possibly need, but what use had that been if I couldn't even remember the essentials when I headed out to explore?

Despite my constant fear that I had forgotten something important, I had managed to pack reasonably light. My backpack contained five pairs of shorts and trousers, a dozen T-shirts and vest tops, along with a shirt to cover up in temples, two bikinis and some flip-flops, sandals and hiking boots. When it came to tech, I was packing heavy: I was travelling with a laptop, two cameras (a DSLR and point-and-shoot), three lenses, a Kindle, a phone and an external hard drive. I'd thrown in some toiletries, make-up, an enormous first-aid kit, a diary and that was about it: my life for the next year or two.

I entered the Old Town through one of the city's stone gates and felt like I'd wandered into a postcard. It was a scene I'd gazed at on my laptop screen a hundred times by this point, and I couldn't believe I was finally here.

I wandered to a nearby water fountain and gulped at the cold water. It had taken me 2 hours to find my way here, thanks to all my wrong turns, and I was dehydrated, sunburnt and craving a bucket of ice to jump into. I felt like a newly hatched chick, untested and not in any way prepared for the world around it.

I bought a bottle of water from a shop and wandered back outside. In front of me were a series of grey stone steps leading up to the top of the city walls. This was what I was here for; this was the reason why I decided to start my travels in Dubrovnik. I tightened my grip on my bottle and took a deep breath. It was time to start travelling.

I stumbled alongside a sea of terracotta, the tiled skyline a welcome distraction from my weakening body. As I watched daring cliff-jumpers with a mixture of worry and envy, I was reminded of a list I'd written of everything I'd hoped to achieve while I was away – skydiving, bungee jumping, surfing, snowboarding. It wasn't until I had come face to face with adventure that I realised quite how daunting it could be. I continued to gulp from my bottle, wondering how it was possible the water was hotter than the inside of my mouth. After the dizzying highs of yesterday, I was now in a heat-induced slump.

I felt ungrateful for daring to feel less than ecstatic when I'd been afforded such opportunity. I'd been dreaming of this moment for the past five years and I wanted to make the most of it. I rummaged in my bag for my camera, pulling it out and balancing it on the wall opposite with the timer on. As I grinned and threw my arms in the air in an attempt to craft an image of spirited exploration, I could already feel my mood starting to lift. The backdrop of white stone buildings, red roofs and the glistening Mediterranean made for the perfect travel shot.

I studied the photos as I walked, barely able to recognise myself. I was wearing a baggy checked shirt in khaki green with more pockets than I knew what to do with and black zip-off trousers made of a strange material that made me shudder whenever I ran my fingers over it. My flip-flops were designed for hiking, with thick felt straps that were undoubtedly giving me some interesting tan lines. Underneath my trousers, I wore a money belt that was currently glued to my stomach with sweat. I looked like a walking advert for an outdoor clothing store and reminded

Libraries NI

Belfast Central Library
Royal Avenue
Belfast
BT1 1EA
Tel: 028 9050 9150

Borrowed Items 04/08/2018 15:32
XXXXXX0138

Item Title	Due Date
How not to travel the world : adventures of a disaster-prone backpacker	25/08/2018

Thank you for using this unit

==========

Your Library Doesn't End Here
Get Free eBooks And eMagazines
Visit www.librariesni.org.uk
Or Ask Staff For Details

==========

Email: belfast.central@librariesni.org.uk

myself an awful lot of my old geography teacher. I looked wrong, like I was trying to be a person I hadn't yet become.

The one constant was my enormous hair. It didn't take much to render it uncontrollable – a little humidity, a trace of sweat, a couple of raindrops. With just the slightest hint of moisture my carefully styled hair would quadruple in volume, leaving me looking like my face resided beneath a bird's nest. My hair, not unlike the rest of me, was not coping well with travel.

I stumbled into the dorm room and ran straight to the bathroom. I couldn't believe I'd just spent 8 hours walking in the scorching heat and had only drunk one bottle of water.

'You're such an idiot, Lauren,' I mumbled, as I turned on the shower.

The walk back to the hostel had been brutal and I was already convinced I had heatstroke. As I stepped beneath the icy cold water, I caught a glimpse of my naked body and grimaced. I looked like a true Brit abroad: lily-white with splotches of sunburn the colour of raw liver.

The tiles in the bathroom began to spin and I slumped to the floor in a panic, thoughts of contracting fungal diseases far from my mind. When the room continued to whirl around me, I tipped my head back and opened my mouth, taking big gulps of the lukewarm water. *Was the water safe to drink in Dubrovnik?* By this point, I was just focusing on not passing out and giving my dormmates something else to laugh about.

I dropped my head in my hands and burst into tears, desperately trying to fight off the familiar sensation that was rising up inside of me. I felt as though I was choking and I began to gasp at the air around me. The trembling came next, causing me to shiver until I reached the point where I was shaking so violently it would be impossible for me to stand. As I started hyperventilating, waves of nausea washed over me and I retched in the shower with an empty stomach, producing nothing but bile. I was hot and cold and dizzy and afraid.

But I wasn't surprised. Had this happened seven years ago, I would have been convinced I was dying. I'd have thought it was a heart attack or a stroke or a brain haemorrhage. Now, though, I knew it for what it was: a panic attack. These bouts of anxiety had been disrupting my life for years.

From the age of 16, there hadn't been many days where I didn't feel unwell. I wasn't sure what had kicked my anxiety into gear, but after experiencing my first panic attack, I became obsessed with how I was feeling. I was always light-headed, dizzy and nauseated, unable to shake the feeling that there was something wrong with me. I started going to the doctor on a monthly basis, convinced I had a terminal illness.

Over time, I had blood tests for anaemia, diabetes and thyroid issues. I thought that I had a stomach ulcer, stomach cancer, breast cancer, blood clots, IBS, arthritis, leukaemia, a tapeworm, a brain tumour, angina, mad cow disease, scarlet fever, lupus and more.

I'd always been shy and introverted, but as my panic attacks took control over my life, I began to retreat further and further into my shell. At one point, I was so afraid of the outside world that I spent a period of several months unable to step outside my front door.

I attempted to regain control of my life by altering one of the few things still within my power to change. I stopped eating – not because I wanted to lose weight, but because I wanted to have one tiny aspect of my life that I was in control of. Over the space of several months, I lived on nothing but apples and pears, weighing under 40 kg at my lowest point.

'Oh bollocks,' I groaned, shaking myself out of the memory. As I sat on the shower floor, trembling and weak, I noticed my phone was floating in a puddle beside me. I reached for it and tried to turn it on, but the screen remained black.

'I guess I won't be travelling with this then,' I said in a shaky voice.

I sat on the floor for a while longer, drinking the shower water until my legs were strong enough for me to stand. Once I was up, I put my sweaty clothes back on and re-entered the dorm with downcast eyes. Then, surrounded by everything I owned in the world, I wrapped my arms around my backpack and drifted off to sleep.

That evening, I forced myself out of bed and down to the beach because even I was fed up with all my wallowing in self-pity.

I was heading for a row of restaurants I'd spotted on my first day, and I was planning on treating myself to a slap-up meal to pull me out of this funk.

I stood outside the first one, rocking on my heels and struggling to work up the confidence to go inside. *Could I really do this? Was I really brave enough to eat a meal alone?*

I shook out my arms and forced myself to enter, just like I'd forced myself to get on the plane a few days earlier. I stood just inside the entrance, eyes darting around the room.

'Hello!' The waiter strode up to me and seemed to be peering at the empty space that surrounded me.

'A table for one?' I asked. 'Please?'

'A table for *one*?' he exclaimed in mock horror. 'Why are you alone? Where are your friends? Don't you have any friends?'

'I...' I trailed off, thinking of the friends I'd left behind in London. 'I don't know.'

Fifty pairs of eyes focused in on me and I wondered if I should leave. The waiter let out a booming laugh and gestured for me to follow him to an empty table right in the centre of the room.

I pretended to read the menu while I thought of my family and wondered what they were doing. I hadn't expected to feel homesick quite so early on in my travels.

The woman at the table next to mine suddenly threw back her head and guffawed, slapping her knee and cracking up over something her husband had said. As I watched them laugh and squeeze each other's hands, I felt like bursting into tears.

I reached for my Kindle and pressed the power button, but it was out of battery. I looked around the restaurant at happy couples and families on holiday. I didn't have anyone.

I returned to an empty dorm room an hour later, disappointed by how quickly things had changed. My first night in Dubrovnik had been one of the happiest of my life, but now it felt like everything was falling apart. Perhaps the problem was that I'd always expected I'd fall in love with travel. I'd thought that all I needed to do was make a drastic change to my life and everything would magically slot together. I was starting to worry I'd made a huge mistake.

As I scrambled into bed later that evening, I pulled the covers up over my head and squeezed my eyes shut. *Tomorrow's a new day*, I told myself. *Everything will be better tomorrow.*

My forehead rattled against the window of the bus as I watched the dry hills of the Croatian countryside roll past in a blur. I was leaving Dubrovnik after five days of highs and lows and heading north to a new city; one where I was hopeful I'd have greater success.

I pried my eyelids apart, cursing myself for thinking it would be a good idea to take a double dose of motion-sickness pills. It was my first time on a bus and I couldn't allow myself to sleep. I glanced down at the damp ticket in my fist and let a smile cross my lips.

Before leaving the hostel that morning, I'd waited until I was alone to open my laptop and start my research. 'How do buses work?' I'd typed. 'How do you take a bus?' 'What do you say when you get on a bus?' 'How do you know when to get off a bus?' 'Are buses in Croatia safe?' I'd even checked YouTube to see if I could find an instructional video. Then, with a brain full of notes from informed teenagers on Yahoo! Answers, I'd sat and practised my lines.

'A single to the main bus station, please. A one-way ticket to the main bus station, please. Crap, should I say single or one-way? Is it even called the main bus station? What happens if I end up in Albania?'

To my surprise, I didn't crumble to the ground the second I stepped on a bus. In fact, it was easy. I wondered why it had taken me so long to figure it out.

My foray into transportation exhilarated and saddened me. Even the Amish take buses. *Note to self*, I thought. *Be more technologically advanced than the Amish.*

I stared back out of the window with a sigh, unsure whether I could summarise the past five days as a success or a disaster. What I did know was that I was ready for a change of scenery.

I wanted to go to a place where I could make new friends and wear sun cream and not be known as the lunatic who sleeps with her backpack on. After all, wasn't that the beauty of travel? That I could head to a new destination whenever I felt like it and nobody would know who I was? It was time to start doing things differently.

CHAPTER 2

The door of the hostel swung open and I was hit by an icy wall of air conditioning. *Cold*. I hadn't felt that sensation in weeks. I'd been on the road for a month by now and was still acclimatising to an Eastern European summer. Temperatures had been consistently in the thirties, and now that I was in Ukraine, it was promising to be even hotter. I stretched out my tanned arms, revelling in the frigid air. Around my wrist, I wore a purple string bracelet: a memento I'd bought to remind me of Croatia.

I'd visited four countries over the past four weeks, spending time island-hopping my way up the coast of Croatia, improving my fitness through Alpine hikes in Slovenia, getting lost in lakeside towns in Hungary and taking a day trip through the countryside of Bosnia. Now I was in Ukraine: my final stop in Eastern Europe.

I wriggled my shoulders and let both of my bags tumble to the floor.

Clunk.

'Damn it,' I muttered, hoping my laptop had survived its fall.

I'd spent the previous month living on the edge of my comfort zone and was no closer to knowing if travel was right for me. It had been a month of highs and lows; of homesickness and loneliness. I'd had a vision of travel before I'd left, where I'd pictured myself arriving in Dubrovnik as a savvy backpacker who was making her dreams come true. Instead, I'd spent the past month stumbling from hostel to hostel, struggling to work up the courage to eat alone.

Someone cleared their throat, snapping me out of my daydream. I spun around; relieved to see there was someone to check me in. In Slovenia, I had stood and waited silently at a reception desk for half an hour before someone had noticed me.

I picked up my bags and dragged them over to the desk. As I straightened up, I looked into a pair of irises the colour of coal. Above them, a thicket of hair spread across his brow; this man had the biggest eyebrows I'd ever seen.

'Hi,' I said, trying to look at anything but his forest. 'I have a reservation under the name of Lauren Juliff.'

'Lauren Juliff,' he said, rolling my name around on his tongue. 'Lovely name. Yes, yes, very nice.'

He extended a clammy hand in my direction. When does a handshake start feeling uncomfortable? Right around the time the other person starts caressing your hand with his fingers. *You're kind of gropey*, I thought, staring at him. He dropped my hand as if he could read my mind.

'Well, Lauren. Welcome to the hostel. I hope you'll have a very pleasurable stay in Kiev.'

'I hope so, too,' I said to his eyebrows.

'Come,' Gropey said, beckoning me.

I followed him down a white corridor and into a white room. Three steel bunk beds were pushed up against the wall and the smell of bleach lingered in the air. It looked like the kind of place I had worried I'd end up in at the height of my anxiety.

I sat down on one of the bottom bunks and noticed Gropey lingering in the doorway. Loud breathing had always irritated me and he was rasping with the best of them. I balled my hands into tight fists.

Wheeze. Wheeze.

'Thanks for showing me my room,' I said.

Wheeze. Wheeze.

I dug my nails into my palm. 'I'll let you know if I need anything.'

Wheeze. Wheeze. Wheeeeeze.

∿

The following morning, I was shocked awake by an almighty boom. A sudden gust of wind blew my hair into my face and the girl above me let out a blood-curdling scream. In a panic, I reached up and touched my face, relieved to find it was still attached. Next, I twitched my legs and arms to check they hadn't been blown across the room. A low moan filled the air as injured bodies began to stir. I squinted into the darkness to try to make out if our walls were still intact. I couldn't believe it: there had been a bomb.

Someone switched on the lights and they blinded me with their white glow. I held my hand to my eyes and scanned the room for blood.

'Holy shit, man,' I heard a voice say. I sat up and twisted around. There, lying in the adjacent bed was a petrified looking German guy. On the floor were splintered slats of wood and a mess of tangled sheets.

'I fell through,' he uttered, his wide eyes meeting mine. 'My bed collapsed.'

I gaped at him in silence for a few moments, until one of the girls in the room started to giggle.

'Thank God nobody was in the bottom bunk, eh?' a guy called out in an Irish accent. If there had been someone below, I had no doubt there would now be blood. It turned out there were more downsides to choosing £10-a-night hostels than I'd realised. I'd been a strict bottom-bunk kind of girl after my first night in Dubrovnik, but you could bet I was switching to the top tonight.

After witnessing a bed collapse, I was too nervous to fall back asleep and passed the time lying flat on my back in the darkness, ogling the wooden planks above me. As the sun began to rise, I let out a defeated sigh and got up. Today was going to be a difficult day and I hoped my sleep deprivation wouldn't make it worse. I got dressed, opting to wear my only jumper and only pair of trousers. I needed to cover as much of my skin as possible. Today, I was taking a tour of Chernobyl.

The streets of Kiev enveloped me in their silence and I was spellbound as I walked. This was the first place I'd been where English-speaking tourists didn't seem to be catered for in any way. Even the street signs were in Cyrillic. While the brick buildings looked rougher than other parts of Eastern Europe I'd seen, I still fell in love with their dilapidated beauty. What I found even more entrancing, though, was the city's churches. As I made my way towards Independence Square, I stopped every few steps to take photos, dazzled by their golden domes.

The tour company had emailed me a few days ago, and I had everything they'd said to bring except closed shoes. I'd lost my travel sandals on the Croatian island of Brač and my hiking boots had disappeared shortly afterwards. I'd been planning on replacing them, but living in flip-flops had grown to feel strangely natural.

I spotted a small shoe shop that looked to be open and darted inside. I needed something cheap and closed; something that wouldn't let the cancer-infused soil give me a foot rub.

'*Dobrogo ranku!*' an old lady called, as I nervously scanned the shop.

'Hello,' I said, watching her run to me. I felt terrible for not yet knowing any of the language. She stopped and stared at me in confusion. 'Hello?' I said. She looked at me as if I was, well, speaking another language. 'Hello?' I tried again.

She motioned for me to wait and summoned her staff for a huddle. They spoke in quick-fire Ukrainian, occasionally turning to ogle the foreigner. After 5 minutes of this, she walked back towards me and said, 'No English.'

'Oh,' I said, thinking that was rather obvious. 'That's okay.'

I picked up a shoe, on sale for around £10, and held it out to her. 'These?' I asked. She shot me an expression that said, 'I have no idea what you're saying.' I placed it on the floor and mimed stepping inside it. 'Try on?'

She shook her head and cackled, then dragged me towards a wall to show me a poster of numbers. *Shoe sizes. Of course.* I held up four fingers. She shook her head again and jabbed at the poster. *Damn it. European shoe sizes.*

Drastic times called for drastic measures and I signalled for the woman to wait. I'd been using my Kindle to get online while I'd been out exploring without a phone because the 3G version had free worldwide data through an awful, clunky browser. I scrolled through the search results for a few minutes, looking for a conversion chart of shoe sizes.

'Thirty-seven!' I announced, running to slap the number on the porter.

As I sat and waited for her to bring out the shoes, I let a satisfied smile spread across my face. My family holiday tradition of two weeks in an isolated villa in Mallorca had not prepared me for communicating with someone who didn't know the word 'hello'.

I made my way to Independence Square, arriving just as the tour guides were performing the final headcount beside the bus. The sky was an empty, cloudless blue and I was already sweating, despite it being only 8 a.m. On the tour was an eclectic mix of six British guys on a lads' holiday, a couple of Canadians, a Chinese family, a Romanian couple, five South Africans and twelve Americans.

We were heading for Pripyat, the small town that used to house the workmen of Chernobyl, and one of the guides put on a DVD to prepare us for our visit. It was at that moment that I started to wonder why I was doing this. The physicist in me had been buzzing to get there; the hypochondriac wasn't so sure. It was the personal stories from Pripyat that hit me hardest and I almost broke down when I watched a woman returning to her apartment 20 years after being evacuated. Everything had been just where she'd left it.

We pulled up at the Chernobyl Exclusion Zone, which marked a 30 km radius around the nuclear power plant, where radioactivity is highest. Nobody lived inside here and guards marked the entrance. We passed through and continued on to the 10 km checkpoint, and at this point we were taken off the bus and handed waivers to sign. I squinted in the sunlight as I ran my eyes over the page, choosing to ignore the part about not being able to sue if we experienced health issues. With a trembling hand, I signed my life away; it was too late to back out, anyway. As I climbed back on the bus, I pushed my fingers into the sides of my neck to check my glands, wondering if my cells had already started to mutate.

Our first stop was the fairground, Chernobyl's best-known feature. I separated from the group at this point and wandered up to the rusted Ferris wheel, filled with the urge to reach out and touch it. I felt like touching it would make it more real. A gust of wind came out of nowhere and one of the yellow cars on the wheel squeaked in the breeze. Then, silence. There was no sign of life.

'Look at this,' our guide whispered, holding a Geiger counter to a clump of moss and showing us the reading. 'This is thirty-seven times the amount of radiation in Kiev,' he told us, and I wrapped my arms around my shoulders as if that could somehow keep me from harm.

We passed from apartment blocks to hotels; the community centre to the leisure centre, everything a graveyard for past lives and memories. Our tour group decided to spend most of our time in the school, peering into classrooms and stepping over discarded exercise books. With a shudder, I sidestepped an abandoned doll and trudged over newspapers dating from the day before the incident.

It was visiting the leisure centre that hit me hardest: the drained swimming pool, the broken clock on the wall, the smashed windows, the changing rooms and the dated-looking equipment.

I could almost smell the chlorine in the air; hear the faint laughter of children as they threw themselves off diving boards.

Chernobyl was an important place to visit. I'd decided long ago that I didn't want to spend my trip heading only to the easy places; I wanted to educate myself on the horrors of recent history and the reality of others' lives; to put my privilege into perspective. As we made the trip back to Kiev, trundling under the cloudless blue sky, I made a promise to never forget Chernobyl.

Back at the hostel, I showered fully clothed, not willing to take any chances. I was exhausted, nauseated and convinced I was days away from becoming cancerous. I slipped a bar of soap inside my shoes and began to scrub.

'Did you go to Chernobyl today?' a girl asked when I entered the dorm. She looked to be about 30, with sandy blonde hair and a dozen rings in her ears. The night before, I'd overheard her telling Gropey she was from Sweden.

'Yep,' I said. I opened the door to my locker and pulled out a tube of salt and vinegar Pringles. With my arm outstretched, I prodded my armpit in search of swollen glands. 'Have you been yet?' I asked, grabbing my laptop and taking it over to my bed.

'I'm thinking about going but I am a little frightened. My name is Charlotte, by the way.'

'Lauren,' I said. 'And I was pretty frightened, too. But don't worry – they told us on the tour that the amount of radiation you receive from a day trip is less than you'd get from a long-haul flight, so it seemed pretty safe.'

Charlotte walked over and sat on my bed. Open on my laptop was a list of the symptoms of lymphoma. She stared at me in horror. 'Oh, don't worry,' I said. 'That's from this morning. I'm a bit of a hypochondriac. This,' I waved my hand at my screen, 'is what I do.'

'That is what I do too,' she announced. 'I am a hypochondriac.'

'High five for hypochondria!' I cheered, throwing my hand up for her to slap. We exchanged embarrassed grins and I felt a sudden urge to pull her into a bear hug.

'How do you do it, Lauren?' she asked suddenly.

I frowned. 'What do you mean? How do I do what?'

'Travel. Aren't you afraid of all of the illness? I find it hard.'

'I'm terrified,' I confessed and she looked surprised. Seven years of panic attacks had given me plenty of time to figure out how to disguise my anxiety as eccentricity, with not even some of my closest friends having any idea how debilitating it had been. Most people thought I was just chronically nervous. 'I have pretty bad anxiety,' I told Charlotte. 'So I freak out about everything.'

'I know how that feels,' she said.

'Take today, for instance,' I continued. 'The fried eggs they give us at the hostel breakfast? My biggest fear.'

'What? Your biggest…'

'Well, not really. But it's a big one. I've never eaten eggs before and I've been avoiding them like the plague since I started travelling. Why do so many hostel breakfasts contain eggs? I suppose I should really try them at some point but I'd much rather do so under the care of a trained medical professional. What if I'm allergic to them? What if I'm allergic to *rice*?' I was still furious at my doctor for refusing to prescribe me an EpiPen.

'You have never eaten rice?' Charlotte asked, her jaw hanging open.

I shook my head.

'Have you been to Asia?'

'Not yet. I'm dreading the food though. I've never really eaten Chinese food, or Indian food, or Thai food, or—'

'You are too crazy,' she interrupted, looking at me like I was an alien 'What do you eat?'

'Sandwiches, mostly,' I said. 'I like bread.'

An uneasy silence settled over the room.

That evening, my dormmates descended on the room, spreading out across the floor and passing around a bottle of cheap vodka. Charlotte and I hadn't spoken since she'd discovered I was scared of food, but all seemed to be forgotten now we had alcohol flowing through our veins. She clambered up on to my bed and sat beside me.

'Tell me about your travels,' she said. We'd had two shots of vodka and I was searching for something to hold on to. I still wasn't used to the sensation of being drunk.

'What do you want to know?' I asked with a nervous giggle.

'How are they going? Do you like it?'

I froze, wondering how best to answer. It was a question I hadn't been expecting, and one I'd been too afraid to even ask myself. I opened my mouth, then closed it again. 'I think so?'

'You think so?' asked the German guy who'd fallen through his bed the previous night. I realised everyone had heard what I said and my cheeks flushed scarlet.

'I mean yes,' I stammered, trying to save myself. *How could I not like travel? Everyone liked travel.*

'Is it your hypochondria?' Charlotte asked, and I wished that everyone would stop staring at me.

I shook my head. 'No, it's not my hypochondria.'

'It's okay, dude,' the German guy said, walking over to fill up my cup with another shot of vodka. 'Not everyone likes to travel. Maybe travel isn't what you're supposed to do.'

'I guess,' I said in a shaky voice, 'I think it's just not what I expected. Um...' I hated admitting to other people that I suffered from anxiety but I didn't know how else to explain my way out of this situation. 'I'm struggling,' I said in a louder voice. 'I've wanted to travel for as long as I can remember – it's been an obsession at some points – and I spent five years saving up money so I could do it. Now that I'm actually travelling, though, I'm terrified I've made a huge mistake.'

There was an awkward silence and I wondered if I should apologise for being so honest. Admitting that I hadn't fallen in love with travel made me feel like a terrible person. I was doing what so many people dream of doing and I was failing miserably at it. I'd spent more time having panic attacks in dorm room toilets than I had actually seeing the places I was travelling through.

'What are you struggling with?' Charlotte asked. 'Everyone struggles at one point or another – I've thought about going home so many times on my trip, but you get over it.'

'It's my anxiety,' I said. 'Well, it's a lot of things. I guess I'm just scared. Of everything. This all feels like I'm way out of my depth. I'm scared of public transport, of eating foreign food, of talking to people I haven't met in dorm rooms.' I tried to keep it vague but my list of things I was scared of ran into four figures. Even worse, my first reaction to feeling anxious was to stop eating. My stomach let out an angry grumble, right on cue. 'I just think that maybe this isn't the right time for me to travel,' I confessed. 'But what else can I do? My life's revolved around this trip for years. I don't have a plan B.'

'You know what I think would help?' the German guy piped up.

'What's that?'

'Coming out with us tonight. The hostel owner recommended this crazy sounding club that all the locals go to. I'm talking cocktails in buckets, insane Ukrainian tracks and beautiful girls everywhere. Come with us – we'll leave here around midnight and probably stay out all night. It'll be a messy one, for sure.'

My eyes widened and I immediately came up with a thousand excuses for not going. I'd never been to a club before and it sounded like my worst nightmare. 'I can't go tonight,' I told him. 'I've got to get up early tomorrow, but maybe another time.' I was drunk and on the verge of falling asleep and it was only 8 p.m. *Was it any wonder I wasn't enjoying travel if I was refusing to put myself out there?*

I knocked three times on the door of Gropey's office and it opened as if operated by remote control. Inside, he was lounging on a red leather sofa with an old Nokia phone in his hand.

'Hi,' I said.

'Hi,' he mimicked, putting on a fake British accent.

'Would I be able to get you to call me a taxi for tomorrow?' I asked, struggling not to shudder. His eyes were perusing my body like he was at an all-you-can-violate buffet.

He sat up and exhaled a phlegmy sigh. 'You're leaving Kiev?'

'I am,' I said. 'It's time for something new.' *New foods*, I reminded myself, and my stomach cartwheeled.

'I can call for you,' he said. 'Why don't you sit next to me while I do it?'

'I need it for five-thirty a.m.,' I said. 'And I'm going to the airport.'

I perched on the edge of the sofa and watched him mutter down the phone in Ukrainian. His lip movements caused a small drop of spittle to abseil from his bottom lip. It dangled for a few seconds before plummeting to his crotch with a splat.

'It is done,' he said, turning back to face me.

I awoke before my alarm. The dimmed screen of my laptop told me it was 4.45 a.m. – after showering with my phone in Dubrovnik, I'd had to rely on my laptop to wake me up. The night before, I'd downloaded an alarm clock app and set it for 5 a.m. Then, I'd plugged in my laptop charger, turned up the volume, disabled sleep mode, darkened the screen and placed it beside my pillow. It was inelegant but until I accidentally threw my laptop out of my bed mid-dream, it worked.

I got out of bed, pulling on the clothes I'd left folded on the floor the night before. Beside me lay my backpack and daypack, both zipped up and ready to go. I slid my laptop into my daypack, my pyjamas in my backpack and padded outside to wait for the taxi. Easy. Out of respect for my dormmates, I'd learned to always pack the night before. There was nothing more maddening than the rustle of plastic bags at 4 a.m.

Despite the successes of the morning, I couldn't shake the feeling of uneasiness. I wouldn't have been surprised if Gropey's phone call to the taxi company had really been to a friend, arranging for them to pick me up and deliver me to a dungeon. I'd live out the rest of my days as a sex slave, making friends with rats and talking to whips, existing solely on cheese sandwiches and the flakes from Gropey's eyebrows. I wouldn't complain about the sandwiches.

A tingling sensation crept up the back of my neck and I spun around, but nobody was there. The streets were empty, quiet, and nothing had changed.

I'd read over and over about how one of the most important things a solo female traveller could do is listen to their instincts. How could I, though, when mine always told me I was going to die? Intuition was a thing for me to ignore. If I paid attention to it, I'd never leave the house. At that moment, it felt like every part of me was screaming I was moments from death.

I pulled out my laptop and checked the time: 6 a.m. The taxi was half an hour late. I stopped pacing and sat down by the side of the road, wrapping my arms around my knees and rocking to keep myself calm.

When 6.15 a.m. arrived, I was still swaying. Throwing up my arms in defeat, I picked up my bags and walked to the nearest main road to try to flag down a taxi. Trucks and buses and beaten-up cars from the 1980s whizzed past while I wobbled next to them with my arm outstretched. My waist straps were digging into my sides and the breeze kept puffing my hair into my eyes.

It was 6.30 a.m. when I realised I was in danger of missing my flight. I flashed back to a month ago and my traumatising journey to Dubrovnik. *Was this really happening again?* I silenced the voice in my head that told me the plane was going to crash and it was my destiny not to get on it.

'Never trust your instincts,' I whispered, turning on my heel and running back to the hostel. I needed Gropey.

I threw my bags by reception and thundered down the corridor. *Gropey's room… Gropey's room… which room was Gropey's?* None of the rooms had any kind of sign outside. *Did he even sleep in the hostel?* With only my dignity to lose, I pushed on the door of the closest room.

Once inside, I snuck towards the centre, scrutinising the bunk beds and their snoring contents. Even in my sleep-deprived state, I knew Gropey wouldn't be staying in a dorm. I slinked back out and allowed myself to breathe, taking deep, diaphragm-stretching gasps.

I entered the next room. 'Do you work at the hostel?' I whispered.

'Fuck off,' someone mumbled. I quickly flicked the light on and off to check it wasn't him.

'Fuck *off*,' he repeated.

Gropey's room was the last I checked and I recognised his twitching eyebrows that were poking over the sheets. I crept inside and then with no better ideas coming to me, slammed the door behind me. He let out a long and shuddering snore.

'Hi?' I said, marching on the spot to try to stamp him awake. He snuffled. I cleared my throat and tried again. 'Hi? Excuse me? My taxi isn't...' No response. *Damn it.* I really didn't want to have to abandon my passive British roots.

'SORRY!' I bellowed, startling myself. I felt like a lion cub producing its first roar. I tried again. 'SORRY! HELLO! PLEASE WAKE UP! I'M SO SORRY BUT I NEED YOU TO WAKE UP!'

There was a loud groan and Gropey's eyes slid open. 'Lauren,' he murmured, chewing on his bottom lip.

'Sorry! I *know*! I'm so sorry! I didn't mean to wake you. It's just that, well, my taxi didn't arrive and it was meant to be here forty-five minutes ago. I'm going to miss my flight if it doesn't get here soon.'

'The taxi? I did not call... taxi,' he mumbled, eyelids wavering.

'What do you mean?' I spluttered. 'I saw you call a taxi. How could you *not* have called a taxi?'

'I called...' he said.

'What? You did call or you didn't?'

He slipped beneath the bedcovers in response, and I was reminded of all the arguments I'd failed to win, all because I didn't know what to do. I was always the person to roll over and do what I was told; always accepted my fate without question. I wasn't quite sure how to scare someone into doing something for me, but now seemed like the perfect time to try.

'Right,' I said, speaking in an even tone I didn't recognise. 'I have had enough. *Enough!* You need to call me a taxi *right now* or...' I jabbed my finger in his direction while I searched for the right words. 'Or I will be *so* angry with you.'

I rolled my eyes. Even I felt like falling asleep at my feeble attempt at a threat. To my surprise, Gropey nodded and waved me outside. Maybe I was better at this than I'd thought.

Back in the reception, my laptop told me it was 7 a.m. and I was scared I was going to miss my flight. I didn't have time to google what to do in that situation. I slid my laptop back inside my daypack and started to pace up and down the corridor.

After 5 minutes, I was leaning up against Gropey's door, straining my ears to hear. With my heart pounding in my chest, I eased open the door and peered through the crack. The covers were rising and falling as Gropey purred contentedly.

My British sensibilities abandoned me in the corridor and I thundered inside. After scrabbling up on to his bed, I paused. I had no idea what to do.

'Oh, wake up!' I called, bending over and tapping his shoulder.

This time, he was alert within seconds, snatching my wrist and holding it in his fist. He sat up as I fell to my knees beside him, my free hand pulling at his fingers. I raised my eyes to meet his, horrified to see tight slits in their place.

'What are you doing?' I said in a voice that sounded like I hadn't spoken in years.

'Wait.' He lay back in bed and flashed a smile. Then, with his free hand, he peeled back the bedcovers. Time and space lost meaning as I cowered behind his fist. From beneath the covers emerged a very hairy and *very naked* body.

'No!' I shrieked, pulling back. I thrashed my arm in an effort to break free, tugging on his fingers and pushing off his bushy chest.

'Let… go… of… me!'

He loosened his grip and I back-pedalled off the edge of the bed. I lay frozen in a crumpled heap on the floor. *Was instant paralysis a sign you'd broken your back?* Gropey continued to stare at me with a deranged look on his face, his hands moving under the covers like he was making me a birthday balloon animal.

'What are you going to do?' I stammered.

'Whatever you want me to do.' He crawled towards me, stopping when he reached the edge of the bed.

'I want to go home,' I said, sitting up and digging my heels into the floor. 'I just want to leave.'

'I want to celebrate your last day in Kiev,' he said.

'You think this is what I want?' I shot back, keeping my hands pressed into the floor so he couldn't see me tremble.

'Yes.'

'Please,' I begged, growing desperate with every passing second. 'Just call me a taxi. Don't rape me.'

'Silly girl,' he spat, suddenly sitting up and reaching beneath his pillow for his phone. 'I'm not going to rape you.'

As he dialled the number, I scrubbed away my tears. Recalling YouTube videos on how to use body language to gain confidence, I stood up and placed my hands on my hips. I wondered if Gropey thought I was looming.

'Fine,' he said, hanging up. 'It is booked. The taxi will be here in ten minutes. What do you want to do?'

'I want to go,' I said, storming out of his room and slamming the door behind me.

Ten minutes later, I was sat breathless in the taxi, assured by the driver I would make it to the airport in time. In my hand, I clutched a boarding pass for a flight to Shanghai that was growing damp in my fist. A Ukrainian heavy metal song drowned out my panting as I traced the swirling lines embroidered on the seat.

CHAPTER 3

The flight gave me a chance to reflect on my travels so far. My month in Eastern Europe had been a rollercoaster ride full of adventure, joy, mishaps and fear. I had broken through some long-standing barriers, like riding a bus and eating alone – things I knew I should have figured out how to do before I was a teenager – but I still felt like I had hundreds lining up ahead of me. *At what point would I start feeling as if I had some semblance of life experience?* I still had no idea what I was doing.

Now that I was in a brand new continent, though, something felt different. I decided I'd label my Eastern Europe stint as my introduction to travel. It was there where I'd figured out how hostels worked, learned to take buses, faced my fear of eating alone and been sightseeing with my feet firmly on the beaten track. In China, I decided I was going to try to be more like a normal traveller – one who wasn't full of anxiety and fear. I was going to talk to strangers, meet the locals, try the food and no longer resort to taking a taxi to my hostel.

'*Ni hao!*' I sang out to the stern-faced immigration officer. He cocked an eyebrow before taking my passport from my outstretched hand.

I watched him run his eyes over my visa. *Why is he so angry?* I wondered. *And why is he frowning at me? He's not going to throw me in jail is he?*

I'd paid a company in London to arrange my Chinese visa for me, not giving a second thought as to whether it would be legitimate. Now that the immigration officer was glaring daggers at me, I was convinced it was fake.

He pointed to the yellow footprints painted on the floor, and I stepped backwards until my feet were above them. I watched him angle a small camera towards me while I gave my best impression of an innocent person who would have never even thought about buying a fake visa. He held my passport up to my face and compared it with my photo. It was the photo that everyone said made me look like Morticia Addams. I held my breath.

He slammed a stamp against my passport and held it out to me.

'*Xie xie,*' I mumbled, quickly pocketing it before he could change his mind.

I was in. Next step: successfully navigate an unfamiliar public transport system and find my hostel.

I wandered through the arrivals hall to the metro station with my head held high, buzzing with newfound confidence. It was 7 p.m. and the airport was packed.

I bought my ticket for the metro and pushed my way on to the platform, sucking at the suffocating air. It was claustrophobic down here, especially when everyone around me was jostling for space. Announcements rang out in Mandarin and the unfamiliar smell of Chinese food hung in the air.

I heard the rumbling of an approaching train and the frantic pushing of the crowd reversed. Instead of being forced towards the platform edge, I was now being shoved backwards. A knock to the ribs caused the right-hand strap of my backpack to slide down my arm until my bag was hanging sideways from one shoulder. I started to topple over and grabbed on to angry limbs to stay upright.

The doors of the subway train whooshed open and the thousand-strong crowd surged with a united grunt. I tried to take a step backwards but stood on the toe of a small girl who let out a blood-curdling scream.

'I'm so sorry,' I yelled down at her.

She pummelled the back of my thighs with her fists and I lurched into the woman in front. The London Underground this was not.

'So sorry!' I shouted.

I watched in open-mouthed awe as the doors of the train repeatedly banged into the heads of passengers. Parents battled to wrench their children inside and a couple of elderly ladies started whacking people out of the car with their walking sticks. When the doors finally closed, a hundred sweaty faces were squished up against the glass.

I hoisted up my backpack and waddled forwards like a penguin, knocking people to the side so I could fill the spaces they left behind. I was still inching forwards when the next train arrived.

I braced myself. When the doors hissed open, pandemonium resumed. A teenager shoved me from one side and I took a shoulder to the face from another.

'Oi,' I grunted, shouldering them back. I began to perform a kind of breaststroke through the crowd, pushing off bodies as I swam my way forwards.

I stubbed my toe on something cold and metal and tottered the final few inches inside.

'Ah ha!' I grinned, throwing my fists in the air. Or, at least, I would have done if there hadn't been several hundred people pressed into the carriage with me. I couldn't even raise my hands above my waist.

My backpack was hanging at an awkward angle, resting diagonally across my back so that one of the straps was slicing through my shoulder. I winced as the metal frame dug into my left hip bone, and when I tried to shift into a more comfortable position, I discovered my backpack was jammed between too many people. We were packed so tightly in this claustrophobic carriage that I couldn't even move to take it off. I glanced at the map above the doors and counted 21 stops. Piece of cake.

By the time we reached the station, I was convinced I was dying. For 90 minutes, I had stood in a train-sized coffin while my backpack had slowly sanded away the skin from my shoulders.

With a final burst of energy, I fought my way on to the platform and immediately let my bags fall to my feet. Rather than waiting for the platform to empty, I lay down on the ground beside my backpack. Letting out a moan, I spread my limbs like I was making a dust-and-grime angel.

I rolled on to my side and searched through my daypack for my camera. Before leaving Kiev, I'd taken a photo of the hostel directions on their website. It was a 10-minute walk away. I picked myself up and dragged my bags along the station floor.

'*Ni hao*,' I called to a man in uniform stood a few metres away from me. 'I'm looking for exit seven?'

He shook his head. 'No.'

'What?'

'No seven.'

'But my directions say to take exit seven,' I said, holding out my camera. 'What am I supposed to do?'

Without saying a word, he turned and walked away.

I froze to the spot, squinting at my camera screen. *What was I supposed to do?* With no ideas coming to me, I chose exit six and pulled my bags to the steps outside. My directions were now useless. It was 9 p.m. and the pavement was glistening from the rain. I eased my backpack over my blistered shoulders, all the while cursing myself for thinking this journey would be easy. My legs were on the verge of collapse, but at least I'd be at the hostel soon. All I had to do was find a taxi.

Three hours later, I gave up on finding one. I'd stopped feeling pain about an hour ago, grateful for my abundant adrenaline reserves that had numbed my bloody shoulders and aching back. It had been raining non-stop and my hair was plastered to my face. I'd approached several dozen people by now, but none of them had even heard of the hostel. I'd walked in circles for hours, and even tried searching for a different hostel, or even a luxury hotel – anything to prevent me from sleeping in someone's doorway. It was midnight in Shanghai and I had no idea where I was.

As I traipsed back and forth in front of flickering living rooms lit by television screens, I couldn't shake my homesickness. I wondered what my family were doing. If my mum could see the state of me right now, she'd be ordering me to turn around and head straight back to the airport.

I don't know why I felt an urge to follow an unkempt-looking man down a series of alleyways. He looked like a backpacker, I guess, with his tangled dreadlocks and baggy fisherman pants.

I limped across the still road in swaying pursuit of the man, following him down a quiet street and through a small park. He disappeared through a gate up ahead and I quickened my steps, my fingers crossed by my side.

'Oh my God,' I breathed when I saw the sign for the hostel. 'I've found it. I've finally found it.'

I hobbled up the path and pushed through the door, overcome with a sudden burst of energy.

'Your directions are wrong!' I announced, staggering inside. 'It says to take exit seven but there isn't an exit seven! It's taken me three hours to find you. *In the rain.*'

'Oh,' the receptionist said, not looking up from her computer. 'I am sorry about that. Do you have your passport?' I handed it over, too exhausted to argue.

She pressed a key into my palm and I hobbled down the narrow red corridor that was lined with blue doors. The smell of fried chicken filled the air and my rumbling stomach reminded me I hadn't eaten in 24 hours. On the walls were signs advertising tours to Tibet and warnings about scammers in the area. I reached my door and bared my bottom row of teeth: it was the closest to a smile I could manage.

After unlocking the door, I crept inside and clambered into a spare bed. I didn't even have the energy to brush my teeth or change out of my wet clothes.

The next day, I awoke to a cacophony of horns. Fragrances of unknown spices floated through the window, turning my stomach when I realised I'd have to eat Chinese food today. I wasn't even sure what Chinese food *was*. I checked the time and gasped: it was 6 p.m.; I had managed to sleep for something like 17 hours.

I slipped out of bed and busied myself with rummaging through my backpack for a clean outfit; I didn't want to waste a moment more in bed. *I was in Shanghai*, I reminded myself and my heart beat faster. Not even jetlag could keep me from exploring.

'You're finally awake,' a girl's voice called out from the bunk above mine.

'I know,' I groaned, craning my neck to grin at her. 'I don't know how it happened; I've never done anything like that before.'

'Aww, you must be tired,' she said, clambering down the ladder to sit with me. 'I'm Bula. Where have you come from?'

'Ukraine.'

'Wow,' she exclaimed. 'That's unusual. I was expecting you to say somewhere like Vietnam.'

I wish, I thought to myself. Southeast Asia was the region I was most excited about visiting.

'Fancy grabbing dinner with me?' Bula asked, and I eagerly agreed.

The restaurant was stark and white, with steel furniture, and teenaged locals grabbing dinner while taking selfies on their phones. I'd been quiet on the walk over here, psyching myself up to tackle Chinese food for the first time. It didn't help that Bula intimidated me. She was a Canadian–Pakistani girl with bags of confidence and several years' worth of travel experience.

This time around, she'd been travelling for a similar amount of time to me, but had spent most of it in South Korea. Against the odds, she'd met a guy in her hostel on the first day of her trip and they'd quickly fallen into a relationship. It wasn't what she was expecting or hoping for, she told me, and she wasn't sure how it would change her travels, especially as he'd be living in South Korea for the foreseeable future.

A plump elderly lady rushed to our table and handed us some menus. I ran my eyes down the page, widening them when I realised there was nothing in English. The entire menu aside from the word 'beer' was in Mandarin.

'So, what sort of thing do you feel like?' Bula asked me.

I froze. *What could I say?* So far I had done a pretty good job of hiding my lack of life experience but this was going to give me away. I glanced around the room to see if there was something I recognised – a pizza, a burger, or anything I wasn't afraid of.

'Lauren…?' Bula waved her hand in front of my face. 'What sort of food do you like?'

'I, um…' I started, racking my brains for a way to come out of this situation without sounding like a freak. 'I think I'll just have what you have?'

'You'll… have what I have?'

'Yep.' I turned bright red. 'I'm not picky.'

Bula ordered something called ramen, which I'd never heard of before, and a couple of beers. I just hoped it wasn't going to be spicy. I gave her a nervous smile and continued to stare at the table.

Our food arrived. It was a steaming bowl of what looked like noodles in a brown broth. There was an egg floating in the middle of it and several chunks of dark brown meat. I inhaled for 5 seconds and exhaled for 7. Then, I picked up my chopsticks. I had no idea what to do with them.

'So what are your travel plans?' I asked Bula, dipping my chopsticks in my soup and then letting them rest there.

'I'll probably head back to South Korea for a while,' she told me. 'And then Southeast Asia. Three months in India and then maybe three months in the Middle East. Something like that.'

I opened my mouth to tell her about my original plan to visit India and then closed it again. She'd ask me why I wasn't going now and I'd have to tell her it was because it scared me. Bula didn't seem scared of anything.

I picked up my chopsticks – one in each hand – and started fishing for noodles, making scissor-like movements. Somehow, I managed to hook some between the two utensils and gingerly raised them up to my mouth.

It was then that I noticed half of the restaurant was staring at me. This was not, apparently, an alternative way to use chopsticks.

'Lauren,' Bula said, staring at me incredulously. 'What the hell are you doing¿'

I dropped my chopsticks back in the bowl and looked her straight in the eyes. 'So, confession,' I said. 'I've never eaten Asian food before.' I reached for my glass of beer and took a gulp.

'You…¿'

'I know. This is my first time and I'm terrified. I have no idea what I'm doing.'

'Lauren,' she repeated.

I had a feeling she'd think I was less strange if I had dropped my face into the bowl and started slurping the soup through a straw.

For some reason, my inexperience with food excited Bula and I was astonished when she didn't suddenly come up with a reason to leave. Instead, she explained what ramen was and patiently taught me how to use chopsticks. Within the hour, I was slurping down the last of my noodles and high fiving Bula over my achievement.

That night, I lay in bed with my laptop on my stomach and waited for the room to stop spinning. I'd had three small glasses of beer with Bula that night – my new record – and I was distracting myself by drunk tweeting.

Something on Twitter caught my eye: a sarcastic response to my poorly worded tweet and a wink. It was from a guy called Dave, a travel blogger I'd been chatting to every so often for the past five months. He was from New Zealand, had been travelling on and off for the past 15 years and was always teasing me. He was also drop-dead gorgeous. With alcohol coursing through my veins, I giggled at his tweet and sent him a direct message.

'Hi!' I typed. 'I would like to know how old you are.'

His reply came within minutes. 'I would like to know lots of things…' he typed. My heart beat faster. *Was he flirting with me?*

'Mysterious,' I wrote, and my stomach started tumbling. Maybe this wasn't such a good idea. I was terrible at flirting. 'What would you like to know?'

'I suspect I'm far too drunk to be having this conversation.'

I grinned. 'I'm drunk, too!'

'So why do you want to know how old I am?'

'Because I'm inquisitive.'

'I'm barely a day over 74. I think I hide it well.'

'I'm not sure I believe you. Stop being so enigmatic.'

'I turned 36 last month.'

I stared at the screen, racking my brain for a suitable response. I'd always found myself attracted to older men once I'd discovered I had so much more in common with them than guys my own age. I was a strict classic rock kind of girl who rarely listened to anything recorded outside of the 1960s and 70s, and I wasn't one for staying out late and partying. I'd dated plenty of guys my own age, but always struggled to connect with them, especially the ones who collected Lego and owned *The Simpsons* underwear. As I typed and deleted and retyped a dozen responses, the room spun faster and I decided to take a chance.

With trembling hands, I typed, 'Dateable.'

'Totally.'

I sat up in bed and stared into the darkness, trying to think straight. I wasn't sure what I was trying to achieve with this conversation. I'd decided months ago that this trip wasn't going to be about meeting cute guys. It was going to be about me learning to be happy with myself.

'So when do you get to Thailand…?' Dave typed, and my heart began to race.

'Not sure,' I replied. 'I have four days in Shanghai and then five in Beijing. I'm going to Xi'an for another five days, and then I'll be heading to Southern China for 18 days. After that, 13 days circling South Korea. Then 5 days in Hong Kong.'

'Wow. Have you booked all that already?'

'Everything up until Xi'an.'

'Can I make a suggestion?'

'You can.'

'Fuck the route. That's way too fast to be travelling, and not having fixed plans is fun. Why don't you try not booking anything after you arrive in Xi'an?'

I frowned for a moment, indignant that he was trying to tell me my way of travel was wrong, but if I was being honest with myself, I was exhausted. I'd been powering my way across Eastern Europe and was craving spending more than a few nights in a place.

'Okay,' I typed hesitantly, unsure whether to listen to him or not. 'I'll try that. I guess it'll be fun to see where I end up.'

'Great,' he replied. 'And I'm going to bed. Talk soon?'

'Of course. When we're less drunk.'

'Something like that.'

A spark of electricity shot through my nerve endings as I closed the lid of my laptop and lay back down in bed. I had no idea if our conversation had simply been harmless banter, or whether it had been something more. All I knew was that I was tired, confused, exhilarated and scared.

The following morning, I found myself in the heart of Shanghai, on the city's biggest shopping street: Nanjing Road. I'd expected to be frozen with culture shock in China, but Shanghai didn't feel anywhere near as foreign as I'd expected. In fact, it reminded me of London.

'You wan' jewellery?' a tout called out to me.

'No thank you,' I said.

'Karaoke?' another tout shouted.

'No thank you.'

'Buy watch?'

'No thank you.'

I knew then that Nanjing Road was not where I wanted to be. It was full of glassy skyscrapers and glossy shops, like every major shopping street I'd ever been to. I was looking for something more authentic. I reached up and slapped myself across the face for using such a tired and meaningless travel cliché.

A tout ran up to me and tried to snap flashing wheels on to the bottom of my shoes. *Why were they targeting me?* I wondered. They seemed able to detect my naivety from a mile away.

I spotted a bench beside a park up ahead and hurried towards it. I'd only been outside for an hour and was already feeling sore. I suspected it would take weeks for my muscles to recover from the other night's hardship.

'Excuse me!' A squeaky voice interrupted my self-pity. 'Can we take a photo with you?'

I looked up and saw two Chinese girls smiling down at me. They were around 18 years old, with identical silky black hair and tiny frames.

'Sure,' I said. 'I guess?'

They cheered and one of them pulled me to my feet while the other held out her camera. I wondered what they were going to do with a photo of a foreigner who was more hair than human.

'We are students and we are from Beijing,' said the girl who took the photo. She held her camera up to her face and examined the photo. 'We are spending the weekend visiting Shanghai and then we will go back to school on Monday. How long are you here for?' Her words were rapid and disjointed, making it sound as if she was reading from a script.

'I'll be in China for just over a month,' I said.

'So great!' she gushed. 'And how long in Shanghai?'

'Four days.'

'What is your name?'

'Lauren. What's yours?'

'Ah, pretty name!' she exclaimed. 'My name is Veronica. That's my English name. My friend is called Tiffany. She doesn't talk much.'

'You are so beautiful,' Tiffany said, squinting at me through her glasses. She reached up and tugged on my face. 'I love your big nose,' she shrieked as the pair dissolved into laughter.

My big nose? I reached up and rubbed it, which caused them to laugh even harder. I joined in with them this time, bewildered by these two friendly strangers. I gestured for them to sit with me on the bench. This was shaping up to be a far better day than I'd expected.

'Are you married?' Veronica asked.

'No,' I said with a laugh. 'I don't even have a boyfriend.'

Her face grew serious. 'You look old. You must marry soon or you will not find anyone. You will be alone.'

'You will be alone,' Tiffany echoed.

'I have three boyfriends,' Veronica told us. 'I will choose which one to marry soon.'

'I will get married at twenty-one years old,' Tiffany said.

'Well,' I said. 'I'm not quite ready for marriage yet. That's why I'm travelling. I'm trying to grow happy with being by myself before I start looking for a boyfriend. I have plenty of time.'

The girls didn't look convinced and their concern had me replaying my conversation with Dave from the previous night. I'd awoken that morning, convinced I'd never hear from him again, but instead found a message from him wishing me a fun day of exploring. I shook my head and reminded myself that this was the last thing I needed right now.

'I have a question,' Veronica said, after half an hour of talking about anything that wasn't marriage. 'It is our final day in Shanghai and we are going to go to a traditional Chinese tea ceremony. Today is a big tea festival in China, where we celebrate by trying many famous teas. Would you like to come?'

'Absolutely,' I said, overjoyed at the prospect of experiencing traditional Chinese culture with a pair of friendly locals. 'I'd love to.'

I followed as they led me through a series of dimly lit alleyways with crumbling buildings on either side. I barely even noticed the flashing lights and determined shoppers fading away as we ventured further away from the shopping district.

'We're here,' Veronica said, striding inside what looked to be an abandoned shopping mall. Shutters were pulled down over every storefront and there was nobody in sight. Tiffany and I followed her up an escalator and towards a nondescript store. Inside, I could see a burgundy entrance room lit by harsh fluorescent light.

'This is it?' I asked, failing to mask my surprise. I'd always expected Chinese tearooms to look so grand, but this building looked like an abandoned old people's home.

'This is where the locals go. The other tearooms are for tourists and they are expensive. This place is good. Very cheap.'

'That makes sense,' I said.

A stern woman greeted us from behind the reception desk. She wore her grey hair in a tight bun and smiled warmly when she saw me. She ushered us into a gloomy room, where our host was waiting for us. She was wearing a beautiful green and yellow silk robe, and her red fingernails looked like talons. The room was bare apart from a low wooden table and a few stools. Peeling wallpaper was adorned with Chinese symbols and landscapes. I sat down and wrapped the strap of my handbag around my ankle.

Veronica turned to me. 'The host can only speak Chinese but I will translate for you. I hope you do not mind my Chinglish.'

Tiffany burst out laughing.

We were handed a laminated menu with a list of items written in Mandarin. I turned to Veronica. 'Well, despite being British, I don't really know anything about tea. Do you want to choose?'

'Yes please, thank you. The tea sampler is very good. It is six cups of tea. It is the best teas in the teahouse.'

'Perfect,' I said, flashing a wide grin. This was exactly what I'd hoped for when I'd left London but believed I was too shy to accomplish. I was thrilled to be gaining a local's insight into traditional Chinese culture.

The host handed me a tiny cup containing no more than a mouthful of tea and I took a sip of the fruity liquid, enjoying the warmth that slipped down my throat and into my chest.

'It's good,' I said, licking my lips.

'It's *very* good,' Veronica corrected me. She held true to her promise and began to offload information about the teas in a robotic manner, translating the host's words for me. She spoke quickly and in fragmented phrases, as if she knew how to pronounce all the words but wasn't sure how to structure a sentence.

After we finished the final tea, Veronica let out a squeal. 'Money toad!' The host fumbled under the desk and brought out a small metal toad with colourful beads on its back and a coin resting in its mouth.

'This is my favourite part,' Veronica told me. 'We splash our tea over the toad and rub the coin and also its back. The more that you stroke, the better fortune you will have with your money. Watch.'

She threw a full cup of tea over the toad and began to fondle it. I sat transfixed as she quickly stroked back and forth, running her fingers over its back. Her eyes rolled into her head as she flicked the coin in its mouth. 'Look,' she croaked. 'Look how much money I am going to make.' She swung her head back and cackled while the host observed in silence.

'Money!' Tiffany suddenly burst out, rubbing her hands together.

'You're next,' Veronica shrieked, poking me in the ribs.

I turned to the toad and cringed. *Dear toad. I am so sorry for what I'm about to do.* The host handed me a cup of tea and I drizzled a few drops over its back.

'More!' Veronica cried. 'More!'

With all the reluctance of a person who'd been told to pleasure a helpless pond animal, I dumped the rest of my tea on the toad. Veronica and Tiffany gave each other high fives.

'Rub please!' Tiffany sang out and I dutifully began to massage the toad. In an effort to distract the girls from my burning cheeks, I concentrated all of my energy on showing the toad a good time. When I was finished, I patted it on the head. *Sorry, toad.*

The host gave a curt nod and left the room.

Veronica gestured to the row of teas on the table. 'This second tea was my favourite tea,' she said. 'What was yours?'

'I liked the chamomile,' I replied.

'You should take some home. It is five hundred yuan. Very cheap.'

'It's a bit too expensive for me,' I said. 'But thanks.' Fifty pounds for a bag of tea was extortionate. They chose two bags each.

The door swung open and the host re-entered the room. She sat down and pulled out a calculator, and began tapping out a few numbers before writing the price on a piece of paper. She slid it across the table to us, and my throat immediately tightened. My share of the price – including the gifts for their families – was 750 yuan. I was going to be paying £75 for six mouthfuls of tea and a grope of a toad.

I suddenly remembered the posters I had seen pinned up around my hostel. That morning, I had breezed past them, barely noticing their warnings of well-spoken Chinese students and something about a scam involving a tea ceremony.

Shit.

My heart sank. *How could I have been so stupid? Of course they'd been scamming me. Why else would two people have shown such interest in becoming friends with a complete stranger?* I'd been rejecting the touts all morning, wondering how on earth they ever succeeded with such transparent tactics, but it turned out all it took was someone investing 30 minutes of their time to chat to me.

'Okay,' I said in a voice far steadier than the torrent of emotions racing through my veins. 'Why am I being charged for the gifts for your family? I'm not going to—'

'It is tradition,' Veronica interrupted. 'In China, we always split the bill equally. This is what friends do. Are you not our friend?'

'I thought you were our friend,' Tiffany said, narrowing her eyes. Together, they stared me down as if they could tell I hated saying no. For a moment, I considered backing down and taking the easy way out.

'I—Sure,' I began to stammer. 'I'm your friend. But I won't pay for your presents. I'm sorry.' I grimaced as the apology slipped out.

Tiffany looked at the host. 'Recalculation, please,' she said in a cold voice.

The host tapped a few buttons on the calculator and handed me a piece of paper with 500 yuan written on it: a week's worth of accommodation in China. *I've just lost a week of travel.* I realised, overcome with grief.

There was nothing I could do. With a defeated sigh, I handed over the money.

'I have to pay by credit card,' Veronica said. 'So I will go with the host.'

I had a sneaking suspicion she was about to receive her share of my money. The anger I'd been consumed by earlier was replaced with sadness and I couldn't even work up the energy to confront her. I felt like crying.

Tiffany waved a leaflet above her head. 'Excuse me,' she squeaked as if I were a teacher. 'This is a ticket for an acrobatic show. Would you like to buy it from me? We can go together.'

I stared at her in disbelief. *Was she trying to scam me for a second time?* I shook my head, wondering if my bad luck would ever end.

'I have a present for you,' Veronica announced when she returned. She held out a bright yellow tassel and dangled it in front of my face. Seizing my bag from my grasps, she threw it on the table and attached it to the straps. 'This is a lucky charm in China,' she announced, taking a step back and admiring her work. 'It will bring good fortune to your life. I am sorry we asked you to pay for our tea. I hope this makes us friends again.'

I forced a smile and gave a nod, keeping my eyes on my bag. I was furious with myself for letting them think it was okay. I wanted to tell Veronica and Tiffany they were disgusting people for taking advantage of innocent tourists, but I hated confrontation.

We left the teahouse and they began to lead me through a different set of alleyways. I wanted to scream, run, pull their hair, punch a wall, but I settled for doing nothing. Betrayed wasn't a strong enough word for how I felt.

I blinked at the bright lights and commotion. We were back on Nanjing Road and surrounded by tourists and shops; scammers and businessmen.

'Follow us,' Veronica said. 'I will take you to the park where we met.'

I wondered why they were still hanging around, then I reminded myself I was letting them. *One day, I'm going to learn to stand up for myself.*

I felt a tug on my left shoulder and stopped in my tracks. I turned around to free it from whatever it had snagged on, but Veronica stood directly behind me, blocking my line of sight.

'What are you doing?' I asked. I tried to shift her to one side so I could free my bag but her arms kept getting in the way. *Why was she making this so difficult?* 'Get out of my way!' I snapped, losing my temper and slapping at her wrists. I pushed her away from me and she pulled me back towards her.

I suddenly realised what was happening. My eyes worked their way down, from her cold eyes to her sneering lips; from her outstretched arm to her hands. One of them was wrapped around the lucky charm she'd given me as a present; the other was halfway out of my bag, gripping on to my purse. My eyes met hers again. She flashed a guilty smile.

A sudden rush of fury caught me by surprise. I'd had a nasty temper as a teenager and struggled for years to control the unfamiliar hormones that raged within me. At my lowest point, I'd ripped my curtain rail from the wall and kicked a door from its hinges, infuriated by the injustice of my parents telling me I had to do my homework.

This was different. I was justifiably livid. This girl had befriended me. She'd tricked me into believing that she wanted to get to know me at a time when it felt like no one else did. She'd scammed me out of a week's worth of accommodation when all I'd wanted was a cultural experience. She'd given me a present with the promise it'd bring good fortune but was using it to steal my purse. I lost it.

With all the wrath of fourteen-year-old Lauren, I pulled back my hand and flung it forward, hitting her square in the jaw.

CHAPTER 4

'Bloody hell, Lauren. I can't believe you hit her!'

A month had passed since I'd thrown my first punch, and I was sat in a stranger's apartment in Hong Kong. I giggled into my can of beer, shaking off my irrational fear that it was spiked with something. When I'd sent out a tweet two days earlier about struggling to find accommodation in Hong Kong, I'd had no idea that a response from a pretty girl would lead to an invitation to crash at her place. But here I was, sat on the floor of her living room and getting drunker by the minute.

Her name was Ally; originally from France, lived in England, travelled through Southeast Asia and was now studying in Hong Kong. She had long, wavy brown hair, a sexy accent and dozens of envy-inducing tales of partying around Southeast Asia. Talking to her made me feel like an amateur. I'd been travelling for three months by this point and the only interesting stories I had were seeing a hostel owner's penis and punching a girl in the face.

I let out an embarrassed groan, flashing back to the horrified look across Veronica's face. 'I still feel guilty about it,' I told Ally. 'I'm not usually so reckless.' It was seconds after throwing my fist at her jaw that I realised what a colossal mistake I'd made. Punching a local in broad daylight on one of China's busiest streets? I was lucky not to have been arrested.

'Nothing to feel guilty about,' Ally insisted, shaking her head. 'And anyway, I think you're like this secret badass. You come across as being all quiet and polite, but I can tell you've got a definite dark side to you.'

'A badass?' I snorted. 'A dark side? Come on. You're crazy.' I held my hand up to the light and examined my knuckles. They'd been sore for weeks. Not only had Veronica thrown her head back and started laughing once she recovered from the shock, but I'd ended up bent over double, clutching my purse with what felt like a broken hand. I couldn't even manage to punch someone without hurting myself.

'It's always the quiet ones,' she warned, taking a sip of her beer.

'A badass would have been able to handle China, though,' I protested, 'I just gave up and ran away.'

From start to finish, my time in China had been a disaster. The optimism I'd felt after arriving in Shanghai had quickly faded as I'd attracted one disaster after another: standing in the pouring rain for an hour trying to flag down a taxi, having the driver drop me off in the middle of nowhere, suffering from food poisoning, seeing children crapping on the streets, being approached by scammers everywhere I went. Each new city had led to tougher challenges while I'd just struggled to remember what a comfort zone felt like.

The toughest part had been the food. After trying the noodle soup in Shanghai, I'd been knocked down with agonising stomach cramps for several days, and after such a traumatising first experience, I'd resorted to eating junk food from the local grocery stores for the rest of my time there. I'd told myself that things would be different in China; that I'd start throwing myself into travel and shunning my anxiety. As it turned out, it was a lot harder than I'd expected.

After our drunken conversation in Shanghai, Dave turned out to be one of my biggest cheerleaders. We'd been messaging each other practically every day over the past month and I was starting to really like him. He was currently busy packing up his life for a move to Thailand but still managed to take a few hours out of his days to have a chat and check that I was doing okay.

I'd been certain Beijing would be different. I'd managed to convince myself that Shanghai hadn't worked out for a reason. It was a big shiny city that reminded me of London and I wasn't travelling to feel like I was at home.

To my surprise, Beijing had reminded me of home in a different way: it had been cold. Temperatures in Eastern Europe had rarely dropped below 40°C so arriving in Beijing had been a shock. It had reminded me of a crisp spring morning in England, but with thick clouds of pollution rather than bright blue skies.

On my first day, I'd shivered as I climbed from the bowels of the subway and into a scene I'd seen a thousand times before. Tiananmen Square stretched out before me, lined with fluttering Chinese flags and guards with guns in khaki uniforms. I'd stood and watched, overcome with emotion. I'd wanted to savour that moment forever and commit to memory how it felt to achieve a travel dream. An impatient local had then shoved me from behind and I'd fallen to the ground, scratching my camera lens against the pavement. That moment summarised my time in China: moments of wonder that were ruined soon afterwards.

I had a good feeling about Hong Kong. Ally was the kind of traveller I'd always hoped I would be – fun, savvy and free of worries. She ate the local food, she wasn't anxious, and she had dozens of travel tales about wild adventures and tight friendships. I'd foolishly managed to convince myself that all I had to do was get on a plane and I'd be just like her. I'd be Lauren 2.0. Drinking, dancing, partying, no panic attacks, living in the moment. But here I was, still waiting for the transformation to start. Lauren 1.0 wasn't even out of beta yet; Lauren 1.0 was still waiting for someone else to fix her bugs.

A shrill alarm jolted me awake.

Beeeep! Beeeep!

I stared into the darkness with terrified eyes, wondering if this was an early warning alarm for a nuclear bomb.

Beeeep! Beeeep!

I wriggled on the vinyl sofa, unpeeling my sweaty skin from its surface.

Beeeep! Beeeep!

'A nuclear attack!' I whispered.

I yanked my blanket over my head and ran over my contingency plan for unexpected warfare. I had a box of saltine crackers at the bottom of my backpack, carried all the way from London for a rationing situation like this. I remembered reading something about having a shower to wash the radioactivity from your body, and getting in a car to drive as far away from ground zero as you could get. *Damn it, I had already been coated in radiation at Chernobyl. I was more vulnerable than everyone else.*

I squeezed my eyes shut and tried to recall where I was. I needed to get my hands on a car. *I'm in Shanghai! I'm in that dorm with the lesbian couple that kept sneaking into the same bed once they thought I was asleep. Oh no, I left Shanghai already. Beijing? No, I left there and went to... Xi'an! I must be in Xi'an with the Japanese guy who doesn't speak a word of English, but spent 3 hours trying to understand where I was from. No wait; I left Xi'an, didn't I?*

'Lauren!' Ally's voice interrupted my meltdown and she wrenched the blanket from my fists. 'What are you doing under there? It sounded like you were performing some kind of ancient ritual.'

'Ally,' I breathed. 'I'm in Hong Kong!'

'Yeah?'

I paused, wondering why her apartment was so silent. 'Why's the beeping stopped? Is it over?'

'Is what over? And what beeping? Are you talking about my alarm?'

'Ohhhh,' I groaned. *'It was your alarm!'*

'What did you think it was?' she asked, walking over to her mirror. She had a towel wrapped around her chest and her wet hair was dripping on the floor.

I hesitated for a moment before shrugging. 'A nuclear bomb,' I said, trying to downplay my tendency to always assume I was moments from death.

'A nuclear bomb,' she repeated, spinning around to frown at me. 'How do you even...?'

I started to laugh. 'I don't know. Can I blame it on my anxiety?'

'How long have you been travelling again?' she asked.

'Two months.'

'Two months and still anxious.'

'Less anxious,' I corrected her. 'You should have seen me before I left. I'd have thrown on my favourite hazmat suit by now.' I was only half-joking. Over the years, I'd found myself on websites selling survival kits for nuclear warfare more times than I was willing to admit. And while I had yet to have a panic attack after that day in Eastern Europe, I was still struggling to convince my brain to follow more logical thought patterns.

Ally's jaw dropped. 'Your... favourite...'

'I'm joking,' I said in an unconvincing tone.

'Well, even with the anxiety, I think you're pretty damn lucky. I'd love to travel like you are. Even if it meant sounding like a lunatic whenever I woke up in the morning.' She wandered into the bathroom, chuckling at her own joke.

As I watched Ally race around the apartment at 7 a.m., it struck me that I hadn't had to wake up at a set time for months now. It had been so easy to focus on all the things that were going wrong in China that I had forgotten to appreciate the positives. I had all the freedom in the world and now was the time to start appreciating it.

In the golden morning glow, Hong Kong had little in common with Mainland China and I warmed to the locals immediately. They were quiet and polite, moving out of the way when I passed rather than sticking an elbow to my ribs. People smiled when I made eye contact and nobody offered to take me to a tea ceremony. Unlike Shanghai, where I felt like I was in just another big city, Hong Kong felt different. It was the dizzying skyscrapers that gave me claustrophobia if I stared skyward for too long. It was the horrifying piles of dried shark fins piled up outside Ally's apartment to make controversial shark fin soup (Ally, a diving instructor and staunch believer in saving the oceans above all else, told me that living directly above these scenes helped to keep her focused on her goal to get it banned). It was the bamboo scaffolding that looked on the verge of collapse at any moment.

As I walked past temples, my nose was exposed to the scents of jasmine and incense, and a few steps further I was hit by a pungent wave of stinky tofu, smelling similar to the pair of sweaty gym socks I once left in my school locker for six months. Hong Kong was foreign in a way that was more exciting than terrifying. I felt more alive than I had in months. As I descended down the steps of a nearby subway station, I surprised myself with an all-too-rare thought: *I love travel*.

I'd been all about the planning over the past couple of months, spending a few minutes of every morning researching places to go and things to do. I decided that today was going to be different. Today, I wasn't going to look up anything about Hong Kong. I was going to step outside with no plans and see what I could discover. It felt like the sort of thing Ally would do.

I walked through the station, my pockets containing Ally's key and a handful of Hong Kong dollars; my camera slung over my shoulder. I paused at a map of the subway and ran my fingers over the stops. *Kwai Fong, Fo Tan, Wan Chai, Lai Chi Kok… How was I supposed to know which stop to choose?* I decided to head to *Tung Chung* station because there was a picture of a cable car next to it.

Cable cars, it turned out, were something I could add to my ever-growing list of terrifying activities I shouldn't repeat. From Tung Chung station, I had boarded the Ngong Ping Cable Car, which takes tourists over the ocean to a nearby island. I had been taking occasional peeks through my fingers at the jungle-clad hills and glassy skyscrapers, but the nauseating swaying of the car and crashing ocean waves below had me convinced this was a situation I'd be unlikely to walk away from. *Try something new*, I thought, berating myself. *When has that ever worked out well for me?* I squeezed my eyes shut and clung on for dear life.

'Are you scared, dear?' A shaky American accent pulled me from my terrified trance and I cracked open my eyes in the direction of the voice. The elderly Chinese lady reached over and touched my arm, smiling sympathetically. I winced and gripped the metal bar tighter, convinced her slight movement would cause us to detach from the cable and plummet into the sea below.

'What gave it away?' I said in a high-pitched falsetto.

'Oh, I don't know. Perhaps your white knuckles and you not opening your eyes since you got in here,' she laughed. 'And the fact you sound like a little mouse.'

'Oh,' I said, forcing the tone of my voice to drop to that of a constipated ogre's. I let go of the bar and rested my hands in my lap. 'Better?'

'Much.'

I smiled. 'I've actually never been on a cable car before. I don't know why I thought it was a good idea.'

'Oh, you must keep challenging yourself, dear. Cable cars? They're *nothing*. I've lived here my whole life and no one's ever died on this. It's perfectly safe. It's when you decide to throw yourself off a cliff to chase an adrenaline rush that you really have to worry.'

'I think I'm a long way away from that,' I laughed, a little less anxious. Her compassion was showing me what I'd been missing out on during the first few months of my trip. It wasn't that I'd been actively avoiding these small connections, I'd just been so concerned with keeping myself alive that I hadn't been seeking them out. The backpackers I'd met in hostels always seemed to glorify meeting the locals and, for many, it was seen as a sign that you were a 'real traveller'. I'd lost count of the number of stories I'd heard from people who managed to connect with a local who was living in the depths of poverty, but who offered them everything they had even when what they had was so little. The few experiences I'd had with locals had been limited to guesthouse owners, taxi drivers, and aggressive touts and scammers.

What was I doing wrong? I'd found myself wondering on more than one occasion. Deep inside, though, I knew exactly what I was doing. I was suffering from crippling shyness and hoping that someone else would make the first move. I'd never been great at making friends back home – I had my university friends who, like me, all studied physics, I had my work friends and I had a couple of old school friends I'd known for years – but very few others. Because, when it came to starting a conversation with someone I didn't know, I kept my head down and shied away.

It was why dorms had been a revelation for me. Dorm rooms were fantastic places for meeting people and never did I have to make the first move. They were full of travellers looking to meet other people, and when you're sharing a room with half a dozen of them, it was impossible not make friends. I'd been honing my conversational skills through daily chats with my dormmates, but it was brief moments like these – where a stranger reached out to comfort me during a hair-raising cable-car ride – that showed me I should be trying to leave the backpacker bubble more often.

I stepped off the cable car and on to steady land with a shudder, and squinted into the hazy air. The sun was just starting to break through the clouds, revealing rolling hills and jagged mountain peaks, shrouded in a coating of mist. The weather looked to be celebrating my safe arrival on leafy Lantau Island, which was far greener than I'd imagined anywhere in Hong Kong to be. This was less concrete jungle and more actual jungle – a scene straight out of *Jurassic Park*. Remembering my cable-car companion, I turned to thank her but she'd merged with the crowds.

A sudden surge of tourists led me along a palm-lined pathway to the foot of the Tian Tan Buddha. I paused in front of a sign, noting that I'd need to climb 250 steps to reach it. I swallowed that piece of information with a gulp when I realised I'd forgotten to bring a bottle of water with me. Mirroring the group of senior citizens up ahead, I gripped the handrail and began to haul myself up the steps.

For half an hour, I whimpered and wheezed, leaping vaguely upwards like a frog in a sock. Halfway up, I'd let out an embarrassed laugh when I'd remembered how I used to complain about humidity back in England. *'Oh, it's so humid today,'* I used to groan. *'The air feels so close.'* I rolled my eyes at a younger me, dreading to think how I'd have reacted if I'd decided to head to Hong Kong as my first stop on this trip. I continued to drag myself up the steps, cringing whenever someone 40 years my senior swanned past. This thick and suffocating heat had me feeling as if I was wading through custard.

Reaching the top somehow felt like my biggest achievement to date. I stood breathlessly, wobbling, staring in disbelief as the Buddha towered over me. The chattering of my fellow stair climbers echoed around me and was almost enough to distract me from the pins and needles that were creeping across my face. *This wasn't good.* I searched for something to hold on to as the scene began to swim before my eyes. The sound of laughter drifted further down the tunnel, as bile rose in my throat and my legs buckled beneath me.

I lurched towards a quiet area and lay down on the cool ground. In an attempt to move the blood from my throbbing calves to my equally throbbing temples, I began to jiggle my legs in the air. It was one of the few times in my life where I didn't care about what I looked like or what people were thinking of me. My thoughts grew foggy as the world faded to black.

Two hours later, I shuffled into the lift for Ally's apartment with a paper McDonald's bag in hand, eager for air conditioning and the coldest shower of my life.

I'd regained consciousness a few seconds after fainting, relieved to find nobody had even noticed my episode. Moments later, I'd sat up and hung my head between my knees, focusing on my breathing and waiting for my vision to clear. Still suffering from light-headedness, I'd begun to laugh – anything to stop me crying. I'd been so convinced that flying to Hong Kong was all it would take to turn my troubles around and here I was on my first morning: passed out beside a giant Buddha.

I'd dragged myself to my feet and shuffled in circles around the bronze statue, gaining strength and stability with every step. In a weird way, fainting had given me a burst of confidence. Something terrible had happened to me and within 10 minutes, I'd picked myself back up again and was forcing myself onwards. I didn't even feel like I was anywhere near having a panic attack.

In the lift, I tapped my feet impatiently. I happened to catch a glimpse of myself in the mirror and cocked an eyebrow. The last time I'd checked, I'd been a timid, defeated girl with bad posture and ill-fitting clothes. The woman staring back at me looked taller, stronger and happier. I barely recognised myself.

By anyone else's measurements, today had been a disaster. For me? It felt incredible. I was exhilarated by the realisation I'd flung myself far from my comfort zone but somehow managed to return unscathed.

I searched through my pockets for my key, mentally composing a list of everything I needed to get done that night. I'd gulp down several gallons of water, have an ice-cold shower, spend a couple of hours chatting to Dave and put on more make-up than mascara for the first time in weeks. Ally had mentioned something about going out for drinks and I was determined not to look like a grotty backpacker. I wondered which of my two pairs of shorts would look more glamorous. While I busied myself with planning my outfit, I slid the key in the lock and twisted.

Crack!

'Shit,' I shrieked, my hands flying to my mouth. Something sharp hit me in the face and I squealed even louder. I watched in horror as dozens of metal chips settled around my feet.

'No, no, no, no, no,' I murmured, dropping to my knees and peering into the lock. 'Please don't let this be happening.' I replayed the moment in my mind, certain I hadn't done anything unusual. I prodded at my scrawny arms for a second, trying to understand how I possibly could possess the strength to shatter a key.

I paced back and forth with my hands over my head, trying to figure out what to do. I didn't have a phone so I couldn't call Ally, and I couldn't get inside to google what to do. I paused and rested my head against her door, racked with guilt over how I'd abused Ally's hospitality. *Hey, Ally! Thanks so much for letting me stay with you for free. Oh, by the way, I broke the key to your apartment and now you can't get inside. You're welcome!* I sighed and banged my already dizzy head against the wood. Suddenly, something clicked in my memory.

'The doorman!' I cried out, remembering the frail man Ally had introduced to me the day before.

'Hello?' I called to the doorman as I raced across the lobby. 'I'm staying in room 2004,' I panted. 'Ally's apartment?' He looked up from behind his desk and nodded. 'This is my key. Well, the remains of my key.' I placed the fragments on his desk. 'It's broken,' I said, stating the obvious.

I watched him rub his chin, showing no sign of comprehension. After a few seconds, he shrugged.

'I need a locksmith,' I tried, and he shrugged again.

I mimed putting a key in a lock and turning it as a last resort. I threw my arms in the air and moaned, picking up a shard of the key and waving it in the air. 'Oh no,' I said. 'Look what happened to my key! I am locked out of my apartment!'

He broke into a toothless grin then leant over and put his hand on mine. He took the shard from my palm and ran his finger over it, nodding.

'Can you call a locksmith?' I asked. 'New key?'

He picked up the phone. I held my breath and crossed my fingers behind my back, hoping he wasn't calling the nearest psychiatric ward to have me committed. He muttered down the phone in Cantonese, sounding agitated about something. He began to shout, spittle flying from his mouth as he banged his fist on his desk.

He let out a groan and shook his head in frustration before holding out the phone to me. I gulped hard. I hated talking on the phone at the best of times. If an angry locksmith was about to shout at me in Cantonese, I wasn't sure I'd be able to keep it together.

'Hello?' I said.

'Key?' I could barely make out the man's voice on the other end.

'Yes! I have broken the key to my friend's—'

'Key?'

'Yes! Yes! Key! I need a new key.'

'Key?'

'Yes!' It was becoming clear why the doorman had been so shouty. 'Can you hear me? I need a locksmith.'

'Key!'

'Yes! Can you get me a new key?'

Bzzzzzzzz.

'Oh!' I gasped. 'He hung up!'

The doorman fired off a stream of rapid Cantonese while I stood dumbfounded, clutching the phone as if the locksmith – if he had even been a locksmith – would call back.

'He hung up,' I repeated.

The doorman pointed at me and then the chair beside him. I sat down. He gave me a sympathetic look and offered me a fruit pastille. When I declined, he reached over and rubbed my leg, all while giving me that same sympathetic look. I pushed his hand away and stood back up.

I spent the next hour pacing in the lobby while the doorman eyed me with interest. I wasn't sure what I was expecting to happen but I had nothing else I could do. Either a locksmith would magically appear to save the day or Ally would return home and kick me out of her apartment.

When the door next swayed open, it revealed a man in blue overalls with a silver toolkit in his hand. *Could it be?* I held up a piece of my key, which he promptly ignored, and he walked over to the desk. I sidled over and watched from a few metres away as the two men berated each other. *What was going on?* I wondered, perplexed. *Why was everyone shouting?*

The doorman waved in my direction. I waved back. He pointed at me and then he pointed at the man in overalls.

'Key?' I asked, miming turning one in a lock.

'Key.'

The locksmith worked quickly and quietly while I sat on the floor and watched as he wriggled different sized tools through the keyhole and rattled them around. Every so often he'd let out a sigh and shake the door so hard I was convinced he'd tear it from its hinges. Though I was worried he might be up against an impenetrable door, my shoulders relaxed for the first time since breaking the key. I'd come up against a problem and I was solving it. I was too tired to waste energy on stress.

'Key!' The locksmith's cheer jerked me from my musings and I looked up to see the door wide open.

'You did it!' I cried out, wondering if it would be inappropriate to pull him into a bear hug. 'Thank you! Thank you *so* much!'

I rushed into the kitchen and poured myself a glass of water, my desperate gulps causing me to spill it down my front.

'Key¿' The locksmith held up a new lock as a way of asking the question.

I nodded, wringing out my top. Ally had warned me she only had one key to her apartment.

While he busied himself with replacing the lock, I searched through my daypack for my laptop. As much as I wanted to avoid telling Ally what had happened, and as much as I was contemplating trying to replace her key without her noticing, I knew I had to tell her as soon as possible. I began to draft out an email.

Just like my phobia of phones, I also had a phobia of sending emails. I wrote and rewrote that one paragraph message a dozen times over, analysing every word to try to make it sound like having her apartment broken into by a man who could only say 'key' was an everyday occurrence. Just as I was preparing to press send, I was struck by a horrible realisation. I didn't have any money left.

I cleared my throat and the locksmith looked over. 'How much is this going to cost¿' I asked.

He looked confused.

'Money,' I said.

He nodded and turned to his toolbox. Pulling out a notepad, he scribbled for a few seconds and held it up for me to see.

HK$500.

My stomach dropped, HK$500 – roughly £40. I searched through my pockets and smoothed out what little I did have. I had a hundred dollars to my name, perhaps enough to pay for the wriggling he'd done with his tools.

'Excuse me,' I said, crouching down beside him. 'I need to go to an ATM. Money? I don't have money. Not enough, anyway. Is it okay if I just pop out to an ATM?' He stared at me and I had no idea if he understood. 'Hang on,' I muttered. I stood up and searched through my daypack for my debit card. I held it out to him and mimed putting it into a machine. He nodded.

I hit the streets of Hong Kong the second the sky opened up. It was late afternoon – rush hour for the city's commuters and students – and it was starting to get dark. I stood outside the apartment block being jostled from side to side by impatient people. Their umbrellas provided sporadic shelter from the increasingly powerful droplets. I wrapped my arms around my shoulders, my flimsy strappy top doing little to protect me from the downpour.

'Okay,' I whispered. 'You can do this. Find an ATM and it'll all be okay.'

Hong Kong felt like a different world after sunset. It was a world illuminated by neon signs reaching several stories high. A world that was dizzying and thrilling all at the same time. I began to run.

A minute later, I came to a main road. It was raining heavily now and my top was threatening to fall to my waist at any moment. I crossed my arms over my chest to protect my modesty.

'Yes!' I cheered, spotting an ATM across the street. I dashed into the road and straight into oncoming traffic. Weaving through the cars and scooters was like taking part in a real life game of *Frogger*, and I pretended the blaring horns weren't aimed at me.

I celebrated my survival by throwing both arms in the air and slapping my hands together as a way of giving myself a high five, then thrust my card into the machine. 'Come on,' I murmured, tapping my fingers as it whirred into life. I punched in my PIN and selected HK$500.

Error. The transaction could not be completed.

I pushed my card back in and tried again.

Error. The transaction could not be completed.

'What do you mean, it can't be completed?' I wailed at the screen as if expecting a response. I snatched my card and scowled at the machine for letting me down. Fortunately, there was another ATM within running distance. I hurried towards it, apologising as I ricocheted from person to person.

I trembled as I sheltered beneath the welcoming glow of the second machine, marching on the spot as if I was about to wet myself.

Error. The transaction could not be completed.

My heart pounded against my ribs, threatening to jump out of my chest and abandon me for the next plane out of here. I took my card from the machine and frowned. A sinking feeling settled in my stomach when I realised my bank must have blocked my card. *How was I supposed to pay the locksmith when—*

Shit.

I'd left the locksmith alone in Ally's apartment. I'd left him alone with everything I own in the world; with everything Ally owns. Our laptops, our cameras, our valuables – everything but the clothes on my back and the debit card I held in my hand. I'd just given him the perfect opportunity to steal everything that was important to us.

'What the fuck is wrong with me?' I hissed at myself. 'Fuck my stupid life and my stupid… *Argh*!' With my tears joining the rain in puddles on the pavement, I turned on my heel and ran.

'Is he still here? Tell me he's still here!' I panted as I hurled myself into the lobby. The doorman offered a cheery wave in my direction.

I jabbed the button for the lift and went back to marching on the spot as if that was going to make it arrive any sooner. When it reached the lobby, I leapt inside. The vertigo-inducing ride was nauseating at the best of times but my stomach was somersaulting like never before. Visions of a ransacked apartment raced through my mind as I paced back and forth.

By the time the doors slid open, I was circling the lift like a hysterical vulture. I tripped over my feet in my panic to stop the burglary and flew face first into the apartment.

'Stop!' I squealed, the floor muffling my voice. I was a hysterical vulture with broken wings.

'Hello.'

I looked up and there was the locksmith, sat on Ally's sofa.

'Hello,' I said, still lying on the floor. 'You're here.'

He stared blankly back at me.

I picked myself up and rubbed my head. A quick survey of the room revealed everything was how I left it. *Our laptops? Check! The TV? Check! My Kindle? Ally's hair straighteners? My backpack? Check! Check! Check!* I darted between the rooms, combing the apartment for anything different but it was just how I'd left it. I glanced over my shoulder at the locksmith, still sat on the sofa, and was flooded with guilt and relief. After being scammed in China, I'd been treating everyone I'd met with more suspicion than usual and it turned out this came at a price. I had stopped trusting strangers.

I took a deep breath and walked towards the locksmith, terrified about what would happen next.

'So, I have a confession,' I said, hoping my mascara-stained cheeks would elicit sympathy rather than dread. 'My card doesn't work. I think my bank blocked it or something. So... I can't pay you. I only have a hundred dollars.' I reached into my pocket and held out the crumpled notes.

He looked me dead in the eyes. 'No money?' he asked.

'No money.'

Back in the lobby, the doorman and the locksmith barked at each other in Cantonese as I stood beside them, weighing up the pros and cons of making a run for it before they called the police.

'No money!' the locksmith bellowed, clenching a fist at the doorman.

'No money!' the doorman shouted, balling his palm right back at him.

'I'm so sorry!' I moaned, but neither of them paid me much attention.

I wondered if this was travel karma for punching Veronica. *Maybe they were arguing over who would get to punch me in the face?* I thought. I puffed out my cheeks and pressed my knuckles into them, trying to find an area that wouldn't feel pain. If one of them was going to hit me, I wanted it to be where it would hurt least.

The doorman pointed in my direction, startling me as I attempted to pummel my cheeks numb.

'No money?' he asked.

'No money,' I echoed. 'Well, I have a hundred dollars. I gave it to him.' I pointed at the locksmith. 'But I can't pay five hundred dollars. Well, not yet. I can tomorrow. Or maybe even tonight. I have to call my bank to get my card unblocked.' I wondered when my brain would let my mouth know that neither of them could understand me.

'I pay,' the doorman said.

I paused. 'I'm sorry, what?'

'I pay. You pay me. To…' He stopped and thought for a second. 'To… morrow!' He glowed at his successful pronunciation.

'You're going to *pay* for me?' I asked in disbelief.

I watched him pull out a wallet and take HK$500 from it. He handed them over to the locksmith, who counted them out before giving me back my hundred dollars.

'Thank you so much,' I burbled, overcome with emotion. 'Thank you! Thank you! I'll pay you back tomorrow, I promise!' I decided I would give him an extra hundred dollars as a way of saying thanks – I couldn't bear to think about what would have happened if he hadn't stepped in to save me.

Back in the apartment, I opened my laptop and finally pressed send on my email. It didn't feel quite as daunting as it had an hour ago.

'Lauren, open up,' Ally shouted, battering the door with her fists. I ran to let her in.

'Oh, hey Al—'

'Lauren!' she shrieked, latching on to my wrists. 'What have you done? You *broke* the *key* to my *apartment*?'

'I'm so sorry,' I told her, surprised to see she was so angry. 'I feel like such an idiot. Honestly – I feel terrible.'

'As you should.' She looked furious, staring me down in a way that had me convinced I was about to be kicked out of her apartment.

'And I do. But it's all sorted now so you don't need to worry. We got a locksmith and—'

'*We* got a locksmith?'

'Yeah.' I said, finally managing to untangle myself from her grip. 'Me and the doorman.'

'You and the—wait, what?'

I walked over to the kitchen table. 'Yeah, he called out a locksmith for me. Look – I've got your new key here. And don't worry, I paid for everything, and I can pay for you to get copies made.' Now didn't seem like the best time to tell her I owed her doorman HK$500.

She chewed on her bottom lip, staring at the key in my hand. I held my breath and waited for her next move. *Was she going to tell me to leave? Scream at me for abusing her hospitality? Tell me I'm the worst person in the world?*

'The locksmith was legit, right?' she asked with a concerned look on her face.

'He was legit. He was very professional. And, well,' I started laughing. 'He's a locksmith. He could break into your apartment without needing a key.' *And he had already been left alone with everything you own and taken nothing*, I silently added.

'I guess.' She took the key from me and ran her fingers over the grooves. 'And you're okay?'

'I'm fine,' I said. 'A little stressed, but fine.'

Ally dropped her shoulders and smiled; seemingly satisfied her apartment was safe. I walked over to the sofa and opened my laptop. I couldn't wait to tell Dave about my latest incident.

That evening, card unblocked and doorman repaid, I ventured out for drinks with Ally. The rainstorm from that afternoon had long passed and the air was denser than ever. I arrived at the bar feeling just as soggy as I had during the storm. It seemed strangely quiet for 8 p.m. on a Friday. Or was it Thursday?

'What day of the week is it?' I asked Ally as we wandered inside.

'Tuesday.'

'Ah,' I said, amused by my lack of connection to the real world. *And what did I know about bars anyway?* I wasn't about to admit it but this was my first one. I sat down on an empty stool and swung my legs to try to dry the layer of perspiration that was coating them. 'It's hot today, huh?' I said, hoping I looked like I belonged. A bead of sweat rolled down my back, tickling me as it fell.

'Is it?' she asked. 'You get used to it after a while. It feels weird now if I'm walking around and not drenched in sweat. Fancy a cider?'

'Please.'

I watched her walk up to the bar where she began chatting with the bartender as though they were best of friends. She gave off an air of confidence I was longing to attain.

'Phew!' she said with a laugh as she reached the table. 'I was certain I was gonna spill these drinks. You know – do a Lauren?'

I rolled my eyes.

'No, wait,' she said. 'If I were you, I'd have probably tripped over, cut my face open on broken glass and be on my way to the emergency room.' She collapsed in hysterical giggles.

'Very funny,' I said. 'No, really. You're *hilarious*.'

'Aww, I'm sorry, chick,' she said, her tone softening. 'You know I'm just messing with you. You're an easy target, though, what with all your mishaps and disasters and punching of scammers.'

'I know,' I said. 'And it's true. Did I tell you I fainted today?'

She shook her head and I replayed the events of that morning for her.

'Lauren.' She was staring at me as if she was trying to process how I was still alive.

'I know.'

The pulsing bass from the loudspeaker drowned out our laughter, and I took a gulp of my cider. It was easy for me to laugh about my mishaps once they were over, and I loved being able to tell such ridiculous stories, but I couldn't help but feel a tinge of sadness when I reflected over my travels. Nobody else seemed to be as unlucky as I was and no matter how much I tried to remain optimistic, everything still seemed to go wrong. There were only so many times that I could buy a plane ticket and convince myself my luck would change.

'So what's next for you then?' Ally asked. 'Back to China to seek revenge on more nasty scammers?'

I shook my head. 'I don't know. China is just so... different? Challenging? Terrifying?' I laughed. 'Likely to result in my death? It wasn't just the scams, it was everything. I was miserable there. But that's not a reason not to go back, is it?' I took a sip of my cider. 'Shouldn't I be travelling to widen my horizons? To challenge myself and leave my comfort zone?'

'Not if it makes you miserable,' she said.

'Well, then the question becomes,' I continued, 'where do I go instead?' My stomach back-flipped at the realisation I had more freedom than I knew what to do with. *I could go to Australia or South Africa or Argentina or...* how could I possibly know which country was the right decision and which ones would lead to my imminent demise? *What if I went to Australia, got stung by a jellyfish and died?* I imagined my parents weeping, all because I had got lost while trekking in Malaysia and ended up eating poisonous berries in a futile attempt at survival. Whatever decision I made now had the power to alter the course of my life. I felt a searing pain beneath my ribs and was reminded that there could be such a thing as too many options.

'What are you thinking?' Ally asked.

'That choosing where to go next feels like the biggest decision of my life.'

She shook her head. 'Jesus, Lauren, *relax*. Just buy a flight to wherever you've always dreamed of going. It's not hard. I've done it and – trust me! – it's the best.'

I got lost in my thoughts for a moment, flicking through the pages of the atlas that resided inside my head. In my heart, I knew there wasn't any question about where I'd end up. I'd always been transfixed by Southeast Asia.

'Vietnam,' I said, finally. 'It's close to here and it's in Southeast Asia. I'm desperate to get there.'

'I'd pick Thailand,' Ally said, nudging me. I knew she loved it there. 'Head to the islands, hook up with a hot Australian guy. Or two.' She laughed. 'But seriously – it's beautiful there and I think you'd like it a lot.'

'Well, it's funny you say Thailand…' I felt my cheeks turn crimson. My mind had jumped immediately to Dave. ''Cause there's kind of this guy…'

'A guy?' She raised an eyebrow. 'Why haven't you said anything about a guy before?'

'Because it's not a big deal,' I lied, choking out a laugh. 'I've never even met him. I've barely even spoken to him.' I groaned inwardly, convinced I was coming across as a weirdo that wanted to travel to a new country for a guy she'd never even met. The pesky voice in my head reminded me that that was exactly what I was thinking about doing.

'Come on,' she grinned. 'Spill the beans.'

I opened my mouth, but then shook my head. 'It's ridiculous. He's just a guy I've been talking to for a while. Just a guy I kind of find insanely hot.' I paused and focused on a dark stain on the table. I scratched at it, summoning up the courage to share the most important detail. 'He just quit his job to move to Thailand.'

I held my breath as Ally began to grin. I could feel my cheeks flushing and attempted to cool them by reciting the alphabet backwards in my head. It was a trick I'd once read about in a self-help book but it never seemed to work for me.

'You're going to go to Thailand,' she declared.

'Stop it,' I laughed, fanning my face. 'Yeah, maybe. But I won't go for him. This whole trip is about me – *not* about meeting guys. I decided to travel alone because I wanted to prove I didn't need a man to make me happy. I've only been going for a few months. I don't want a boyfriend. I want to be happy by myself first.'

'Dude, who said anything about a boyfriend?' she said, frowning. 'Just meet up with this guy and see what happens. Have a harmless fling and move on. It doesn't have to be a big deal.'

'I don't *do* harmless flings,' I insisted. I was the type of girl who jumped from one long-term relationship to the next without so much as a few weeks in between. I wasn't good at not getting attached. I *always* got attached.

'Maybe now's a good time to start,' Ally suggested. 'Live a little, Lauren. Bloody hell, you've been through enough. Get your arse over to Thailand and start having some fun.'

I couldn't stop shivering that night, as I lay sprawled out on Ally's sofa. My mind was dancing with indecision; my extremities icy cold from adrenaline. I pictured the moment when I'd show up outside Dave's apartment: *Oh, hi! It's Lauren. You know, that travel blogger you've been speaking to online? You told me that if I made it to Thailand you'd love to buy me a drink? Oh… you don't remember… Ha ha, oh no, it's fine. I'm fine. I'll just… leave.*

I shuddered and pulled my laptop towards me. I doubted I'd be getting any sleep tonight. I clicked absent-mindedly through the open tabs in my browser, stopping on Facebook when I saw Dave was online. Still buzzing from my pint of cider, I clicked on his name and began to type.

'So, I have a question…' I wrote, skipping the small talk entirely. I waited breathlessly for several minutes.

'Go on…'

I buried my face in my hand as I typed. 'I think I want to go to Thailand.' My finger hovered over the send button; my knees were trembling and I could feel the heat radiating off my cheeks. As I began to wonder if travel was turning me insane, I remembered Ally's advice: *Live a little, Lauren.* I nodded. Before I could find a reason not to, I sent the message into cyberspace. I sat in silent contemplation as my heart beat at the speed of a terrified rodent's.

'Great! I'm leaving for Chiang Mai tomorrow. When are you thinking of getting here?'

'Within the next few weeks,' I typed. 'I won't be going straight to Chiang Mai but I'm sure I'll make it there at some point.'

'Sweet! Well, if you're still up for that drink… just let me know when you get here.'

'I will.'

My body swelled with a muddle of anxiety and elation. I was certain if I could see myself, I'd think I looked just like a rabbit caught in the headlights: wide eyes, hair on end, body rooted firmly to the sofa. *Am I really going to go to Thailand to see a guy?* I shook my head and reminded myself that I was absolutely not doing that.

I busied myself with thoughts of Thailand that didn't involve handsome men from New Zealand: lying on gorgeous white sand beaches, dipping into warm turquoise waters, riding scooters past glittering temples and losing my inhibitions as I partied under the full moon.

Yes, I thought, a sense of calm washing over me. *Yes, this feels like the right decision.*

CHAPTER 5

I delved into the pockets of my faded denim hot pants, searching for a torn-up receipt. Shifting the weight of my backpack to my hips – I was still getting used to carrying my life on my back – I smiled as pounding dance music blared out from a nearby bar and shook my insides. A plume of smoke from a nearby street cart wafted through the air and I inhaled the smell of frying sausages. I sidestepped a glassy-eyed backpacker in hippie pants. It was a Tuesday morning on Khao San Road and it was unbearably humid.

I located the receipt and squinted at my handwriting on the back – one of those scribbles was the address of my hostel. It was at the end of a *soi,* I'd written – the name given to a side street in Thailand. I made my way to the side of the road, ducking past a vendor selling unidentifiable lumps of skewered meat. She offered a melodic *'Sawadee ka!'* when I made eye contact and I sang it back at her – hello was now the one word... Travellers of all ages and nationalities reeled past, wincing from their collective hangover, and hundreds of signs soared above me, advertising guesthouses for a pound a night and bars that don't check for ID.

I was buzzing. *This* is what I'd hoped for when I'd left London four months ago: something that was so far away from anything I'd ever experienced. This would usually be my idea of hell, but after spending every second of my student years in the library studying, I was ready to try something new. I reminded myself of Ally's words: *Live a little, Lauren.* I grinned and picked up the pace.

I passed a guy who looked to still be a teenager and he tipped his bowler hat when he saw me. 'G'day,' he said in an Australian accent. He pointed to my backpack. 'You coming or going?'

'Coming,' I said.

He cracked up. 'Well, welcome to paradise, then,' he winked. 'You may never leave.'

I smiled. 'We'll see.'

'See you around,' he said, touching my arm. I watched him fade back into the chaos and my heart beat a little faster. I shook my head and laughed. I felt like I was on another planet.

I'd booked myself into a two-bed dorm at my hostel. The idea of sharing a dorm with one other stranger felt so much creepier than seven, but I was hoping that nobody else would be strange enough to book the other bed. After a week spent in Ally's apartment, I had grown accustomed to having some privacy.

I pushed open the door and my heart sank. In front of me was the disappointing sight of a pale girl with dark brown hair throwing her clothes around the room.

'Oh, hi ya!' she sang out in a strong Irish accent. 'I'm Jen. Don't mind me. I'm jus' trying to find something decent in this bloody suitcase to wear.' She picked up a grey vest top and examined it.

'No worries,' I laughed, setting my backpack down in the corner of the room. 'I'm Lauren, by the way.'

'Oh, you're from England!' she exclaimed.

'Yep. And you're from Ireland?'

'You bet.'

I stood for a moment, watching her rifle through her suitcase.

'So, are ya travelling, Lauren?' she asked, pausing to look at me with bright green eyes. 'Or is this jus' a holiday?'

'Travelling,' I said. 'This is my first stop in Southeast Asia, though.'

'I'm a bit of both. I've been doing this thing called a working holiday visa in New Zealand – ya heard of it?'

'Yeah, I—'

'Yeah, you get to live and work for up to two years in Australia and New Zealand and I jus' finished my time in both o' them. Fruit picking and stuff. I'm heading home, *finally*, but figured I might as well stop in Thailand on the way.'

'Absolutely.'

'And I've been to Thailand before, but stayed mostly in fancy hotels then. That doesn't count as proper travel, does it?'

Jen's words gushed out like a waterfall and I barely had time to agree before she had moved on to the next topic. I immediately warmed to her bubbly personality; her chattiness meant that I didn't have to worry about what to say next.

'How about you then?' she asked as she finally reached the bottom of her suitcase. 'Where've you been so far?'

'Eastern Europe,' I told her. 'And parts of Eastern Asia, but I'm just so excited to finally be in Southeast Asia.'

'Ah, you'll love it here.'

'I hope so.'

'She'll be right!' she said in a fake Australian accent.

I spent the afternoon getting to know Jen better, neither of us making any kind of effort to head outside and explore. I'd proven to be abysmal at making friends on the road, but meeting Ally had done wonders for my self-esteem. Saying goodbye to her had been tough and I was still feeling down about it. We'd hugged, and I'd apologised again for breaking her key, while she'd made me promise I'd stop worrying so much. I was already worrying I wouldn't meet anyone like her.

Jen and I were going to be overlapping for two nights in Bangkok. After that, she'd be heading to Vang Vieng in Laos, a notorious party town fuelled by drinking, drugs and tubing: the act of floating down the Nam Song River in an inner tube. I still hadn't decided if I was going to head south to the islands or north to see Dave, but my plans for a month of island-hopping were looking less likely by the day. Dave and I had been furiously messaging each other for 6 hours a day since I'd told him I was coming to Thailand and it felt like my stomach would never stop fluttering. Talking to him reminded me of how things used to be with Jeremy in the early days, back when we never ran out of things to say.

'What are your plans for tonight?' I asked Jen, eager to grab a beer and drown my butterflies.

'I was gonna go out for a little wander and a drink. Nothing messy. You wanna come along?'

I nodded. 'I'd love to.'

I shielded my eyes to protect them from the strobe light. The last thing I wanted was to have an epileptic fit in front of all of these people. Not that I had ever been diagnosed with epilepsy but it would be just my luck to spontaneously develop it now. I took a few steps forward and stopped to soak it all in. Hundreds of drunken twenty-somethings milled around me, snacking on fried crickets, guzzling beers, and arguing with touts trying to sell T-shirts, fake IDs and entry to the loudest bars. I stood in the middle with my mouth agape, feeling more alive than ever.

'Fancy a smoothie?' Jen asked, pointing at a rickety stand a few metres away. It was in the middle of the road in front of a lively bar and beside a group of local teenagers who were breakdancing in front of a large crowd. I nodded and followed her over there, bewildered by the colourful array of fruits I had never seen before.

I went for the dragon fruit, falling for its hot-pink horned skin. It looked like an alien and I couldn't imagine what it would taste like. When I was handed a plastic cup of grey sludge and black seeds, I was less enthusiastic. Was dragon fruit code for frogspawn-infused cement? A gulp of the liquid confirmed my suspicions.

'Bleurgh,' I gagged, searching for a bin.

'Yeah, it's not very nice, is it?' Jen said.

'You could have warned me,' I laughed, pointing at her pineapple smoothie. 'You definitely came out better from this.'

'Don't be silly. Tryin' new things is what travel's all about. You might have liked it.'

'Not so much.'

As I walked with Jen towards the end of Khao San Road, the throbbing bass from a nearby bar resonated in my chest, and for the first time in my life, I felt an urge to get drunk. I beamed at passing backpackers, deliberately meeting their eyes and finally feeling like I was one of them. My mind turned again to Dave and I wished he were here with me.

'So what do ya feel like doing?' Jen asked, interrupting my daydream. 'We could grab some drinks somewhere if ya like?'

'You read my mind,' I said; glad that she couldn't. 'Where do you want to go?'

'Well, last time I was here I always went out drinking in Patpong. It's super touristy but a lot of fun. You want to go check it out? We can take a tuk-tuk.'

Tuk-tuks, the ubiquitous method of transport in Thailand, were kind of like a motorbike with three wheels and a small carriage welded on to the back. With a roof but no doors, you were susceptible to strong winds and perilous levels of euphoria.

I followed Jen to a nearby driver and watched as she negotiated like a pro. My idea of bargaining was to offer half the price, worry I'd offended, and then agree to pay double the amount they'd originally quoted me.

'What're ya doing dawdling, Lauren?' Jen called out. 'Jump in already!'

I crawled in beside her and squeezed the foam seat for good luck. With a deft manoeuvre from our driver, we sped off into the night, the wind whipping my hair across my face and stinging my eyes.

'I love tuk-tuks,' I shouted before inhaling a gustful of hair.

'Me too,' Jen yelled back.

Our tuk-tuk left us stood by the side of the road, our eyes level with the breasts of a beautiful woman. She was handing out leaflets to passers-by. Jen yanked on my arm and pulled me towards a nearby night market.

'She was hot,' I said.

'She,' she laughed, 'was a *he*. Or a she. I forget which they prefer.'

'They?'

'That was a ladyboy, Lauren.'

I frowned.

'You know, it's a—'

'Yeah, I know. It's just that, well, it was a bit unexpected, I guess.'

'Patpong is the red-light district,' she told me. 'I forgot to mention it. You'll see things far crazier than that here.'

I wasn't sure that the red-light district was quite where I wanted to be, but I decided I might as well throw myself in at the deep end. I pretended to take an interest in some knock-off Ed Hardy dresses at a nearby stall, running my fingers over the sparkly fabric and acting as if I wasn't out of my depth. A man walked up to us and handed me a laminated menu listing items like 'smoke cigarette', 'shoot balloon', 'write letter' and 'open bottle'. I shot Jen a quizzical look and the man grinned at me through yellowing teeth.

'Don't ask,' she sighed, handing it back to him and dragging me away.

'What was that menu?' I asked her a few minutes later.

'For the ping-pong shows,' she said. 'It was a list of what you can pay the girls to do with their, uh, ya know.' She pointed at her crotch.

'Oh, cool,' I said, glad the darkness was masking my red cheeks. I'd never come across a place like this before and I wasn't sure how to behave.

'Drink?' she asked, pointing at a cocktail bar that was spilling pink light on to the pavement. Outside, there were several couples furiously making out with each other against the wall, a loud group of 20 guys, and a couple of girls who were shouting obscene comments at them. My heart raced as I struggled to take it all in. This was unlike anywhere I'd ever been.

'Yes, please,' I said.

As I sipped my drink – a cosmopolitan, my first one – I felt a sense of serenity drifting over my shoulders. I sank into my chair and smiled as the tension in my neck floated away. Patpong was intimidating but I wasn't on the verge of a panic attack. For the first time, I felt like I'd slipped off the shackles of anxiety and taken a running jump into a world where fear didn't rule my life. Maybe this was how it felt to be free.

'I think I'm dying,' I moaned the following morning. I squinted at Jen, who was already up and dressed and typing on her laptop.

'What's up?' she said.

'I feel terrible. My mouth is dry, my head is pounding, I feel sick, I feel dizzy… how many cocktails did I have last night?'

'Two.'

'That's it?' I replied weakly.

'Yep. You spent half an hour telling me how much you loved cocktails and almost fell asleep on the table!'

I groaned. 'Really?'

'Really.'

I dove beneath the covers and attempted to piece together the night before. I remembered thinking about Dave an unhealthy amount of times. I remembered the cosmopolitan and I remembered… a rose? And a rugby player? A rugby player giving me a rose? I frowned. *That can't be right.*

I popped my head back up. 'Hey, Jen! This is going to sound stupid, but… did a rugby player—'

'Give you a rose? Yep.' She rolled her eyes. 'He said he was from the All Blacks – ya know, the New Zealand rugby team? I doubt it though.'

'Yeah, I doubt it,' I echoed, suddenly feeling light-headed. It was like I was a different person. The pre-travel version of me had never even been to a bar, let alone been given a rose from a rugby player. Maybe the travel version of me could become someone who goes after what they want.

I sat up in bed, pulled out my laptop from under my pillow and pretended I had something very important to do. Behind the screen my eyes were sparkling.

'So, there's a flight to Chiang Mai for £30 and I'm thinking about buying it,' I typed in a message to Dave, startled by my newfound confidence.

'Lunchtime,' Jen announced as I breathlessly waited for him to come online. 'What do you feel like?'

A McDonald's, I immediately thought, but I remembered eating with Bula in Shanghai, and how I'd embarrassed myself over my inexperience with food. *What if Jen expected me to know all about Thai food?* 'I don't mind,' I told her.

'Well,' she said. 'Don't judge me but…'

'But?'

'I'm kind of craving a massive McDonald's,' she said with a grin.

My heart skipped a beat and I plastered a triumphant grin across my face. 'I'm craving one, too,' I sang out.

It turned out that Jen was just as much of a picky eater as I was. As we sat in the air-conditioned McDonald's, surrounded by Thai teenagers and attracting judgment from passing tourists who were all about eating the local food, we compared our lack of experience.

'I've never had rice,' I told her.

'Me neither,' she beamed. 'What about eggplant?'

'I used to think it was a plant that tasted like eggs! Never had it.'

'I was once judged for having never eaten a curry before.'

'Me too,' I gasped. 'My friends once held a curry night to try to introduce me to some mild versions, but I couldn't eat any of them. They all had peanuts in!'

'I hate peanuts as well.'

We paused for a moment and suddenly I no longer felt like the worst traveller in the world. I wasn't the only backpacker who was a picky eater, and Jen seemed to be coping just fine.

We wandered back to the room after lunch because I couldn't focus on anything until I'd seen if Dave had replied.

'Remind me again,' Jen said as we walked into our room. 'You want to go to Chiang Mai to meet up with a perfect stranger?'

'He's not a stranger,' I said, walking to my open laptop. 'We've been talking to each other pretty much every day for the past month. And anyway—' I stopped what I was saying when I spotted he'd replied.

'That's great!' Dave had typed to me.

I looked up at her and grinned. 'He wants to see me,' I whispered and she gave me two thumbs up.

'The flight is for tomorrow,' I wrote as I tried to swallow the lump in my throat. My heart began to gallop.

'Even better.'

'Do you mean that?' I asked, and then frowned. I wanted him to think I was self-assured, like a girl who'd accept a rose from a potentially famous rugby player.

'Yeah. I mean, we've been talking practically every day for what? Weeks now? It's rare I find someone I instantly connect with and I think you'll really like Chiang Mai. So, what I'm trying to say is that this city's awesome, I like you a lot and I'd love to see if there's something there. But, no pressure, of course. It's your call.'

I slammed the lid of my laptop shut and opened it again. Closed it and opened it. My head spun ever faster. *Was this ridiculous? Was I insane, or following my heart?*

'What're you doing?' Jen asked, staring as I flapped my laptop lid with abandon.

'I think I'm going to Chiang Mai.'

Suddenly, this was now my last full day in Bangkok and I was hungover. I felt like the worst kind of traveller – a cliché I'd always promised myself I'd avoid. I reasoned with myself that with several months planned in Southeast Asia, this wouldn't be my last visit to Bangkok, but I couldn't help feeling disappointed. I had seen barely anything of the city.

Right on cue, Jen turned to me. 'What do ya want to do today?'

'Not much,' I said, letting out a yawn. 'I'm feeling pretty fragile.'

'How about a massage then?'

I hesitated, chewing on my lip. 'Maybe.' My lack of life experience happened to also include massages.

'Maybe?' Jen repeated in disbelief. 'They're like, two pounds a pop here. Why *wouldn't* you want one?'

'I've kind of never had one before,' I mumbled beneath my breath.

'No,' she gasped, staring at me as if I'd grown an extra head. 'Like, never?'

I shook my head. 'Never. Is that weird?'

'Um, yes,' she laughed before letting out a gasp. 'I get it. So, like, you know how neither of us have tried many foods? You're like that with everything?'

'Pretty much,' I said.

She burst out laughing and dragged me off the bed. 'Right, missy,' she said, pulling me towards the door. 'Let's get you a massage.'

Ten minutes later, a woman holding a sign advertising £2 massages was leading us down a *soi*. We were ushered through a squeaky wooden door and greeted by two elderly Thai ladies.

'Massaaaage?' one of them called.

'Yes!' Jen said. 'An oil massage if possible?' She turned to me and whispered, 'Thai massages can be brutal if you've never had them before. We'll start you off easy.'

My laughter turned to coughs as I inhaled the strong incense fumes. I looked around the room and waited for my eyes to adjust. It was empty aside from a picture of the Thai king and a few bottles of massage oil on the floor. Velvet curtains were pulled across the door, with plumes of incense furling around the edges.

One of the women gestured for us to follow her behind a partition where she pointed at two faded mattresses lying side by side.

'Please take off clothes,' she said. 'Then I will come.' She gave a curt nod and walked away.

My eyes met Jen's and we shared timid giggles to cover up our embarrassment. She slipped out of her T-shirt and I averted my eyes to the mattress. Following her lead, I eased off my top, folding it into a neat square and placing it on the floor. I unbuttoned my shorts and wriggled out of them. *Z, Y, X,* I chanted to myself. *W, V, U, T, S, R...*

Our masseuses entered the room. They cackled and shook their heads when they saw us.

'No, no, no,' one of them said. 'You take off everything. This.' She reached inside her shirt and pulled out her bra strap, letting it go with a ping. 'This is clothes. No clothes. You will get oil on them.'

'Naked, please!' the other woman sang out.

They began chattering in Thai, probably discussing the two *farangs* who were now stark naked and looking at anything that wasn't each other.

Without saying a word, I lay down on my front and closed my eyes. I hoped Jen was doing the same thing and not ogling my ghostly white behind.

One of the women clutched my ankles and began to crawl up my body until she was straddling my hips. I felt every movement as her greased-up fingers slid along my spine and over my shoulders and it was not relaxing in the slightest. I peeked over at Jen to see if she was struggling but she looked to be asleep. I pressed my forehead into the musty mattress and forced my eyes shut. I felt like I was going to sneeze.

Ten minutes later, the woman had clambered off my back and was moving towards my face. She took a shoulder in each hand and performed a manoeuvre not unlike a wrestler, flipping me over in one fell swoop. I lay flat on my back, stark naked, clutching at my body in an attempt to cover everything at once. The giggles from the next mattress told me Jen was in the same situation.

The masseuse then wrapped her hands around my chin and pulled my head towards her, pressing it into her crotch as she sat cross-legged behind me. I squirmed as her hands worked their way down from my neck to my chest. I was helpless, lacking in strength and weak from laughter, unable to remove her pinching fingers from my nipples. For the next 5 minutes, she caressed my breasts while I convulsed in her lap. I couldn't believe that people actually paid money for this. Massages were even weirder than I'd expected.

'Okay,' she sang to me. 'On your front.'

I complied, letting the waves of relief billow over me. She crawled towards my feet and began to rub my calves while I wiped my tears of laughter away on my wrists and tried to get myself to relax. The worst was over; the end was in sight. My shoulders dropped and I lost myself in thoughts of how I would spend my final evening in Bangkok.

A slap to the bum cheeks shocked me out of my daydream. I felt a pair of hands caressing my backside, moving in opposing circles. I lay motionless as my cheeks were gently spread and squeezed back together. *Spread and squeeze. Spread and squeeze.* Her hands slid back down my thighs and stroked back and forth.

It was then, while she was sliding her hands up and down the inside of my thighs, that it happened. Before I could say 'sexual assault' her fingertip was in my vagina.

And then it was out again.

I gasped and she continued to massage my thighs.

'And then she poked me!' I finished, crossing my arms and leaning back against my pillow. I'd pulled Jen back to our room after the massage and spent 10 minutes trying to work up the courage to ask her about my unhappy ending.

'I—she—she what?' she spluttered, her shoulders starting to tremble.

'She poked me,' I repeated. 'She put her finger inside me!'

'What? Her entire finger?'

I shook my head. 'Just the tip.'

'Why didn't you say anything?'

'Well, because it's *Thailand*. And because it was my first ever massage.' I raised my eyes to the ceiling. 'I didn't know if it was normal.'

'Lauren.' Jen had stopped laughing and was staring at me in disbelief. 'That is definitely not normal.'

'And it was over with so quickly that I assumed it was just an accident. I didn't have time to think. And what about the boob massage? Tell me that happened to you, too.'

She waved her hands dismissively. 'Oh, that's normal. It happens all the time here. Well, it's not normal for a massage in Ireland or anything, but it's pretty common in Thailand. I just cover myself with my hands and they get the message.'

'That's what I tried to do!' I exclaimed. 'But she kept pushing my hands away.'

'Well, love,' Jen said. 'You're not the most forceful of people. She probably thought you were encouraging her.'

'I'm blaming you for this,' I said with a shy smile. 'This is all your fault.'

'Well, how about we go out for dinner and you can yell at me over a plate of spicy noodles we'll both be too afraid to eat? My treat?'

I shook my head. 'I'm not hungry. But you go. I'll join you later.'

Travel was a rollercoaster and it felt like my lows were so much lower than everyone else's. Every traveller I'd met had gushed about their wonderful experiences whereas all that seemed to cross my path was bad luck and misadventures. *Why did Jen get a normal massage experience while I walked away feeling violated?*

I reached for my laptop and opened Skype. I knew that speaking to my mum would make me feel worse but I was missing her so much. I'd been emailing every day since I'd been away, bashing out thousand-word extracts of my life, but talking over the phone was different. I knew the sound of her voice had the power to tug my heartstrings all the way back home. What I needed right now was someone to tell me to stop feeling sorry for myself. My mum was not that person. I tapped my nails on the keyboard as I waited for her to pick up.

'Lauren!' she squealed when she heard my voice, and I could tell she was beaming from ear to ear. 'Where are you?'

'I'm in Thailand, Mum. I'm in Bangkok.'

'Ah, lovely,' she sighed. 'I bet those beaches are incredible compared to rainy old London. They're predicting an Indian summer this year, mind you.'

'There aren't any beaches here,' I giggled, rolling my eyes at my laptop. My mum was the sort of person who could happily return to Mallorca on holiday every year and I was certain she would never decide to visit Thailand. Southeast Asian geography was not her strong suit.

I listened as she updated me on everyone's news – her and my dad were bumbling along at work and my sister was currently studying for her exams. It sounded like nothing had changed since I'd left.

'How's Thailand?' she asked me.

'It's hot,' I said, choosing to stick to my British roots and describe the weather. 'But I like it a lot here – much more than anywhere else I've been. I made friends with a girl from Ireland and we've been hanging out over the past few days.' Now didn't feel like an appropriate time to tell my mum I'd just been molested by an old woman.

'Wonderful!' she gushed. 'It sounds like you're having so much fun.'

'I am,' I lied and fell silent. My bottom lip began to quiver. I wished I was having the time of my life.

'Lauren? You okay, honey?'

I sniffed. 'Yeah, I'm okay. I just think I'm a bit homesick. It feels like everyone I meet is having all of these incredible travel experiences while I'm sidestepping from one disaster to the next. I hate that nothing ever seems to go right for me.' I felt like an awful person just for saying those words. I was so privileged. What right did I have to visit poverty-stricken countries and complain about how I'd had a bit of bad luck, especially when my definition of bad luck involved being scammed or breaking a key? It wasn't like I was worrying about how I could afford to feed my family today.

'Oh, Lauren. You know you can come home at any time.'

'I know,' I said. 'I don't want to give up, though.'

'It's not giving up. You tried something and it didn't work out. There's nothing wrong with that,' she said reassuringly.

'But it's not that it's *not* working out. Sometimes it's great and I feel like I'm doing exactly what I've always wanted. I just wish I could avoid all the horrible bits. Nobody else seems to have them. What am I doing wrong?'

She sighed. 'I don't know what to say to you, Lauren. You decided to travel alone. We told you it wasn't a wise decision. But you wanted this so much that you wouldn't listen.'

'I know,' I groaned, running my fingers through my hair. 'And I do still want it. I'm just frustrated that I kind of suck at it. I don't know why I thought travel would solve all of my problems.'

I had a feeling my mum would take this opportunity to try to convince me to return, and it filled me with a blend of guilt and frustration. Guilt for leaving her and frustration that she wasn't encouraging me to follow my dreams – even though my travels weren't playing out quite how I'd dreamed.

'Honey, you know that coming home doesn't make you a failure, don't you?' she said. 'Your dad and I, we're just so proud of you, no matter what you decide. And, of course, we'd be delighted to have you home with us. Don't force yourself to stay and spend your precious savings if you're not enjoying it.'

I nodded through the tears. I could tell she was hoping I was days away from returning, but I wasn't able to tell her I didn't want to. Like tossing a coin and discovering you were hoping for an outcome all along, talking to her had made me realise I wasn't ready to go home. Going home would mean giving up on my dream. Going home would feel exactly like failing.

CHAPTER 6

'What am I doing?' I muttered, crouched beside a row of suitcases at the airport in Chiang Mai. In front of me was the arrivals hall; beside me was my backpack. I was minutes away from meeting Dave and I was currently hiding behind a wall of luggage.

I'd spent my final morning with Jen planning for this moment. A sunrise stroll through Bangkok had resulted in me returning to my room with armfuls of new clothes, everything carefully chosen to make me look less like a grubby backpacker and more like a sophisticated traveller.

With a nervous gulp, I picked myself up off the floor and brushed the dust from my knees. I was wearing tight denim hot pants and a baggy Rolling Stones vest top. Around my neck was an enormous pair of headphones and on my wrist were a dozen multicoloured string bracelets. *Who was I trying to kid?* I looked exactly like a grubby backpacker.

I threw my backpack on to my shoulders with ease and hoisted my daypack up on to one shoulder. During one of our conversations, Dave had confessed he was a big believer in packing light so in an attempt to make a good first impression, I'd thrown out half of what I owned before leaving Bangkok. I'd already been travelling lighter than most people but my backpack now weighed just 7 kg. The biggest mistake I'd made when it came to packing was copying the lists I'd found online: the clothes I'd been wearing had been hideous, shapeless sacks in neutral colours with dozens of pockets and zips. It wasn't me and it was a relief to throw them away. With my heart pounding in my ears, I took a deep breath and began to walk.

Things seem to happen at warp speed on the road, from friendships to relationships, and this was proving to be no exception. In the two months I'd been talking to Dave, we'd jumped from a drunken conversation to speaking every day to me deciding to fly to Chiang Mai to see him. On the plane, I'd imagined how this would play out a thousand times over. *Would he kiss me¿ Shake my hand¿ Give me a hug¿ Would it be awkward¿* As I walked into the arrivals hall, the sensible part of me was demanding I flee the airport before he could see me; the other part was telling me to grab on with both hands.

I scanned the sea of blurry, unfocused faces in front of me, feeling more nervous than when I'd stepped on the plane to leave England. Taking a deep breath, I shuffled through the crowd, searching for a familiar-ish face. *Where was he¿ What if he looked nothing like his photos¿*

'Lauren!' I felt a hand on my arm and looked up.
Dave.

I stepped back and took him in: shaved head, gorgeous blue eyes, warm smile. He looked *good*. He'd told me that morning that he was 5 ft 9 in when I'd had a sudden panic I didn't know how tall he was. It turned out to be the perfect height. He looked toned and tanned, not surprising as he'd recently run a half-marathon.

'Hey you,' he said, and my stomach transformed into a thousand butterflies.

'Hi,' I said in a trembling voice, dropping my bags to the floor, not in the slightest bit concerned about the thud of my laptop. I held out my hands for a hug and he pulled me close, wrapping his arms around me so I could feel his heart beating against my cheek. I leaned back and looked into his eyes just as he leaned down to kiss me. It was a minty kiss; one that left me breathless and dizzy.

This was undoubtedly the weirdest thing I'd ever done but somehow it felt like the most natural. It felt as if I'd known Dave for half my life, not like I was stood in the middle of an airport kissing a complete stranger.

'You look younger than I thought you would,' I said, interrupting the kiss to examine his face. There were no signs of wrinkles and none of his hairs were grey. If I didn't know he was a decade older than me, I'd have guessed he was in his late 20s.

'I do?' he asked with a smile. 'I guess I have travel to thank for that.'

I leaned my body into his, suddenly feeling faint. As I pressed my head against his chest again, I noticed the slow and steady beat of his heart. *Wasn't he feeling nervous, too?* We stayed stood in that moment as if time had paused, my hands glued to his hips, and whenever we made eye contact, every one of my nerve endings tingled.

'Shall we go?' he asked after a few minutes, reaching for my backpack when I nodded. 'Hey, I'm impressed,' he commented. 'You travel light.'

'Oh yeah,' I said, pretending to brush off the compliment. 'I only travel with what I need.' *Mission accomplished.*

I'd landed at 8 p.m., a deliberate decision that would ensure I wouldn't have to eat dinner with Dave. I didn't want him to take me to a night market and force me to eat a live rooster, or whatever people eat there. I followed him through the airport and outside, where we were greeted by a wave of thick, hot air, like walking behind an exhaust pipe.

'Do you have a guesthouse booked?' he asked, pulling open the door of a taxi for me.

'Not yet,' I said, sliding inside. 'I figured I'd just turn up and find somewhere when I get here. There'll still be lots of availability, right?' There was no way I'd be arriving in Chiang Mai without a guesthouse booked if I hadn't been meeting Dave. My seemingly relaxed attitude to travel was all part of my attempt to convince him I was more experienced than the reality.

'Yep. And there are loads of guesthouses near to my apartment, too. Why don't we drop your bags off there and then we can find one together?'

I followed Dave up the steps of his apartment complex, surprised to find I didn't feel in the slightest bit nervous. I silenced the logical part of my brain that was screaming that this was weird. *Live a little, Lauren*, I reminded myself. *You're just hanging out with a guy you like. And he likes you, too. It's no big deal.* I laced my fingers through his as we walked down the corridor to his room, our flip-flops squeaking against the polished white tiles.

'Here it is,' he said, stopping outside a black wooden door with a golden 315 hanging above it.

I took a few steps inside and swivelled. His apartment was like an Ikea showroom, all white walls and black cupboards. There was a double bed, a desk, a fridge and not much else. Dave's beaten-up backpack lay in a corner with a pile of neatly folded clothes beside it. He didn't even have a wardrobe.

'It's pretty small,' he said, coming to stand beside me. 'The bathroom is in here.' He opened a door to reveal a wet room lined with grey tiles. 'And there's a small balcony out through those patio doors.' I followed his line of sight and eyed up the outside space where you'd struggle to fit more than a chair.

'It's great,' I said, and I meant it. Living in dorm rooms for the past few months made Dave's humble apartment look like a palace. 'How much would you pay for something like this?' I asked.

'One-hundred and eighty pounds a month,' he said. 'That's excluding bills. But it includes a weekly cleaner, and there's a rooftop gym and swimming pool I get access to as well. I think it's pretty good value.'

'It's amazing value,' I insisted. A quick calculation told me that I could pay for a ten-year stay with my savings. *How could I ever return to London?*

My nerves caught up with me and I suddenly felt awkward and shy, not sure what the protocol was for being in a guy's apartment you met 15 minutes ago. If I thought I was out of my depth in Patpong, it had nothing on this. Dave carried my bags to the corner of the room and placed them on top of his empty backpack.

'So how was your flight?' he asked, sitting down on the edge of his bed and looking up at me. *Was I supposed to join him?* I was bad at this. I decided to stand in the middle of the room instead.

'Not too bad,' I said. 'Well, actually, it was terrifying. I'm scared of flying – I know, ridiculous, right? I'm travelling. How can I be afraid of flying? I have this playlist on my iPod that I listen to when I fly. The first song is "Don't Fear the Reaper". It calms me down because, you know, seasons don't fear the reaper. Why should I? So anyway, there was this massive bang halfway through the flight. I was certain we were going down.' I knew I was jabbering but couldn't seem to stop. Dave said nothing so I continued to fill the silence. 'And *then*! When we started to land, the clouds were so thick I couldn't see anything outside the window. It was all white. I was worried I'd died or something. I don't believe in an afterlife but damn, being stuck in a plane for eternity? That's got to be what hell is like.' I took a deep breath. 'But it was okay in the end. Well, obviously. You can see it was okay because I'm here and I'm alive. Well, maybe I'm not okay because I can't seem to stop talking.'

'Are you nervous?' Dave asked and my cheeks turned pink.

'A little,' I confessed, wiping my palms on my shorts.

I walked over and sat on the bed beside him and he draped his arm around my shoulders. I felt nervous, awkward, terrified and longing.

'So, what do you do for a living?' I blurted out, and then looked at him in shock.

Dave stared back at me and frowned.

'Whoops,' I said quickly. 'I don't know why I asked that. It's possibly the strangest question I could have asked someone who's just quit their job.'

'It is rather,' he said with a sparkle in his eye. 'But to answer your question anyway, I'm trying to find a way to fund my travels and travel blogging seems like the best way to do it. I'm already making a bit of money here and there, so I figured I'd quit my job, move somewhere cheap and give it a go.'

I knew from our previous conversations that Dave had been travelling on and off for 15 years. He'd told me about how growing up in New Zealand – right at the bottom of the world – had helped instil a love of travel in him.

'So your plan is to keep travelling full time?' I asked him. 'No going back?'

He nodded. 'I started travelling after I graduated from university and eventually fell into corporate IT. I grew to hate it after a few years – I always wanted to be journalist – but it paid far better than writing. It also made it easy for me to pick up a contract for a year or so, build up my savings, travel for a bit and then do it all over again. Having to go home and reintegrate into normal life just gets harder and harder the more you do it, though.'

I gaped at him in awe, noticing our age gap for the first time. I had no idea how to reply – I'd never even had a full-time job before.

'I'd like to try the travel blogging thing, too,' I said eventually, cringing at how I'd turned the conversation back towards me. I had so much I wanted to ask him, but didn't know where to start.

'You should,' he said. 'I have a few advertising contacts I can share with you and you only need to make a few hundred pounds from it to cover your costs in Chiang Mai.'

My head was spinning from information overload and the dizzying idea of being able to fund my travels. As I pondered it over, I noticed Dave watching me with absolute attention. I swallowed hard and in a panic over what to do, leaned over and pressed my lips against his. He kissed me back and the world faded away until there was only him and me. Until there was only desire and fear.

The evening passed in a blur, full of kisses and flirting. We shared travel stories and nightmares, Dave winning with the former and me the latter. At 3 a.m., we finally passed out, collapsing into each other's arms, exhausted and exhilarated, thoughts of finding me a guesthouse far from our minds.

My stomach rumbled, stirring me awake. I hadn't eaten in 24 hours. While I'd managed to avoid having the 'food frightens me' talk with Dave last night, there'd be no avoiding it today. I shuddered at the thought, disturbing him from his slumber.

'Good morning, beautiful,' he mumbled, pulling me towards him. He kissed my forehead and any worries I had melted away. 'How did you sleep?'

'Pretty good,' I said with a sleepy smile. I felt like I'd slept for days. 'You?'

'Yeah, not bad.' He rolled on to his back and held out an arm so I could snuggle into him. His chest hairs tickled my nose as we lay together in a tangled mess of limbs and I arranged my lips into a downward chute to funnel my morning breath from his face.

'Tetris,' I announced.

'What?'

'Tetris,' I repeated. 'Our bodies fit together so perfectly.'

He burst out laughing and squeezed me even tighter. 'Tetris,' he repeated. 'I like it.'

My heart felt full enough to burst.

'So, how do you feel about scooters?' Dave asked as we made our way downstairs.

Vehicles of death, I immediately thought but the words, 'They look like fun,' somehow left my lips instead.

'You fancy a ride?' he asked.

I stopped in my tracks, a thousand perilous scenes flashing through my mind. Dave driving into a wall, me toppling off the back, thick red blood, my bone sticking out of my leg, my mangled body, a coffin, my parents crying, a funeral full of friends saying they'd warned me not to travel. I shook my head, stubbornly wanting to prove them wrong.

'You know what?' I said, running to catch him. 'I think I do.'

'Great,' he said with a grin, leading me to a black and orange scooter. 'I picked up a spare helmet when you told me you were coming to town.' He handed me a yellow one with 'Golden Hamster' printed across the front. 'They're not particularly well fitting, so let's hope we don't fall off.'

I let out a strangled laugh and fastened the strap below my chin. It wobbled as I climbed up behind Dave, feeling about as protective as a cardboard box. I dug my fingers into his waist and closed my eyes.

With a roar of the engine, I was thrown out of my comfort zone and into the path of oncoming traffic. I pressed the side of my face into Dave's back and peered out at the chaos. Tuk-tuks veered dangerously close, cutting us up as we weaved in and out of dozens of scooters. A couple of pick-up trucks on either side threatened to crush us as we squealed down the centre line of the road. It felt perfectly choreographed but I had no idea what was going on.

'This is Chiang Mai's moat,' Dave shouted over the cacophony of horns. 'It surrounds the Old Town.' I winced as he let go of the handlebar with his right hand and pointed at the murky green water.

'It's beautiful,' I choked out, tightening my grip as we followed it around a bend, trying not to picture us riding straight into it.

~~~

'How was that?' Dave asked after we came to a standstill.

'So much fun,' I croaked, wiping my hands on my T-shirt. Our 10-minute ride through Chiang Mai had been one of exhilaration and fear. From the dozens of golden temples, glinting in the morning light, to the brick ruins scattered around the corners of the moat, there was no denying this was a beautiful city and I could see why Dave had chosen to make it his home. I just wished he wasn't showing it to me from the seat of a death trap.

My legs wobbled as I followed Dave into a restaurant, wondering why I felt so light-headed.

He pulled out a wooden bench for me and I sat down at the table. I looked around: the restaurant contained a haphazard array of wooden tables and benches, and was already full of chattering locals and tourists. Beside me was a lamp in the shape of a man playing a guitar. I liked it a lot.

A waitress handed me a menu and I began to leaf through it, my stomach lurching when all I could see were eggs: boiled eggs, fried eggs, poached eggs, scrambled eggs, omelettes. Every kind of egg and all I wanted was toast.

'Dave?' I whispered.

'Yep,' he replied, staring at his menu.

'I have a confession.'

'Go on.'

When I didn't say anything he looked up, his eyes warm and reassuring.

'Okay,' he laughed. 'Come on. Spill.'

My heart was pounding as I took a deep breath and dug my nails into the damp bench. 'Okay. I'm just going to say it,' I said. 'I'm just going to say it.'

'Okay.'

'I'm scared of eggs.'

There was a long pause as Dave waited for a punchline that wasn't going to emerge. 'You're... scared of eggs?'

I nodded.

'What do you mean by scared?' He was staring at me as if I'd told him I had an egg for a foot.

'I've never eaten them before. I think I'll hate them. In fact, I'm pretty sure I'm allergic.'

'I see.'

'Now you think I'm weird.'

'A little, yes.'

'Let me explain,' I said. 'When I was growing up, my mum would never give me eggs. She didn't like them so never bought them. I didn't get to try them so now the thought of eating eggs is really intimidating. And, well, everything on this menu has eggs! I don't know what to order.' I was relieved to see Dave was laughing, hopefully not at the poor choices he'd made to lead him to this point.

'I've never met anyone like you,' he said.

'Me neither,' I sighed. 'But I promise I'm working on it. I'm much better than I used to be.'

'Well then why don't you start with an omelette?' he asked. 'Look – you can get one with cheese and ham in it. Then you'll barely be able to taste the egg.' He paused and squinted at me. 'Wait – you've eaten cheese and ham before, right?'

'Of course I have,' I said.

'Of course you have.'

My ham and cheese omelette arrived a few minutes later, looking nothing like I thought it would. 'Oh,' I gasped. 'It's all of the yellow! I thought the white and the yellow would stay separate.'

'Oh, Lauren,' Dave said, and I could tell he was struggling to keep a straight face.

I realised then that I'd ruined any possibility of Dave thinking I was normal. Me not eating eggs was the tip of an iceberg the size of Antarctica. There was a whole continent worth of fears hiding beneath my surface.

'An omelette is a combination of eggs and several other ingredients, all mixed up and cooked in a pan,' he told me. 'So – as you would say – the "white" and the "yellow" are mixed together.'

I could feel Dave's eyes on me as I played with my food, cutting it into tiny slices and sliding it on and off my fork.

'Are you actually going to try it?' he asked.

'Yeah, I am. I'm just preparing myself, you know?'

'No. I don't know.'

I winced at his confusion. There were so many things to like about Dave but if hanging out with him was going to mean facing an everlasting line-up of my fears, I wasn't sure I was ready for it. When I travelled alone, I could have cupcakes for breakfast and baguettes for dinner.

I stabbed the smallest sliver of egg and the largest slice of cheese and shoved it in my mouth before I could talk myself out of it. It tasted like a cold, wrinkled toe.

'It tastes like feet,' I announced with a shudder before gulping the mouthful down whole.

'It tastes like feet?' he repeated, letting out a snort. 'Have you eaten lots of feet then?'

'You know what I mean,' I said. 'It tastes how I'd *imagine* feet to taste.'

'But hey, you tried it, and that's an important first step. You conquered your – admittedly weird – fear. That deserves a high five.' He held out his hand and I swung my arm towards it, but misaimed and slapped the air next to him. I quickly picked up my fork and hoped he wouldn't comment on it. 'Maybe you wouldn't have even tried eating eggs a few years ago?'

I nodded. 'That's true.'

'Try some more – you'll get a taste for it. Here—' he handed me a bottle of hot sauce. 'Try it with some of this.'

'Hot sauce!' I exclaimed. 'I can't eat that. I can't eat anything spicy.'

Dave exhaled and I had a feeling he was counting to ten.

'I'm sorry,' I said in a desperate attempt to make everything okay again. 'I really am trying to change. I've run into so many travellers who tell me their favourite part of travel is getting to sample local delicacies. It sucks that it's my biggest obstacle.'

'I'm one of those travellers,' he muttered.

'I think I could be,' I said, despite knowing that if it were possible to exist without needing to eat, I'd never have another meal again. I wanted to like different dishes if only to stop everyone I met from judging me.

'So, you just don't like food at all?' Dave asked.

I began to reel off the list of foods I had never tried but was certain I wouldn't like. I couldn't blame my mum for all of my food-related issues – a lot of them resulted from my fear of trying anything new.

'But what about when you lived alone?' Dave pressed. 'Or with a boyfriend?'

I shrugged, thinking back to mealtimes with Jeremy. We'd always eaten plain foods – burgers, pasta, shepherd's pie, pizza, sandwiches – there was never any Asian food in our house, although I knew he liked it. He'd never pressured me to try anything new. 'I just ate what I was comfortable with, which wasn't a lot.'

'Well, at least you're open to trying a few new things now,' he said, taking a sip of his coconut juice. I hoped he wasn't about to offer me some.

'Yep,' I said, scooping another mouthful of foot into my mouth. 'I know it can be annoying to hang out with someone who's nervous to try new food but I do want to change. And I think a good step would be learning to enjoy it again.'

'Again?' he asked, picking up on my misstep.

I paused for a few seconds, wondering whether to dismiss it as a slip of the tongue. I wouldn't dream of sharing this information with a guy I'd just met – most of my friends still had no idea – but something about the way Dave looked at me made me want to tell him everything.

'I used to have a bit of an eating disorder,' I blurted out.

'Damn,' he murmured, sitting up straight and removing his sunglasses.

'Yeah,' I said, waving my hands dismissively. 'Sorry. Awkward topic. Let's talk about something else.'

'Oh, no,' he said. 'It was just a shock to hear. You can talk to me if you want.'

'I'm okay.'

'I really don't mind.'

'Are you sure?'

'I'm sure.'

I took a deep breath to steady my voice. Part of me wanted to pretend I was just a traveller who happened to be a picky eater, but the other part wanted to explain why I was this way.

'Well,' I started. 'I don't know if you've been able to tell from the short time you've known me, but I'm a bit of an anxious person.' Dave nodded and my stomach filled with butterflies. *Oh. I thought I'd been hiding it pretty well.* 'So anyway,' I continued. 'It used to be pretty bad. At the height of it, I was having ten panic attacks a day, unable to go into work, hadn't seen my friends in months and couldn't even step outside the house.'

Dave looked incredulous. 'You literally couldn't step outside the house?'

I nodded. 'Pretty much. I spent about six months of my life mostly inside, not really able to leave. I think I probably had a panic attack once when I stepped outside so I started associating leaving the house with feeling like I was going to die. My life was a mess.'

'No shit.'

'I've only realised within the past few years that it was all about control. I was having panic attacks because I didn't feel in control of any part of my life. Except eating. So I stopped.'

'Ah.' He was starting to look uncomfortable.

'But I wanted to eat,' I said with a nervous laugh. 'I used to put food in my mouth but start retching until I spat it out. I wanted to eat more than anything in the world but my brain just couldn't seem to let me swallow.' I waited for Dave to make some kind of innuendo but he kept quiet. I cleared my throat. 'I weighed under six stone at my lowest point. I used to buy protein shakes and vitamin tonics to try to get nutrients into my body but when it came to solid food, I had a mental block.'

Dave reached across the table and took my hand in his. It was rare for me to be this open with someone I'd just met and this simple gesture had me feeling like I was on the verge of tears.

'Did you see a doctor?' he asked.

'Too scared,' I said. 'I didn't want to admit anything was wrong and didn't want to be put on medication.'

'I can understand that.'

The truth was, my parents hadn't wanted to admit that anything was wrong with me, and I had been just as much in denial. We'd all just pretended nothing was wrong for over a year, like it was a small quirk that would fix itself eventually, like I hadn't become skeletal in a matter of months.

'The turning point was my sister's birthday,' I told Dave. 'My family and I went out for a meal at her favourite restaurant but I was so consumed by anxiety I could barely function. I'd only ordered a bowl of chips but couldn't even eat that. I'd put one in my mouth and start retching until I spat it out. I tried again and again, tears streaming down my face as everyone in the restaurant stared at me. I was so hungry but I just couldn't swallow. My sister told me I'd ruined her birthday. That was when I knew I had to do something.'

'Bloody hell, Lauren,' he said after a moment. 'That's awful.'

I didn't know how to respond, so I stayed silent, staring at my half-eaten eggs. Despite sharing some of my biggest secrets, the silence was more comfortable than I'd expected and Dave seemed more concerned than anything else.

'I'm much better now,' I reassured him, detailing how I'd overcome the worst of it in an attempt to lighten the mood. Telling him how I'd set myself daily targets – making myself eat a chip one day, two chips the next day, and increasing it until I could eat them without issue – filled me with pride. I was a long way from overcoming my issues with food, especially when my first reaction to fear was to stop eating, but I was starting to realise that trying new things could take me one step further from regressing.

'Can I make a suggestion?' he asked.

'You can.'

'How about you let me introduce you to some Thai food while you're here? I think you'll really like it. We'll find some dishes without any spice or whatever else you don't eat and see how it goes. Hopefully we'll be able to find a way to wean you off those cheese sandwiches.'

'I'd love that,' I said, breaking into a grin. 'Thank you.'

It hadn't escaped my notice that Dave had just used an awful lot of 'we's. *Were we a 'we' already?* I looked down at his hand, still holding mine, and realised I didn't want him to let go.

I spent the day lost in a whirlwind of scooter rides, temples, handholding and stolen kisses, not ready to say goodbye to a wonderful guy who hadn't been scared by my crazy. I liked Dave a lot. He was inspirational, funny and handsome, and he seemed to like me, too. *Was this how dating on the road worked?* Was it about meeting someone new and exciting, immediately forming an intense connection and revelling in the freedom that meant we didn't have to have a conventional relationship? Part of me wanted to ask Dave what we were doing but the other part was happy knowing we were doing whatever we wanted. We had nowhere to be and no one to please but ourselves.

As the sun began to set, I was on the back of the scooter again, careering through a labyrinth of alleyways as I watched the sky turn pink.

'This is Chiang Mai Gate,' Dave told me as we eased into a gap between a hundred parked scooters. 'It's my favourite night market. Here – take a seat over there and I'll get us some food.'

I sat down on the blue stool he was pointing towards and rested my elbows on the plastic table. I looked around: there were roughly 50 stalls lining this part of the moat, each of them looking just as intimidating as the next. Plumes of smoke hung ominously in the air and I was struggling to recognise any of the smells.

Dave reappeared a few minutes later and sat down opposite me. In his hands were two plastic cups. 'A smoothie from Mrs Pa,' he announced, handing me one. 'Chiang Mai's best smoothies and they're less than fifty pence.'

I took a sip of the yellow liquid. It was sweet, tart and delicious. 'Wow!' I said. 'This is amazing. What is it?'

'Mango,' Dave announced with a twinkle in his eye.

'But I don't—'

'Like mango,' he finished for me. 'Right.'

I shook my head and laughed.

A cheerful teenage boy dropped two plates on our table. On top of them were rolling hills of rice speckled with chunks of white meat and green leaves. There was a fried egg on top that I immediately shifted to the side.

'This is *pad krapow gai kai dow*,' Dave told me. 'It's stir fried rice with chicken and basil. The *kai dow* means you get it with an egg on top.'

'A risky move after this morning,' I laughed.

'I figured you needed more challenges in your life.'

I scooped up a spoonful and sniffed it. It smelt like the sort of thing my friends used to eat while I would tuck into a Happy Meal.

'Go ahead,' he encouraged me. 'Don't worry – I got you the non-spicy version.'

I unclenched my jaw and pushed the spoon inside, keeping it as far away from my tongue as possible. I noticed Dave was giving me another strange look so I forced myself to taste it. When you've spent your whole life convinced you won't like any new food, it can be tough to suppress those misconceptions, especially when you can't recognise the flavours you're tasting; I'd spent my whole life equating unfamiliar with bad. I squished the rice against the roof of my mouth and tried to work out if it was a sensation I liked. It was savoury and mushy, and the garlic tingled in my mouth. I was relieved to find that basil didn't taste like trees.

'Ooh,' I murmured, gaping at the clean spoon. 'I actually like it.'

I shovelled another spoonful into my mouth, less afraid this time around.

'I can't even imagine how it feels to experience all these flavours for the first time,' Dave said. 'In a way, I'm kind of jealous. I can't remember the last time I tried a new dish.'

'So, you have the spicy version?' I asked.

'Yep. Look over there.' He pointed towards a Thai woman guarding a huge pan of sizzling meat and herbs, a surgical mask pulled over her mouth. 'She wears that mask to protect herself from the fumes. It's funny – when the wind blows in the right direction, you'll see everyone at the market start coughing.'

As he talked, I eyed the chilli peppers on his plate and was struck by a craving to try one. My *pad krapow gai kai dow* had given me confidence. I reached over to Dave's plate and grabbed a red one. Before he could say 'big mistake', I popped it in my mouth and bit down.

'What are you doing?'

'Trying something new!' I beamed, surprised to discover it tasted just like a bell pepper. 'Hey, I actually quite like—'

The heat hit my tongue and I tried to spit it out. *Get out, tongue! You don't belong here any more!* I tried to inhale but my mouth was a cul-de-sac; my throat had closed up; my body was no longer accepting oxygen. *Anaphylactic shock! I can't believe it – after all these years of panic, it was finally happening to me.* A blend of tears, snot and sweat glided down my face.

'What—hap—ing?' I choked out. The heat travelled to my chest and centred over my heart. 'Think—I—dying,' I gasped. 'Ana—phy—lac—tic shock!'

'Lauren.'

I looked up and saw Dave calmly observing me. 'It's a chilli,' he said. 'It's not a big deal.' He pushed my smoothie towards me. 'Have some of this and it'll pass within a few minutes.'

He was right. My tongue had already started to recover and now I was just hoping he'd think my red cheeks were from the heat of the peppers. I sniffed and rubbed away my tears. 'So that probably wasn't the smartest idea I've ever had.'

'Not really,' he said with a bemused smile.

Then my eyeballs caught fire.

'My eyes,' I yelped, covering my face with my hands. 'I'm blind!' 'What?'

'Argh!' I gargled, throwing my head back as everything turned black. 'I'm blind! *Anaphylactic blindness!*'

'Oh, Lauren,' Dave chuckled, handing me a fistful of tissues. 'I don't suppose you managed to rub your eyes with the same finger you touched the chilli with, did you?'

Back in Dave's apartment, we sat in bed with our laptops in a comfortable silence. I was emailing Jen and Ally to tell them what had happened; he was writing an article – hopefully not about the unstable girl he just took on a date.

'So,' I said, staring at my screen. 'That probably wasn't the best way to impress you tonight, huh?'

'You think?' he said, cracking up when I fiercely nodded. 'Well, I think you impressed me with your inability to eat chillies.'

'Such a disaster,' I groaned, wiping a stray tear from my cheek. 'You must think I'm insane.'

'Not insane,' he said, reaching over to squeeze my hand. 'But put it this way – it's a good job I like you as much as I do.'

My stomach dropped and I felt like I was falling. 'I like you too,' I said.

For some reason, Dave made me want to try new things. He made me want to fight my anxiety and challenge myself and prove I wasn't afraid of everything. He made me want to gain life experience and discover what I'd been missing out on. As I finished sending my emails, a thought crossed my mind.

'Dave,' I said.

'Yeah?'

'I think I'm going to try fried eggs tomorrow.'

CHAPTER 7

I dangled my legs over the sides of the scooter, letting the cool breeze tickle my ankles. Pushing up the visor of my helmet, I leaned my head back and smiled as the sun warmed my face. It was another beautiful day in Chiang Mai. I leaned into the turn as we rounded a corner of the moat and wrapped my arms around Dave.

Today marked six weeks in Chiang Mai and, despite my protestations that this trip was going to be a solo endeavour, I now found myself with a boyfriend. Dave and I had spent close to every second together since I'd moved into his apartment 30 minutes after meeting him and I had a good feeling about this. For once, I was paying attention to my intuition. We'd spent more time together over the past month and a half than I had during 18 months with Jeremy, and we had yet to argue or run out of things to say.

My inbox was filling with emails from friends back home, asking if I was still travelling, and I'd had to explain that I was slowing down for a few months to get to know a city more than superficially. Not many people decided to go travelling then spent three months not moving, and while it was never in my plans, it hadn't taken much convincing for me to stay. My travel blog was growing in popularity and now that I was accepting advertising and starting to make a profit, I was one step closer to being able to work from anywhere.

'We're here,' Dave announced, pulling up beside a giant yellow statue of a dog wearing glasses. Like many of our lunch dates, he had wanted to visit a small Thai restaurant and fill his stomach with chillies and rice. Unfortunately for him, it was my turn to choose where to eat and that meant we were going for cake.

'This looks like fun,' I exclaimed as I fastened my helmet to the handlebars. I wandered inside, pretending not to notice Dave dragging his feet behind me.

I pushed open the glass door and a wave of chilled air swirled around us. Inside, brown leather sofas were pushed up against the walls and the low wooden tables were packed with people nursing cartons of gelato. Just like every other cute cafe in Chiang Mai, it looked to be the haunt of Thai hipsters taking selfies.

'What do you fancy?' Dave asked me, as we loitered in front of a display of cakes.

'Something new,' I said. It was a phrase that had left my mouth several dozen times since arriving in Chiang Mai. After prodding my eye with chilli-soaked finger, I must have tried over 20 new dishes.

'Okay,' he said, squeezing my shoulder. 'Well, have you had cheesecake before?'

'Nope. I don't like it, though. Cheese on a cake? I prefer to keep my cheeses and cakes separate.'

'Lauren,' he interrupted, giving me 'the look'. The one that told me I'd said something ridiculous.

'What?'

'What do you think a cheesecake is exactly?'

'A sponge cake with a slice of cheese on top?'

Dave struggled to rein in his laughter. 'No,' he said, ruffling my hair. 'That's not what it is. How about you try your first cheesecake then? I promise there'll be no slices of cheese on top. Just cream cheese.'

I pictured a cake topped with Dairylea and reluctantly agreed. Dave ordered two chocolate cheesecakes, which was enough to turn my stomach. Chocolate and Dairylea sounded like a terrible combination.

'So, you said you had something to ask me?' I said, as we carried our cakes to a table. I sunk into a sofa while Dave perched on the wooden stool opposite.

'Oh, yeah,' he said, his face splitting into an infectious grin. 'How would you feel about going on a road trip?'

'On the scooter?'

'Yeah.'

My smile dropped. I didn't want to die.

'I don't actually know much about it,' he continued, not commenting on my frown. 'My friend, Stuart – you know him, don't you?'

I shook my head. 'Nope.'

'Oh, well, he's coming to Chiang Mai and dropped me a message to see if I was up for a road trip around northern Thailand. He owns Travelfish, right? The huge resource site for Southeast Asia?'

'Right,' I said, despite having never heard of it.

'So he knows the region better than pretty much anyone and wants to go for a ride. He sent me a list of places he wants to go to and I've never heard of any of them. It'll be amazing.' Dave's eyes lit up as he spoke; adventure was his passion.

'That sounds great,' I said, cutting a slice of my cake and popping it into my mouth. It tasted like creamy chocolate. 'Hey, this isn't bad. It doesn't taste like cheese.'

'I told you,' he said. 'I knew you'd like it.' I loved seeing Dave's reaction whenever I discovered something new that I liked and his enthusiasm was helping expand the size of my comfort zone.

'So do you think you'll want to come then?' he asked, studying my face. 'You can say no if you want.'

I looked at my cheesecake – something I'd expected to hate – and knew I had to keep challenging myself. 'I think I do,' I said. 'It sounds incredible.'

'I think it *will* be incredible and I'd love to have you there with me. And I think doing something like this will be a good introduction to an adventure for you. Then we can work up to doing something bigger.'

'Something bigger?' I gulped, picturing him throwing me into a coffin full of rattlesnakes. *'What an adventure!' he'd cheer, while I was slowly bitten to death.*

'Yeah, I've always wanted to buy one of those old American school buses,' he told me. 'My ultimate dream is to convert it into a liveable space and then drive it the length of Africa. I could get some of my friends involved and have people hop on and off along the way.'

My head was spinning. 'That sounds... impractical,' I said, running over the logistics of such a long and dangerous journey. *How did I end up with someone so different to me?* I'd thought Jeremy was insane for suggesting we travel to India, but now Dave was talking about driving the length of Africa?

~~~

'I think I'm ready!' I shouted, zipping my daypack shut. It was the morning of the road trip and we were going to be spending the next eight days with a single 20-litre bag between us. In it, we had two Kindles, five changes of clothes, some shower gel, a razor and, at my insistence, an enormous first aid kit.

'You sure you've got everything?' Dave asked, in a voice that said he knew I was forgetting something.

'Yep.'

'What about your toothbrush?'

'Packed just now.'

'Your motion-sickness pills?'

'Got about eighty in my bag.'

'Some warm clothes?'

'What?'

'Some warm clothes,' he repeated. 'For when we're up in the mountains?'

'Wait, what? There are going to be *mountains*?'

He rubbed his eyes and stared at me. 'Did you even pay attention to our conversation with Stuart yesterday or were you too focused on your cheese sandwich?'

'Of course I did!' I lied. In reality, I'd spent much of our conversation worrying about my likelihood of surviving this road trip.

We had arranged to meet Stuart the previous day in a coffee shop. 'We're looking for a guy who looks like he's been living in Southeast Asia for the past twenty years,' Dave had told me. I had been nervous: while being in Chiang Mai had helped boost my confidence, I was still awkward around strangers I hadn't met in dorm rooms. I was still unsure about how to have a conversation that didn't focus on 'where have you been?' and 'where are you going?'

I'd turned around and focused on the guy in a black T-shirt with Travelfish emblazoned on the front that was strolling towards us. He'd looked a little older than Dave: unshaven face, lightly tanned, messy greyish hair and a serene expression, just how Dave had described him.

'Hey guys,' he'd said in an Australian accent.

'Oh hey, Stuart,' Dave had said.

'Hi,' I'd mumbled, offering a wave. 'I'm Lauren.'

'Hi Laura,' he'd said, waving back. I'd opened my mouth to correct him but then shut it again, too concerned about scooter crash statistics to worry about being called by the wrong name. I'd zoned out after that and spent the next couple of hours coming up with a plan for how to tell him I wasn't called Laura.

'Well, do you have any warm clothes?' Dave asked, pulling me back into the moment.

'Nope. I threw them all out in Ukraine in case they were still radioactive.'

'Come on, Lauren,' he groaned. 'What are you doing? Why haven't you replaced them? Can't you just go to the market at the end of the road and get a jumper or something? I can meet you there with the bike.'

I grabbed a handful of cash and rushed out of the room in a flurry of panic. 'Stupid Dave and his stupid warm clothes,' I muttered as I ran.

Faced with a market full of options, I decided to buy the most hideous jumper I could find for no other reason than I was feeling petty. Dave would come to rue the day when he'd told me I'd need warm clothes.

'Got it,' I shouted, when I spotted Dave parked up beside the market. He handed me my daypack and helmet, and I leapt on the back. 'Done.'

I hooked my fingers around the belt loops of Dave's jeans and rested my head against his back. I'd grown fearless when it came to scooters after over a month of riding them every day. Now, I wore shorts and a T-shirt so I could work on my tan from the back of the bike. Tempting fate? Absolutely.

We met back up with Stuart and within half an hour, our small procession had left the city and merged with a congested motorway. When visualising this road trip, I'd imagined us flying down lonely dirt tracks lined with glowing rice paddies, with leafy palms on either side, waving to local children who'd try to chase us down when we passed through their villages. A lorry shot past us, blaring its horn as Dave slammed on the brakes to avoid hitting another scooter. I inhaled a toxic cloud from its exhaust and broke into a coughing fit. Just as my heart rate began to calm, we hit a rock with our front wheel and I caught some air, hovering over my seat and falling back down with a thump. My daypack mirrored my movement, grating the skin from my back as it slammed down behind me. *No, this was not what I'd imagined at all.*

We stopped for lunch in the chilly mountain town of Chiang Dao. By most people's standards, it had been an easy 90 minutes of riding but I was already feeling road-weary. I dug a dozen flies out of the corner of my eye and looked around: dense jungle; soaring limestone peaks; the glint of a golden pagoda poking through the tree line; a cloud of black smoke rising from a nearby farm. The air was thick with the smell of damp grass and burning.

I'd thought this trip would be easy, especially as all I had to do was sit on the back of the bike and take photos. Jumping on a scooter for a 5-minute trip around a moat felt like the most comfortable thing in the world. Stretch those 5 minutes to 90, add vibrations from high speeds on a rough surface, throw in some nerve-wracking manoeuvres with vehicles 30 times our size, and strap a daypack to my back and you have all the ingredients you need for me staggering into the restaurant like I'd spent the morning atop a mechanical bull.

'How would you guys feel about spending the night here?' Stuart asked, as he tucked into a plate of unrecognisable Thai food.

Relieved! Ecstatic! Euphoric! The happiest girl in the world! I poked at my cheeseburger and looked at Dave.

'I could definitely stay,' he said.

'Yeah, I could definitely stay,' I echoed.

The next day, I awoke with a swirl of steam around my face. It was a sensation I hadn't felt in several months. *Cold.*

'Time to get up!' Dave called out to me while pulling on every item of clothing he'd packed. I hopped out of bed and dragged my new hairball of a jumper out of my daypack. I held it out in front of me. The brown and orange yarn was setting my teeth on edge before I'd even put it on, and the fluffy strands of wool would add several inches to my size.

'What on earth is that?' Dave spluttered as I dragged it over my head.

'My warm clothes,' I said, twirling a pirouette. 'Do you like it?'

'It's quite possibly the most hideous thing I've ever seen.'

I caught a glimpse in the mirror and marvelled at how my jumper looked like it'd been struck by lightning.

I joined in with Dave's laughter, feeling lighter than yesterday. It was a Tuesday: a day when most people around the world were dragging themselves to work. This was my Tuesday: a road trip through a stunning part of a country that few tourists get to see. My pessimism from yesterday was long gone. In its place was a desire to soak up every moment and appreciate the experience.

I pulled on two pairs of socks and forced my flip-flops over the top of them, then slipped another pair over my hands. Travelling light means being creative when you don't have space in your backpack for a pair of gloves.

Two days of riding brought us to Phu Lang Ka, a remote village in the mountains, overlooking a gorgeous valley filled with brown farmland and limestone karsts. There was only one guesthouse here: the eponymously, if optimistically named, Phu Lang Ka Resort. It comprised of a dozen primitive bungalows, all with holes in the walls large enough for a dog to fit through.

'Beer,' the guys panted in unison as we clambered off our bikes.

'Nap,' I gasped, collecting the keys from the owner and hurrying to our bungalow.

I collapsed into bed with a sigh. Not even the clammy sheets could wipe the smile from my face. It had been a spectacular few days of riding. Outside of Chiang Dao, we'd lost the traffic of the first day and spent the next two days puttering along curling roads overlooking sweeping vistas of emerald rice paddies. It was rare to see another white face in this part of Thailand and I couldn't help but wonder just how many tourists do make it out here.

I frowned and sat back up again. This had to be the worst bed in the world. I ran my hands over the mattress, wondering if it had been constructed from wet sacks of concrete.

A few minutes later, the door creaked open.

'They don't have any cold drinks here,' Dave announced with a sigh. I squinted in his direction and watched as he wiped his shoes on the blackened mat outside. 'Stuart's taken his bike to the village to get some beers.'

'Oh,' I said, my eyelids wavering.

'There's a gorgeous sunset out there, by the way. You want to watch it with me?'

I hesitated, weighing the options. A nap sounded wonderful, but I could never resist a sunset. 'Damn you, Dave,' I grumbled, forcing myself out of bed. I sidestepped a cavernous hole in the floor and tiptoed outside, too tired to put on my shoes.

I padded over the wet grass, past a cluster of wooden picnic tables and a small white building. I followed Dave around a corner and there it was. The most incredible sunset of my life. I stood transfixed, mouth agape, staring up at the sky. A hundred shades of yellow, orange, pink and purple, colliding together over layers of rolling jungle-clad hills. A distant gunshot broke the silence just as the colours began to fade. As I turned to look at Dave, I noticed a fluorescent light flickering behind us and illuminating the grassy clearing. It was then that I realised we were stood next to the toilet block. It was one of the most romantic moments of my life.

'I'm happy I came to Chiang Mai,' I whispered, reaching for Dave's hand.

'Me too.'

That night, I tossed and turned, irritated as my sleep was interrupted by the unexplained firing of shotguns and squawking of insomniac roosters. At least the noise made it easy to catch the sunrise. If I'd thought the sunset had been impressive last night, it had nothing on this. In the chilly morning hours, the valley looked almost mystical, cloaked in a thick layer of mist with the tops of limestone karsts poking through. Every so often a gust of wind would shift it slightly, revealing the green countryside that lurked beneath.

I ate my breakfast in silence, awestruck by our surroundings. While Dave and Stuart chatted about the journey ahead of us, I concentrated on watching the sun creep up over the top of the mountains.

I eased myself on the back of the scooter that morning, and held on to Dave as we began our descent down the wide curves to the steamy valley floor. The scenery switched from open woodland and small villages to impenetrable forests and weathered mountain ranges, meeting only with the motorway when we closed in on Nan, our destination for the night.

It took two days to reach Lampang, the only place in Thailand where – bizarrely – colourful horse-drawn carriages replaced tuk-tuks as transport. We had just one night in this small city and, with all of us sweaty and exhausted, decided to spend it drinking vodka on our balcony while we gorged on 12 plates of fried pork.

Tomorrow, we'd be leaving for Chiang Mai, eight days later and with a thousand extra miles on the odometer, and I was already wondering how I'd ever be able to top this travel experience.

Over the past week, I'd seen some of the prettiest vistas of my life, strengthened my back after 8 hours a day on the scooter and taken a much-needed digital detox, all in a part of the world that few tourists get to visit. We'd seen little more than a dozen other Westerners during our trip and I felt grateful to have experienced it for myself.

I awoke the following morning to sunlight streaming in through the window. I rolled on to my back and exhaled, watching the steam rise from my mouth. My back was sore; my face was sunburnt; and I was covered in road grime that had been too stubborn for any of the guesthouse showers to remove. It was a bittersweet feeling. I'd loved every moment of the thousand miles we'd covered, but my weary body had felt every single one of them. I couldn't wait to get back to our apartment.

I reached under Dave's pillow and pulled out his phone. It was 7 a.m., which meant we'd be hitting the road within the hour and reaching Chiang Mai before nightfall.

We got dressed and I pulled on the same denim shorts and pink vest I'd been wearing for three days straight. They felt damp and musty, and my shorts were stained orange with mud.

'You looking forward to getting back?' I asked Dave, pointing at his equally grimy T-shirt – once white but now a distinct shade of brown.

'Not really,' he said with a grimace. 'I'd be happy doing this for months.'

'Oh,' I said, zipping my daypack shut for the final time. I imagined doing this for months on end and winced. *Wouldn't he miss the sensation of freshly washed clothes? Not risking your life on a daily basis? Not feeling like a cripple whenever you move?* I couldn't imagine doing something like this for more than a week at a time.

'Don't you feel the same?' he asked, pulling me in for a hug. 'Wouldn't it be so great if this was our life? We could spend a year riding scooters around Southeast Asia: no plans, just a small backpack and wherever the road takes us.'

'Sort of,' I said, wriggling away. It sounded like a sure-fire way to die.

As it was our final day, we decided to take the longer scenic route that would take us over narrow mountain paths rather than congested motorways. It was during these hours of riding that I forgot about my aching back and could see where Dave was coming from. As we rode through farmland and countryside, and curled around sweeping mountain vistas without another vehicle in sight, I found myself secretly planning an extended scooter trip. *Spend a year riding through gorgeous scenery like this? Yeah, I could do that.*

A couple of hours into the ride, my enthusiasm was beginning to waver. These mountain roads were steep and our scooter was ill-equipped to conquer them with two people on board. As I watched Stuart disappear up ahead of us, we began to slow down. I peered over Dave's shoulder to check the speedometer: 40 kph… 30… 20… the engine was whining now… 10… 5…

'Are we still moving?' I asked, gazing skywards at the enormous tree towering above us. It must have been 30 m high.

We came to a standstill.

'Get off! Get off! Get off!' Dave shouted.

'What?'

'GET OFF THE BIKE!'

'HOW?'

'JUMP OFF!' he bellowed over the whine of the engine.

'I CAN'T JUMP OFF THE BACK OF A MOVING VEHICLE!'

'WE'RE NOT FUCKING MOVING, LAUREN.'

Oops. I let go of Dave and pushed on the seat so I bounced backwards off the bike. My traumatising five years of gymnastics lessons had finally come in handy. I landed on my ankle and collapsed in a heap in the ground. *Maybe not.*

'Argh,' I groaned, watching Dave peel off around the bend.

I stood up and began to stagger after him. I didn't know how high we were, but the chilly air was thin enough to leave me struggling to breathe.

'Come along, plod,' I heard Dave call. I looked up and saw him and Stuart waiting up ahead, watching a forlorn Lauren battle with the steep incline.

'Man,' I panted when I caught up to them. 'That was frightening.'

'And you can't relax yet,' Dave warned, wrapping his arm around my shoulders and kissing my forehead. 'We've still got the downhill part to come.'

'Woohoo,' I said in a monotone. I climbed back on to the scooter and tightened my grip around the back of the seat. Rather than clinging to Dave, I would need to do everything I could to keep my distance. He didn't need my weight pushing him forwards.

The road narrowed and the drops became even more precipitous. As we wove our way around the bends, I dug my heels into the pedals and tried not to focus on the screeching brakes. I watched Dave clench the paddle in his fist and wondered if we'd be riding them the whole way down.

'Thank God we have brakes, hey?' I shouted over the squealing.

At that moment, the smell of burning chemicals filled the air and Dave began to speed up. I let out a joyful laugh, enjoying the cool breeze on my face. It was just like him to pretend the brakes had failed as we were careering down the steep face of a mountain.

'Ha ha,' I called to him. 'Very scary. Can we slow down now please?'

He didn't reply and instead sped around a corner, missing a sheer vertical drop by inches. It was then I noticed the brake paddle flapping uselessly in his hand.

'What are you doing?' I shouted.

'The brakes!' he roared back at me, as we swept around another corner. 'The brakes have gone.'

I screamed as we whipped past some thorny branches, grimacing as they sliced up my legs. 'Please don't let me die,' I wailed, burrowing my nails into the seat.

'Hang…on…' he grunted. He took his feet off the pedals and pressed his trainers into the ground to try to slow us down, but just ended up leaving half of his sole behind on the road.

'Dave!' I gasped as we skidded past another drop without a barrier. There was no doubt about it: we were going to die. I arranged myself in the brace position I'd memorised from aircraft safety manuals.

A loud bang sounded and I was thrown forwards, arcing through the air and collapsing against Dave's back. I waited for the freefall.

'We're safe,' he said in a trembling voice.

I cracked open my eyes, wondering why I couldn't focus on anything until I realised I was face to face with a bush. Dave had somehow managed to steer us into the side of the mountain. He had saved our lives.

'So, I think what's best,' Dave addressed our group after we'd caught up with a nervous Stuart who'd thought we'd plummeted to our deaths, 'Is if, Lauren – you go on the back of Stuart's bike and I'll follow behind, taking it slow.'

I nodded, scrambling off the back of the scooter and on to Stuart's.

'You alright?' Stuart asked.

'Yes, thank you,' I replied. I went to put my arms around his waist and froze. I couldn't just *touch* Stuart. I barely even knew him. I squeezed my thighs around the seat instead and braced myself for the acceleration.

He revved the engine and we shot forwards at a much faster speed than I was used to. He wasn't renting an underpowered £2-a-day scooter. I threw my arms behind me and grasped the edge of the seat, struggling to stay upright. The weight of my daypack began to drag me down and my helmet slid over one eye. As I took a deep breath to try to gain control, a chunk of my hair whipped into my mouth and I started to choke. My bag was hanging off the side of the scooter now and I was seconds away from tumbling off the back. My feet left the pedals. *Oh God*. I watched in horror as they rose up, past Stuart's legs, past his arms...

Screech!

We came to a halt right around the point when my ankles started wavering around his neck. *You were right,* I told myself. *This is much less awkward than touching Stuart's waist.*

'You okay there, Laura?' he called, twisting around to look at me.

'Yes,' I whispered, lying flat on my back behind him.

CHAPTER 8

Dave fiddled with the keys while I impatiently tapped my foot beside him.

'The first thing I'm going to do,' I told him, 'is have the hottest, longest shower. Then, I'm going to go downstairs and wash my clothes. And *then*, I'm going to have a cheese and pickle sandwich for dinner.' I spun myself in dizzying circles, thrilled to be back in Chiang Mai.

'Right, you. Inside.' Dave pushed open the door and my smile stretched from ear to ear.

'Home!' I squealed, throwing my daypack at him and waltzing into the room. 'I missed you,' I sang, stroking the bed, the desk, the windows and the fridge. Nobody would describe our apartment as homely. Thanks to our lack of possessions, it still looked like a page from an IKEA catalogue. I dive-bombed the bed and rolled around in the crisp white sheets.

'You know what I like most about you?' Dave said with a bemused look on his face. He was still standing in the corridor outside.

'What's that?'

'How excited you get at the most mundane things. You're like a puppy discovering the world for the first time.'

I grinned and untangled myself from the bed sheets. 'True,' I said, running to drag him inside. 'But how can you not be excited about this?' I twirled and pointed at our simple room. 'No more sore backs, no more sitting on a scooter for eight hours a day, no more worrying about brake failures…'

'Something like that.'

I stopped spinning. 'Are you really sad it's over?'

'A little.'

'I'm sadder than I'd thought I'd be,' I confessed.

'Liar.'

'No, really. I'm fairly certain that once I've had a shower and my back has stopped aching, I'll be craving hopping on the scooter again.'

'Speaking of showers,' he said, grabbing my shoulders and marching me into the bathroom.

'You're right,' I said. 'I stink.'

An hour later, I wandered out of the bathroom with a stabbing pain in my head.

'Do you have a headache?' I asked Dave, rubbing my right temple.

'No?'

I walked towards him and squatted beside his desk. 'I do.'

'Oh dear,' he said absently, typing a quick sentence on his laptop before looking down at me. 'And you thought because you had a headache I'd have one too?'

I thought about it for a second and nodded.

'You're strange,' he chuckled, reaching down to flick my nose.

'I mean it,' I said. 'What if there was a brain-eating amoeba in one of our road trip showers? That's a thing, you know. That happens to people.'

'Honey,' he said patiently, tucking a strand of hair behind my ear. 'You're fine. It's just a headache. Drink some water or something.'

I walked across the room and rummaged through my daypack for my first aid kit, then gulped down two paracetamols with my fingers crossed. Keeping a watchful eye on Dave, I perched on the end of the bed and opened my laptop. While he focused on catching up on work, I typed, 'headache causes death' into Google to see if I was having a brain aneurysm. My eyes ran over the search results and I slammed the lid of my laptop shut. I bounded back over to him.

'Do I have a fever?' I asked.

'No.'

'How do you know? You haven't felt my forehead.'

'You'd know if you had a fever.'

'No I wouldn't. I've never had a fever.'

'You've never had a—'

'Please?'

Dave reached over and pressed a warm palm to my forehead. 'No,' he said. 'You don't have a fever. You feel colder than me.'

I sat back down on the bed and put on my sunglasses. My temples were throbbing and it ached behind my eyes: classic symptoms of dengue fever. While I examined my fingers for haemorrhaging, I wondered what Dave would do in this situation. He was one of the most logical thinkers I'd met and couldn't seem to comprehend my propensity to jump to the worst-case scenario.

In this situation, Dave would probably drink a big glass of water, swallow a couple of painkillers and take a quick nap. He'd fall asleep with the knowledge that it would all be better tomorrow. I decided that's what I'd do, too. *In your face, hypochondria. I won't let you break me.*

The following morning, I realised I was dying. My head was hammering away like a piston, my jaw was throbbing and there was a searing pain behind my eyes.

'Help,' I moaned, waking Dave up by suctioning on to his back like a human jetpack.

'What are you doing?' he grumbled, untangling himself and turning to stare at me.

'My headache,' I said. 'It's worse.'

His glare softened. 'Oh, I'm sorry, baby,' he said, reaching out to stroke my forehead. 'I guess you should see a doctor if it's that bad. You have travel insurance, don't you?'

'Of course.' I leaned into Dave's chest and sniffed. He smelt like burnt toast. 'Phantom smells,' I muttered. 'The sign of a brain tumour.'

He stopped caressing my face. 'You don't have a brain tumour.'

'I bet that's what people say to people who have brain tumours.'

'So, you're going to go to the doctor?'

I imagined myself walking into a doctor's clinic, full of sterile, white furniture and bright lights. The thought was enough to make me retch. 'I can't,' I said, pressing my fist to my lips. 'It'll make me feel worse. But I think I can handle the dentist.'

'What?'

'Referred pain: pain perceived at a location other than the site of the painful stimulus,' I quoted from a page I'd memorised from Wikipedia. 'Maybe my headache is due to my teeth.'

'Oh, of course,' he groaned, slapping his head. 'That makes sense. I can't tell you how many times I've been to the dentist because I had a headache.'

'*Referred* pain, Dave,' I said, easing out of bed and reaching for my sunglasses. 'My teeth *could* be the cause.' I stood up and started to get dressed.

'I'm sorry,' he said in a strained voice. 'Look – if you think it'll help then go, but I think it sounds like a huge waste of time.'

'I think it *will* help,' I said, pulling on a black T-shirt. 'And if it doesn't, I'll see a doctor next.' I leaned over and kissed him on the cheek. We both knew I was skirting around the issue but I was in too much pain to admit to it.

I stepped into the hazy morning light and grimaced, the breeze in the air cooling my skin and tangling my hair. The restaurants and street carts were just starting to open and the aroma of frying bacon drifted across the street. If I hadn't been suffering from referred tooth pain, I'd be tucking into a greasy fry-up at one of these places and sipping on a pineapple smoothie. I daydreamed about how I'd spend my morning if I weren't at death's door, deciding I'd celebrate my health with a pool day. I manoeuvred my way across the road, taking it one step at a time while the scooters weaved around me like I was a human traffic cone.

When I'd been planning out my dream trip around the world, I'd never imagined it would involve spending several months in one city, but Chiang Mai was starting to feel an awful lot like home. Life was good here and already I was starting to dread leaving in a month's time. *Was I a terrible traveller? Could I even call myself a traveller when I'd spent almost as much time in one place as I had moving?* I shook my head and sidestepped a scooter taking a shortcut along the pavement. I was worrying about what other people thought of me again. If I thought I was a traveller, then I was a traveller. And I could spend as long as I wanted in a place. Chiang Mai was beautiful, it was cheap and being here made me happy.

Things with Dave were going well, too. I liked that he challenged me and, oddly enough, rarely showered me with sympathy. It was what I needed from a relationship right now. Someone who'd call me out when I made excuses and encourage me to challenge myself when it was the last thing I wanted to do. After all, that was part of the reason why I'd wanted to travel.

There was a dentist's surgery a couple of blocks from our apartment and it had everything I didn't need right now: cold air conditioning, bright lights and white furniture. Just like my vision of the doctor's surgery I was trying to avoid. My stomach lurched. Inside, I was greeted with the scent of a hospital and three giggling receptionists. I was the only person in the waiting room this early in the morning. I gave them my details and took a seat.

'Miss La-oo-wen!' a voice sang out.

I looked up from the magazine I was pretending to read and saw a small Thai girl wearing large hipster-style glasses. She waved me over.

'Miss La-oo-wen,' she repeated, as I walked up to her. After greeting me with a smile and a slight nod, she ushered me in through a shiny white door and motioned for me to sit. I was feeling surprisingly relaxed for someone who was convinced her brain was home to a bowling ball-sized tumour.

'How can I help you?' she asked.

I froze. *What was I supposed to tell her? That I had a headache so I wanted her to look at my teeth?*

'My jaw is painful,' I said finally. 'So I wanted to get my teeth checked.'

'Okay, we can do X-ray.'

'Okay.'

She pulled open the door and I followed her down the corridor to another room. It was the only non-white room in the building and it smelt like wet paint. It was warm and stuffy, with scuffed grey walls and a large X-ray machine.

'Miss La-oo-wen, please take jewellery off,' she sang, circling her hands around my ears.

Damn it, I thought. *That was going to be a problem.*

When I was 18 years old, I decided to get my ears pierced. As I'd sat hunched on a stool in the middle of Claire's Accessories, the teenage girl had grabbed my ear and said to me, 'You've eaten today, right?'

'Uh, no,' I'd stammered. I was at the height of my anxiety and hadn't eaten in 48 hours.

'Oh,' she'd said in a monotone. 'Well, I'm sure you'll be fine. Some people faint if they haven't eaten before a piercing.' With that, she'd lowered the gun to my ear and quickly shot two pieces of metal through my lobes.

I'd passed out in a matter of seconds, sliding off the stool in front of a crowd of bemused shoppers. After that, I'd associated my earrings with fainting and had never taken them out.

'I can't take them out,' I told the dentist. 'My earrings are stuck.'

She walked up to me and bent over to get a closer look. I felt her lock her fingernails around the silver stud and she began to tug. My eyes widened; this was terrifying. Her hands were shaking from the force, and I was certain she was either going to rip apart my ears or punch me in the face.

'It won't come out,' I insisted, trying to push her hands away.

She let go and studied my burning ear. 'Wait.'

I watched her totter out of the room in her enormous high heels and started wrenching at my earring with all the strength I had. 'Get out of my ear,' I grunted. 'Come on!' If this earring was coming out, it was going to be me who did it.

All too soon, the door swung open and stood in front of me were the dentist and two of the giggling receptionists. I tried to keep calm as they walked up to me and arranged themselves in a circle. I felt like the cauldron in the opening scene of *Macbeth*.

The dentist gripped the sides of my head, while one receptionist grabbed the front of my earring and the other latched on to the back. Working together, they began to twist and pull while I closed my eyes and waited to be torn a new earlobe.

'No work,' one of them sighed.

The dentist motioned for them to leave. 'We do it with earring.'

I stared at the X-ray in my hands, trying to work out why the dentist was looking so solemn.

'Look,' she said again, tapping it with her pen.

'It's okay?'

'No, is not okay,' she sang. 'We do two fillings. Two big fillings.' She began to recline the chair before I could process what was happening.

'Wait, what?' I said, sitting back up. 'Are you sure?' I'd visited my dentist for a check-up a few days before leaving and she'd told me my teeth were perfect. I was meticulous when it came to my dental health, determined to quash the stereotype that all British people have terrible teeth. I found it hard to believe I now needed two fillings, just six months after leaving.

'You wan' anaesthetic?' she said, ignoring my question.

'No, thank you.'

I watched her walk over to a table and lift up some kind of plastic blanket. She cradled it in her arms and then carried it towards me with both hands, as if she was holding a baby. She waited for me to lie down and then draped it over my face, arranging it so the hole was over my mouth. I felt like a horse with blinders over my eyes.

As my jaw began to vibrate, I thought of Dave and how I should have listened to him. I thought of the wonderful weather and how I could have been outside right now, scootering beneath the sun's warm glow.

'Miss La-oo-wen?' came a nervous voice, 30 traumatising minutes later. The dentist lifted the blanket from my face and stared at me with concern. 'I give anaesthetic now. The filling is big and I think will hurt.'

'Are you sure?'

'Yes, I sure.'

What could I do? We were half an hour in and I was certain she was destroying my teeth. *Was she a rogue dentist taking pleasure in annihilating the teeth of innocent tourists? Was I an idiot for letting her?* I examined her face for signs of rogue-ness, but she looked so young and innocent. 'Okay,' I said with a nod. 'Anaesthetic.'

I flinched at the sharp prick of the needle and the sensation of possible anaphylactic shock-inducing liquid entering my gums. Darkness clouded my vision as she rearranged my blinders.

The drilling started up again and under my sweaty covering, I lost track of time. How long had I been here? Five minutes?

An hour? Six months? Decades could have passed and I wouldn't have known.

The searing light of a halogen bulb interjected my timekeeping challenge and I blinked like a trapped bunny exposed to sunlight for the first time. A trapped bunny with a construction zone in its mouth.

'Very big filling,' she sang and I could have sworn she was full of glee. 'Half finish.'

'Are you serious?' I mumbled incoherently with a drooping lip. I leaned over to check the time on her computer screen. 'You've been working for over an hour,' I exclaimed. 'Do I even have any of my tooth left?'

She cocked her head to one side. 'Is very bad tooth.'

I fought the urge to run to my apartment with a crater in my mouth and opened wide in defeat.

Weeeeeeooooooooooowwwwwwww! the drill shrieked in my ear.

Blaaaaaaarrrrrrrrrrrrrrgggggggggggg! bellowed a different drill, feeling like a road digger in my mouth.

Weeeeeeooooooooooowwwwwwww!

Blaaaaaaarrrrrrrrrrrrrrgggggggggggg!

Weeeeeeooooooooooowwwwwwww!

Blaaaaaaarrrrrrrrrrrrrrgggggggggggg!

I braced myself, waiting for the drill to meet my gums. In a last-ditch attempt at protecting myself, I rolled my tongue alongside her fingers to create a chute leading towards my lips. When the blood started spurting, I'd be able to funnel it away from my throat.

'Is done.'

The drilling stopped and I opened my eyes.

'And then she drilled into my second tooth for another two hours!' I declared, curling my palms into fists. I looked at Dave, who was staring at me with a stunned expression.

He opened his mouth to speak but stopped and thought for a second. 'That's... really weird.'

'Thank God,' I said. 'You think so, too? I was worried it was normal and I was freaking out over nothing.' I sat down on the bed and relaxed my hands. 'And I still have this stupid headache.'

'Why does this sort of thing always seems to happen to you?' he asked gently.

'It's ridiculous,' I snapped, anger rising in my throat. I'd been berating myself over my bad luck all afternoon. 'I mean, what am I doing wrong? Seriously, tell me. Because this kind of thing doesn't happen to anyone else. I'm the common denominator. I can see that. You can see it. It can't just be bad luck, can it?'

'Well, if it was me...'

'Yeah?'

'... I wouldn't have gone to the dentist over a headache.'

I stared at him for a few seconds before letting out a sigh. He was right, as always. If I'd listened to him – if I'd listened to logic – I'd have gone to the doctor's and probably have some idea of what was causing my headache.

'Does it hurt?' he asked. He crouched down in front of me and took my face in his hands. Turning it from side to side, he ran his fingers over my jaw in a way that gave me goosebumps. 'It doesn't seem swollen.'

'It's not,' I said. 'And it doesn't hurt yet. I went to the chemist on the way back and picked up some painkillers as a pre-emptive strike. I asked for the strongest ones they had.'

He stood back up and scratched his head. 'What did they give you?'

I pulled the silver blister pack out of my pocket and squinted at it. 'It says it's something called Tramadol¿'

'Never heard of it.'

'Me neither.'

'Ah well, I'm sure it'll be fine.'

'What do you mean¿' ('I'm sure it'll be fine' was what people said when they weren't convinced it was going to be fine.) 'Why wouldn't it be fine, Dave¿'

He closed his eyes and took a deep breath. Then he walked over to his desk and turned on his laptop.

'Dave...¿'

'What¿'

'I'm frightened.'

He continued looking at his screen. 'Why are you frightened¿'

'In case it's not fine. In case I've taken something really dangerous. In case I have an allergic reaction. In case these pills are going to make me feel weird.'

I replayed the moment when I'd left the chemist. How I'd pressed two pills through the foil and dropped them on my tongue despite not knowing what the dosage was. The pharmacist had handed them over without any instruction and I'd guessed I'd need two to get the full effect. *What had I taken¿*

'Well,' Dave said, showing me the page open on his laptop. 'It says here that Tramadol is an opioid pain medication used to treat moderate to moderately severe pain.'

'An opioid¿ What does that mean¿ Like opium¿ Have I just taken opium¿' I ran my fingers through my hair and wondered if I should run to the nearest hospital to get my stomach pumped. 'Oh God, it's going to make me feel weird, isn't it¿'

'Nah,' he said in an infuriatingly calm voice.

'Your girlfriend is about to start feeling weird and all you can say is "nah?"'

'It's not opium,' he said.

'Oh no,' I groaned, my mind racing. 'What are they going to do to me, Dave?'

'Stop you feeling pain?'

I grabbed his hand and pressed it to my forehead. 'Do I have a fever?'

'No.'

I plopped my tongue outside my mouth and let it hang for Dave to examine. 'Is my tongue bigger? Am I having an allergic reaction?'

'No.'

'I feel weird.'

'Go to sleep,' he said.

Dave's tough love could be maddening, even though I knew how frustrating it had to be for him; that if he'd done what I'd wanted and driven me to a hospital, I'd never stand a chance at beating my hypochondria.

I'd had ten years' experience of thinking myself sick. At the height of my anxiety, one of my favourite pastimes had been rifling through my mum's medical dictionary and diagnosing myself with whatever disease I happened to land on. From skin cancer to scurvy, the next morning I'd wake up with every symptom listed.

I had become a permanent fixture in my doctor's office, eager to tell him about my heart palpitations, swollen glands and general sense of malaise. When every test he ordered came back as an inevitable negative, I'd awake the next morning with undetectable glands and a steadily beating heart, every symptom gone within hours.

I inhaled for 5 seconds and exhaled for 7. *It was just a painkiller. I wasn't going to die.*

A few seconds later, Dave was shaking me awake, speaking in what sounded like another language. I strained my ears to understand, but he sounded like he was underwater.

'Why do you sound funny?' I said, struggling to keep my eyes open.

'I don't.'

'Yes, you do,' I insisted. 'Why did you take me to an aquarium? You know that fish scare me.'

I sat up and the room rose with me. I felt as if I was teetering on the edge of a cliff, flailing my arms to prevent myself from falling. I looked at Dave but his face was moving around too much for me to work out if he was smiling or frowning.

'Dinner, Lauren,' he repeated, his voice echoing in my ears. 'I'm going to the night market. Do you want to come?'

I nodded and the world rocked back and forth with me. I felt like I was trapped in a fuzzy world where all my thoughts were tangled up in each other. *How long had I been sleeping?* It felt like seconds but if we were having dinner it must have been all afternoon.

As I watched Dave glide across the room, I told myself that this was all in my head. I'd been worrying about feeling weird and now I was. It was just my hypochondria.

On the walk to the night market, time and space seemed to lose meaning and I felt as though I was dragging my feet through mud. The market was 10 minutes away but it seemed to take hours. Still, I trudged onwards, certain that pushing myself through this would cure me of my hypochondria.

I gripped on to Dave's arm when the crowds got heavier, disorientated from sensory overload. As I glanced around, the bright lights of market stalls left imprints on my eyeballs, so wherever I looked there were green and purple splotches blocking my view. Loud music blasted out from speakers in the back of a pick-up truck and I held my spare hand over my ear in reaction to it. As I did so, I looked down and saw a trail of arms leading up to my face like I was a Hindu god. Dave led me past the shimmering golden *stupa* of a temple and into a labyrinth of food carts.

'You want to sit down and I'll get the food?' he asked, steering me towards a chair. I didn't reply but sat down anyway, unable to take my eyes off the sea of swirling faces in front of me. I couldn't work out why everyone was staring, or why so many of the faces had black holes for eyes. In the distance, some looked like they were screaming, frozen with their faces stretched and contorted. I watched them with interest, more curious than afraid.

'Here you go,' Dave said, placing a plate of chicken and rice in front of me. The crowds dispersed until there was only me and him. *Where had the ghosts gone?* I missed them.

'Thanks,' I mumbled.

I balanced a chunk of chicken on my fork and watched it pulse on the plastic. Then, I opened my mouth and stabbed myself in the cheek.

CHAPTER 9

'So where do you feel like going?' Dave asked, tilting his laptop screen so I could see the map.

'Anywhere,' I groaned, digging my knuckles into my temple. I'd usually be able to recite a list of 50 possible suggestions when asked that question, but the searing pain in my head was making even going back home look appealing.

As it turned out, a double dose of Tramadol hadn't been the best option for an anxiety-ridden hypochondriac who thinks herself sick. It had taken 24 hours for the hallucinations to fade and another month to realise my headache wasn't going anywhere, no matter how much water I drank.

My current theory was that a small herd of tap-dancing elephants had taken up camp on my brain and was trying to kick me into submission. Dave's theory was far more logical. It was spring in Chiang Mai, the time of year when colourful orchids come into bloom, the temperatures start to soar and a mass burning-off of crops takes place. It was the last fact that was important. As farmers set fire to their fields to start the process of replanting, a thick layer of smog settles over the northern regions of Thailand and, at times, we were barely able to see more than 20 m ahead of us. Dave was convinced it was the source of my headache, so we were leaving in search of clearer air.

'Well,' Dave said. 'We could go to Sri Lanka, India, Nepal, Myanmar, Indonesia—'

'What about Bali?' I suggested, perking up. 'I've always wanted to go to Bali.'

'Hmm,' he said and I could sense his disappointment. 'Well, I was actually leaning more towards India. The Holi festival is on at this time of year. You know, the festival where they throw all those coloured paints over each other?'

I hesitated, my tap-dancing elephants stomping their way into my chest. Celebrating Holi had long been a dream of mine but the thought of tackling India while I was already debilitated sounded like a recipe for disaster. 'I don't know, Dave,' I said, chewing on my lip. 'India is just so—'

'I know,' he said. 'It scares you. But so did eggs a few months ago, and haven't you enjoyed trying new things lately?'

It was true.

I *had* enjoyed trying new things, and I'd noticed a change in the way I thought and behaved. I even found myself looking back on my time in China with disdain, appalled at how I'd been so ill-prepared and spent the entire time complaining things were different. *Hadn't I decided to travel to experience diverse cultures?*

'I've just heard so many horror stories,' I told him. 'A friend of mine was nearly raped and another ended up in hospital with dysentery. I'm just not sure now is the right time. I think India looks incredible but with my headache and my anxiety...'

'If you're waiting for the right time, it'll never come,' he warned, shooting me a knowing look. 'I mean, if you'd waited for the perfect time to travel you'd still be in London, wouldn't you?'

'No,' I lied.

'Okay then,' he said with a sigh. 'Bali it is.'

I knew I was being selfish and I felt terrible about it. Dave had been bending over backwards to accommodate me while we'd been in Chiang Mai and here I was unable to do the same for him. It was embarrassing. 'I promise we'll go to India one day,' I told him. 'I just want to get a bit more travel experience under my belt first.'

'No worries,' he said, skimming his finger down my nose. 'I'm sure Bali will be wonderful.'

Dave had been right about one thing. The air in Bali was just what I needed. On our first morning in Kuta, I awoke to find my tap-dancing elephants had left for the circus.

My celebrations, however, were short-lived. As an apology to Dave that we were here and not in India, I'd booked us on to all kinds of adventure activities that would challenge me and excite him. It was win-win for him and terror-terror for me. Now, on the morning of our first surf lesson, I was starting to panic.

'I think I'm going to throw up,' I moaned, poking Dave in the side. I lay coiled on the bed of our humid, grotty guesthouse, slick with sweat. 'I think I have Bali Belly.' I peeked a look at him, but he seemed to be pretending he couldn't hear me. I tried again. 'I don't think I can go surfing with you today.'

I rolled on to my back and began to writhe on top of the faded pink sheets, hoping I looked like someone who had food poisoning.

Like someone who *definitely* wasn't trying to avoid going out in the ocean today. Like someone who was *so* disappointed she wouldn't be able to learn how to surf.

'I'm not sure I can do this,' I said in a trembling voice. 'Do you want to just flag the lesson and hang out by the pool instead?'

'Lauren.' Dave put down his book and looked at me like I was an injured puppy. 'This was your idea.'

'I know,' I groaned.

'And you know you'll regret it if you don't go.'

'Maybe.'

'And you know that if you try it and don't like it you can stop whenever you want. You don't have to stay in the water for the full two hours.'

I changed my tack. 'What if there are jellyfish?'

'So what if there are? If you get stung, you get stung. I've been stung by a jellyfish before, it's no big deal. Just a tickle.'

I gaped at him in horror. This man was like New Zealand's version of Steve Irwin.

'Well, what about sharks?'

'Sharks are awesome.'

'Sharks eat surfers,' I corrected him.

'Not very often,' he said. 'And not as often as we kill them. Do you really think there's going to be a shark attack ten metres from the beach? Do you know how crowded Kuta is? You'll get plenty of warning if there's any kind of danger in the water. Now, why don't you put your bikini on and we'll head down to the beach?'

Kuta was more than crowded. It was overflowing with loud, intoxicated Australians. On the short walk to the surf school, it felt like everyone we encountered was shirtless and drunk.

'Taxi?' a tout called to us from the other side of the road.

'No thanks,' I replied.

'Taxi?' another guy asked, running alongside me.

'No, thank you.'

'Taxi?' said another guy.

I shook my head and stormed past. We'd only walked 50 m by this point.

'This is ridiculous,' I muttered under my breath. I sidestepped a pile of beer bottles, plastic bags and a beaten-up flip-flop.

'Just a bit,' Dave replied.

'Have you seen that shop?' I asked, staring in horror through the glass window. He followed my line of sight to the shop's display. It was full of stickers reading, 'I shit on fat chicks', 'Dan loves it in the stink', 'Up the bum, no babies', and 'Tongue my ass'.

'Damn,' he said, letting out a low whistle.

Paradise, this was not.

We arrived at the surf school just in time for my anxiety to fade. Now that I couldn't get out of it, my fear had been replaced with a determination to make the most of the experience. When the receptionist handed me my rash vest – a long-sleeved lycra top to protect my chest from abrasions – I threw it on over my bikini top without a moment's hesitation. Linking fingers through Dave's, I took a deep breath and plastered a smile across my face. We were going surfing.

Our surf instructor introduced himself as Wayan. He was 30 years old with deep brown eyes and long hair the colour of coal. He had a silver earring in his left ear and spoke in a deep voice.

'Surfing,' he told us as we traipsed across the gritty sand, 'is all about timing and balance.'

Perfect, I thought, dragging my surfboard behind me. *I have all the balance of a newborn giraffe.* I looked behind me, towards the relative safety of the Kuta streets, and noticed I'd been collecting a small pile of rubbish beneath my board as I walked.

We stopped at the edge of the ocean and Wayan motioned for us to rest our boards on the sand.

'I love to surf,' he told us as the warm water tickled our toes. 'And it is my job to make you fall in love with it, too. I have been surfing for over twenty years, right from when I was a small boy. Catching your first wave is the best feeling in the world and today, I promise that you will both get to experience it.'

I exchanged grins with Dave and rubbed away my goosebumps. Wayan's enthusiasm was infectious and I was eager to get in the water.

He ran through the basics of surfing, making it sound like the easiest pursuit in the world: lie on the board, get on to your feet as fast as you can, keep your knees bent, back straight, arms out and focus straight ahead. Easy.

Dave and I practised on the beach while Wayan swept between us, rearranging our legs and forcing us to squat lower. I tugged my rash vest over my bikini bottoms and wondered whether I should have asked for a full-body wetsuit. As I practised my stance with Dave, I kept one eye on the floating plastic bags in the sea, searching for a glimpse of tentacles.

'Okay, time to surf,' Wayan announced, beckoning for us to follow him into the water. We waded 30 m from the shore and stopped when I was waist deep. 'Who wants to go first?'

I scrabbled up on to my board before Dave could open his mouth. I was never usually the person to volunteer to go first, but the more time I spent out of the water, the better.

'Remember what to do?' Wayan asked.

'Uh huh.' My plan was to fling myself upwards and hope I ended up on my feet. He gripped the back of my surfboard and positioned me perpendicular to the waves. Then, we waited. I clung to the sides of the board, grimacing as the rough surface dug into my fingertips.

It's rare for me to find my panic melting away but in that moment, all I could feel was determination. Determination to find something I was good at; to show Dave I wasn't useless; to prove to my friends back home that going travelling wasn't the wrong decision.

The sounds of Kuta threatened to distract me from my goal and I buried my fingers deeper into the board. The laughter of children on the beach, the screams of inadequate surfers and the groan of traffic all faded into the distance. All that was left was my panting and the pounding of my heart in my ears. I focused on the beach as my board and I became one.

'You ready?' Wayan shouted.

'Yep!' I shouted back, turning my head to look at him.

My eyes met his and then my board was hurtling towards the beach.

'Go! Go! Go!' Wayan yelled.

'Waaaaah!' I screamed and instantly forgot everything I'd learned. In an attempt to do something – anything – I pulled myself on to my hands and knees and remained there, wobbling from side to side. Suddenly, the surfboard twisted to the left and a wave hit me side on, sending me into the water with a yelp.

I smacked my head against the seabed as my board continued onwards, dragging me through a swirling current of foam and plastic bags. As I tried to kick my way to the surface, I somehow managed to end up somersaulting through the water instead; a searing pain in my neck. I was starting to run out of air by this point and in my panic for oxygen, I instinctively inhaled, taking a noseful of briny water to my sinuses. It took a frantic thrashing of my arms to break the surface and I emerged with snot smeared across my cheeks.

Dave hurtled past me seconds later as I fought to catch my breath. I watched him attempt to stand, wincing as he catapulted himself through the air, belly flopping beside me with a slap. *Well, at least he's as bad as I am.*

'Surfing is hard,' I complained to Wayan, looking like a forlorn sea monster.

'You need to remember what I told you,' he said with a chuckle. 'Then you will find your way. Stop thinking so much.'

I clambered back on the board and swallowed. My throat was raw from gulping down seawater and my stomach was churning as it thought about expelling its contents. *Stop thinking so much.*

'Go!' Wayan shouted.

I let out a strangled cry and hauled myself on to one knee, tearing towards Dave like I was in the midst of some kind of surfing-themed proposal. I took my eyes off him and focused on the beach, trying to clear my mind. I pushed down with my hands until my other foot joined the first, then straightened my back and stood upright. My arms helicoptered around me until I face-planted straight into the sea.

'Did you see that, Dave?' I shouted, strings of saliva connecting me to my board. 'I stood up!'

He gave me two thumbs up in reply.

I stayed near the shore to watch his next attempt, holding my breath as he slowly, cautiously, brought himself to his feet and balanced for half a second before falling into the waves. 'Yes!' I cheered, throwing my fists in the air. We were practically surfing champions. I caught a glimpse of Wayan behind us, slapping the water in frustration.

'You did not listen,' he grumbled when I returned the board to him. 'You must bend your legs and don't wave your arms. You still think too much.'

I slid into position and waited for the perfect wave, forgetting about my stinging eyes, my aching stomach and my bleeding fingers.

In a heartbeat, I was off again, careering uncontrollably through the water. I pushed down with my hands until my feet were on the centre of the board. Step one complete. I pushed again until I was standing. Step two. I began to tip to one side and realised I was staring at my feet. I forced myself to look towards the beach and bend my legs. Step three.

'I'm doing it!' I screeched, astounded to be perfectly balanced and racing towards the shore. I was *surfing*.

I leapt off the board when I reached the sand and turned around to see Dave. To my surprise, he was standing too, the same goofy grin spread across his face as he hurtled towards me.

'Yeah!' I shouted at him. My heart was bursting with pride. 'You did it!'

'High five,' he shouted back at me, slapping my stinging fingers.

'Now who's a baby giraffe?' I giggled. I'd never felt more energised. I decided then that I wanted to surf every day. *Finally*. I had found my calling.

The feeling lasted until the following morning.

'How much pain are you in?' Dave asked. He let out a groan as he dragged himself out of bed.

'A hundred,' I said, squinting at him through burning eyes. I held my fingers up to the light and winced when it revealed weeping blisters and sores. 'How are your hands?'

'Torn up.' He held them out so I could examine his wounds. His palms were red and swollen, and covered in small cuts.

'I'm never surfing again,' I told him.

I pulled myself out of bed and began to pack my bag, turning my thoughts to tomorrow's cycling tour. We were heading to Ubud today, said to be Bali's cultural centre. It's a place known for its brilliant green rice paddies, intricate Hindu temples, art galleries, vegan restaurants and yoga retreats. I'd read that it was where people went to find themselves, usually through dubious spiritual means.

We checked into a gorgeous room, a block away from the ominously named Monkey Forest. We had a king-size bed, complete with a duvet – a luxury I'd rarely come across on my travels – and pink hibiscus flowers scattered across the pillows. I stood on the balcony, looking out on our jungle of a garden, where monkeys roamed free and clambered over the lawn furniture.

Within moments of arriving, I had felt a weight lift from my shoulders. There was something about Ubud that immediately made me feel at peace. Perhaps my chakras had aligned the moment I'd left Kuta.

I wandered back inside. Dave was sat on the bed peeling back the brown skin of what looked like a baseball-sized lychee.

'What's that?' I asked.

'Snake fruit,' he replied. 'Want some?'

I shook my head. 'No thanks. I've got a bit of a toothache.'

That was an understatement. In reality, it felt like someone was twisting a knife in my gums. It was so sore that I couldn't brush, eat, or even touch it with my tongue. I was convinced the dentist had drilled into a nerve and I was on the verge of needing a root canal. Despite wanting to google 'death by toothache', I was trying to channel my inner Dave and not jump to conclusions. I'd had enough Southeast Asian dental experiences to last me several years.

I sat down beside Dave and watched him sink his teeth into the white flesh. It was rare that Dave ever came across any food he'd never tried before and the joy on his face was helping me to forget about the pulsing in my jaw.

'What does snake fruit taste like?'

'Sort of like a dry crumbly apple, I guess.' He took another bite and the juice dribbled into his cupped palm.

'It's funny,' he added, turning to stare at me, 'how yesterday you woke up with this so-called Bali Belly and today you're getting a toothache the day before our cycling tour. Bit of a coincidence, isn't it?'

'What are you trying to say?'

'The girl who cried ouch,' he stated. 'How will I know when she's really sick?'

I prodded my jaw with my knuckles, deep in thought. He had a point. I didn't want to be the type of person who used their anxiety as a reason not to challenge themself and I knew just how easy it was to fall into the habit of doing so. I wanted to be able to tell Dave about my throbbing tooth and have him sympathise rather than roll his eyes. I wanted to be able to talk to him about my fear of bicycles, too, because cycling was something that had always led to disaster for me. Like in the spring of 2002.

I was 14 years old and cycling home from school. It was a sunny day, unusual for early April. I soon worked up a sweat and stopped for a moment to remove my blazer, then carefully rested it over my handlebars. The sun beat down on me as I continued to cycle.

It hadn't taken much – just a small bump in the road – to cause my jacket to slip from my handlebars and on to my front wheel. From there, it had shot backwards through the brake pads and brought the wheel to an immediate stop. I was thrown over the top of my handlebars and into the middle of the road.

There was no doubt about it, cycling was dangerous. But I also didn't want to be the girl who cried ouch. I wanted to be the girl who grabbed life by the balls and threw herself at everything that frightened her. I was going on that cycling trip tomorrow, dying tooth or not.

I awoke to the sound of torrential rain lashing against our windows just as Dave's phone started to ring. *Perfect*. That would be the tour guide calling to cancel. I arranged my face into a disappointed expression that quickly turned into a grimace when I brushed up against my tooth with my tongue.

'Hello?' Dave said, failing to suppress a yawn. 'Yep... no... oh, okay... that sounds great... see you in a few minutes.'

Bugger.

Our tour guide's name was Wayan. I shouldn't have been surprised: For most of the population of Bali, names are given based on the order in which people are born. There are four main ones: Wayan (first), Made (second), Nyoman (third) and Ketut (fourth). This Wayan was middle-aged and matched Adidas tracksuit bottoms with a lime green T-shirt.

As we shook hands in the pouring rain, he pushed his aviator sunglasses up his nose.

'Where are you from?' Wayan asked, handing us a water bottle each. He led us to his car and opened the door for us to climb inside.

'New Zealand,' Dave said.

'And England,' I added.

'And how long are you in Bali?'

'Two weeks,' Dave told him. I rested my head against the window and let Dave do the talking. While he spoke for me, I watched the congested streets turn into quiet village roads lined with shelves of rice fields, several stories high. There was even a volcano in the distance.

'And then home?' Wayan asked.

'No,' said Dave. 'Back to Thailand.'

'Oh, Thailand. You live in Thailand?'

'Not really. We're just travelling.'

'Oh,' Wayan said with a hint of sadness in his voice. 'You must not see family much?'

'No. Maybe once a year.'

'I cannot imagine,' Wayan said. 'In Bali, it is very different. In Bali, we live in family compounds with all of the generations together. We have the grandparents and the great-grandparents and the parents and the children. The men will live there forever but when the women get married they move to their husband's compound. Family is very important in Bali.'

I opened my mouth to say something and closed it again. My brain was brimming with questions but my lips were feeling shy. It was something I knew I needed to work on. I'd become comfortable with eating strange food over the past couple of months, and had gained a small amount of confidence when it came to leaving my comfort zone, but when I had the opportunity to talk to strangers, I was still suffering from crippling social anxiety. It was too easy to let Dave do the talking and then answer my own questions through a search online. With my propensity for disaster, I was nervous I'd make a cultural faux pas or say something offensive.

After an hour of driving, we reached the restaurant where we'd be having breakfast. We followed Wayan inside and sat down at a large wooden table. The rest of our tour group were already there, having been picked up by one of the other guides, and all five of them were staring miserably at the rain. I peered out of the full-length windows but there was nothing to see but white.

'Breakfast,' Wayan said, 'will be a typical Balinese meal. We will wait for the rain to stop and then we will bike.'

'Please be something I can eat,' I muttered under my breath. I'd come to find that in Southeast Asia, if you can't eat what's on your plate you'll often come face to face with the person who cooked it. Trying to explain my multitude of food issues to a hurt-looking person who'd spent their life perfecting their dish was a sure-fire way to make me feel like the worst person in the world.

'Coffee for everyone,' Wayan announced, handing out cups of the black liquid.

'Dave,' I whispered. 'I've never had coffee before.'

'I know,' he said, rubbing my back. 'Drink up.'

I put the lip of the cup to my mouth and took a sip.

He raised his eyebrow in question.

I grimaced. 'It tastes like dirt.' It wasn't just that: the heat of the coffee made it feel like someone was pressing a red-hot poker against my tooth, and it started pulsing as if it was trying to throb its way out of my mouth.

By the time we finished a pineapple pancake breakfast that I could thankfully eat, the rain had cleared and cooled the air, and the sky was a delicate shade of blue. Wayan led us into a car park, where we were greeted with a line of parked bicycles. I eyed them with suspicion.

'Who goes first?' Wayan asked.

'Lauren will,' Dave announced, and I frowned at the hint of glee in his voice. He knew I would hate every second of this, but still insisted on challenging me. Afterwards, he would probably insist it had helped me gain confidence.

I felt every eye on me as I tiptoed towards the bikes and pretended to examine them. *What was I supposed to be looking for?* I pulled the smallest one towards me and wheeled it back to the group. Doing my best to look self-assured, like I wasn't the sort of person who gets thrown over her handlebars, I said, 'This one is good.'

'Try it,' Wayan encouraged me. 'Test it out. Is it okay?'

Damn you, Wayan.

'Come on, baby giraffe!' Dave called. He was loving every second of this.

I glanced over at him and found myself thinking, *why am I with you?* I'd thought what I needed from a relationship was someone who pushed me, but this felt like it was bordering on cruel. It was too much. It felt like he was taking delight in my discomfort and refusing to sympathise with my anxiety.

In a way, I understood. He'd told me he'd never met anyone with anxiety before; never seen anyone have a panic attack. To him, I was making excuses not to do things he thought any typical person would love. To him, I was being irrational and freaking out about nothing, and I didn't want to be with someone who didn't want to understand.

I sat on the saddle and readied myself to fall. I pushed off the ground and wobbled a couple of metres as if I was weaving in and out of cones at a driving test. 'It's perfect,' I said, gulping hard. I was going to die.

Once everyone had chosen a bike, Wayan turned to face us: 'The first part of the tour is the hardest,' he said. As he spoke, he fastened his helmet over the top of his baseball cap. 'It has been raining and we are going to be riding through the rice paddies. They will be wet and they will be slippery. Does everybody have good shoes?'

I looked down at my flip-flops I'd bought for £1 in Chiang Mai. They'd lost their grip a week afterwards and, on slippery surfaces, were no better than walking on banana skins. I nodded along with the others. *How important would good shoes be anyway?*

'Okay,' he said. 'We go.'

Dave rode a tight circle around me and pedalled off, leading our group on to the palm-lined road and then following one of the tour guides into the distance.

'Show off,' I muttered. I was wobbling 20 m behind everyone else.

Wayan fell back to accompany me. 'Try it on a higher gear,' he offered, pointing at my handlebars.

I looked down and froze. I couldn't remember how gears worked. As I battled to keep up with the group, I decided to ignore his advice and keep powering through on first gear. My calves were burning and my pulse currently seemed to be centred in my tooth.

I felt a hand on my back and magically, I began to pick up speed. When I turned my head to see what was happening, I saw Wayan grinning out of the corner of my eye. *Oh God, I was so bad at cycling that he was pushing me through the tour*.

'Rice paddy time,' Wayan announced after 10 minutes, patting me on the back and racing towards the first of the group. 'Okay, everyone,' he shouted over the wind, his back to one of the most gorgeous green landscapes I'd seen. 'I warn you: the rice paddies are full of leeches and you do not want to fall in them. They like the taste of tourists.' The tour group let out a collective chuckle and I suddenly began to regret my choice of footwear. The paddies were slick with slippery mud.

I let everyone else go first and followed behind, stepping on to the slimy mud with a squelch and pushing the bike beside me. I tried to tread carefully but my legs were flying in all directions, no matter how hard I tried to balance. I took my eyes off my feet for a moment and immediately one foot slid forwards while the other slipped back, forcing me into a half-split. I gripped my handlebars tighter as I swayed from side to side.

With every step, I sank deeper into the mud until my feet and ankles were covered with gooey slime. Every time I tried to take a step, I would jerk one foot up and end up with sludge pouring across the surface of the flip-flop. When I tried for another step, my feet slid on my shoes, which were sliding on the mud.

I looked up and saw the group 50 m ahead of me, marching steadily with their sensible walking shoes. They were far enough away that I could hear nothing but the wind whipping itself around my face. Visions of me sinking up to my neck in mud flashed through my mind while I struggled to keep my bike upright.

'Yeeeeaaaarrrrrkkkkkkk!'

In an attempt to stop myself falling over, I threw my bike to one side and spun my arms in large circles. I felt less stable than I had when I'd been surfing. I'd lost control. My right foot flew forwards and up into the air, and then my left one jumped up to meet it.

Splash!

Warm water crept over me and for a few moments, I forgot where I was. It was soothing, like having a bath outdoors. Except with leeches. I squealed when I realised I was lying flat on my back in a rice paddy.

'Lauren,' Wayan bellowed, throwing his bike on the ground and rushing to my side. I craned my neck to see what was happening and noticed Dave running with him, camera in hand. 'Are you okay, Lauren?' Wayan asked. He wrapped his fingers around my hands and pulled me to my feet.

'I'm fine.' I started to giggle as the rest of the group made their way over to me. 'Really,' I told him. Dave held his camera up and I wobbled a semicircle to show him my muddy back.

'Perfect,' he chuckled, clicking the shutter. 'It could only happen to you.'

I squelched back around and watched Wayan pull my bike from the mud and raise it over his head like a trophy. 'I will carry it now,' he told me. 'So you can walk.' I stifled another giggle as he began to make his way through the paddies.

'How embarrassing,' I muttered to Dave as we followed Wayan. I reached across to grip on to his handlebars in an attempt to stay upright. As I did so, I could feel the dried mud on my shoulders starting to crack.

'You know I do it for your own good,' Dave said quietly, his feet slipping out with every step.

'What's that?'

'This,' he said. 'I can tell you're terrified of trying these things – surfing, cycling, eating – and part of me wants to tell you not to do them if you don't want to. But not doing things because they're scary isn't who I am, and I'm not sure it's who you are, either.'

After spending three months with Dave, he had come to know me better than anyone else, and I both hated and adored it. Just like how I hated and adored how he was always encouraging me to try terrifying things. On the morning of our surf lesson, when my intuition had been screaming that I needed to get out of this situation, Dave had convinced me to try it and I'd hated him for it. But as soon as I'd managed to stand up and catch my first wave, I'd been hit by the realisation that pushing my boundaries felt incredible.

'It's tricky,' I said, stopping for a moment to grab my flip-flops. Walking barefoot had got to be easier. 'I can see your point of view and, believe me, I annoy myself when I start feigning illnesses to try to get out of things. But you don't know what it's like to have anxiety.'

'I don't,' he said. 'But I do know the look of pure joy you get whenever you try something new and succeed. If you had a panic attack every time then fine, I'm an asshole for making you do it. But it doesn't happen. Look at how much you loved surfing.'

I let out a frustrated groan when I realised that he was right, but still didn't understand. I tried again. 'I guess what I'm looking for is some sympathy and support,' I told him. 'I'm sure that the girlfriends you've had – maybe they haven't been anxious and they've been willing to try new things, or I guess they probably didn't have many new things to try but—'

'I haven't had a girlfriend in several years,' Dave interrupted me. 'I gave up looking a while back.'

'Why?' I asked, surprised by this revelation.

He shrugged. 'I couldn't connect with anyone back home. Everyone seemed to want the husband and the kids and the white picket fence for their house in the suburbs. They thought I was immature for wanting to see the world instead.'

'Funny how neither of us were looking for a relationship when we met,' I said as we finally reached the end of the rice paddies.

'You know what they say,' Dave continued, turning to look at me. 'Focus on doing what you love and the right person will come along – don't look for it. So, that's what I did. Then I quit my job, moved to Thailand, and then eight days later…'

'… I showed up,' I finished.

'Yeah.'

'Wow.'

After Dave's confession, I felt lighter. He wasn't getting frustrated because he didn't want to be with me any more, he was just trying to help me discover my full potential. It was our heart to heart while I was covered in mud that helped us understand each others' point of view. And with a promise from me to try to have more confidence in myself, and a commitment from him to be more patient and sympathetic, our rift healed.

The next two weeks were full of nothing but joy. We quickly shelved our plans to travel around the island, deciding instead to stay in beautiful Ubud in our peaceful hotel. Our mornings were spent wandering around lush gardens and ancient temples; our afternoons working in coffee shops and sipping fruit smoothies; and our evenings at a new Balinese restaurant each night so I could widen my food-related horizons.

I'd even started challenging myself to take solo walks around Ubud with the aim of practising my conversational skills – something that was emerging to be the main cause of my low self-esteem.

'I'm going for a walk,' I told Dave on our final afternoon in Bali. 'You want anything from the shops?'

He nodded yes – he wanted a Sprite – and I set off from our guesthouse in search of a store I hadn't yet visited. It was time to practise the art of talking to strangers. Upon finding one, I then, as usual, had a mildly successful but mostly awkward conversation with the man who worked there. I wasn't sure that asking, 'where are you from?' and receiving the answer 'Bali' counted as getting to know the locals, but it was a start.

I stopped outside Monkey Forest and squinted down the path. I'd been avoiding the enclosure since arriving in Ubud after hearing one too many horror stories from travellers who'd been attacked by monkeys, but I was feeling like giving myself a new challenge. With a shrug, I paid the entrance fee and walked inside.

I wandered down the path for several minutes before I came face to face with my first crowd of monkeys. I stopped in my tracks and attempted to stare them down. The biggest one bared its teeth in a threatening manner until I shuffled past it, wanting to keep my distance. I continued onwards, reminding myself that everything was going to be okay.

I heard a scrabbling sound and turned around to see the monkey a few metres behind me. I sped up; it matched my pace. This wasn't looking good.

'Go away,' I whispered when it reached within a metre of me. I stamped my feet near its face, but it only seemed to anger it.

'Oh bollocks,' I muttered when I felt my plastic bag brush up against my leg. *That was why it was following me.* 'Oh God, I'm such an idiot,' I groaned. It was well known that you weren't supposed to take food or drink – and especially not plastic bags – into Monkey Forest. Just like when I'd been scammed in China, I'd managed to forget about a warning I'd read moments earlier.

I watched in horror as the monkey lunged for my bag. With a single swipe of its arm, it had ripped through the plastic and snatched Dave's bottle of Sprite.

'No,' I cried out. 'I need that Sprite.'

I held out my hand and waited for it to hand the bottle back to me. It picked at the seal, keeping a lazy eye on me.

I stamped my feet again and growled with all the force I could muster. It was a technique I was certain would intimidate it into handing over the bottle. What I hadn't realised was that this monkey was hardened. It was hardened from a lifetime of encounters far more brutal than a small girl tap-dancing near its face. With a frustrated sigh, I turned on my heel and walked away.

A minute later, I heard a snarl and twisted around to see the monkey baring its teeth at me. It began to charge, quickly reaching speeds far higher than I was capable of.

As I ran, my life flashed before me in a series of images: the monkey sinking its teeth into my leg; going to the hospital to get rabies shots; the shots failing; me foaming at the mouth; my funeral. I was about to die.

It took less than 2 seconds for the inevitable to happen.

My gripless flip-flops slid out from beneath me and I fell forwards, landing face first on the cobbled pavement. I didn't have time to react; the monkey was coming for me and I needed to move fast. I dragged myself across the damp ground, wincing as I felt the skin on my hands rip open. I groaned. It was over. There was no point trying to escape. The monkey had won. With my eyes squeezed shut, I held out my leg as an offering and waited for his teeth to pierce my skin.

I squinted behind me and frowned, still waving my leg in the air. Behind me, nothing. There was no sign the monkey had even been there. In its place was a group of American tourists dressed in full safari gear and loudly whispering about me. One of them cleared their throat.

'Hi,' I mumbled, clambering to my feet. *That was embarrassing.* I brushed the gravel from my knees, and stumbled back to our apartment.

I burst into the bedroom, holding up my bloody hands. 'A monkey stole your Sprite,' I whimpered to Dave before bursting into tears.

'What are you talking about?' he asked, getting up from the sofa and running to comfort me.

'Monkey Forest,' I sobbed. 'Never go to Monkey Forest.'

'Oh, baby,' he said, stifling a laugh. 'Why does it always happen to you?'

CHAPTER 10

I thought things had been going too smoothly in Bali, so being attacked by monkeys provided a fitting end to our time there. And when it came time to leave, we already knew where we wanted to go: back to Thailand.

Although we'd spent three months in Chiang Mai, it felt like a huge oversight to have not yet explored its islands. Before travelling to somewhere new, we decided to spend three weeks island-hopping in the south.

Lonely Beach, on Koh Chang, felt like the island where Bob Marley had never died. It was one of the cheapest places I'd ever visited, with £5-a-night bungalows scattered a few minutes' walk away from the beach, and where having a hammock strung up outside felt mandatory. Koh Chang was all about lying on the beach all day and partying all night. It was there where I had my first 'bucket': a child's sandcastle bucket filled with Coke, vodka and Red Bull. Needless to say, it was my first and my last once I experienced my worst ever hangover the following morning.

Next up was Koh Phi Phi Don, one of the hottest party spots in Thailand with a thriving nightlife scene that Dave and I managed to avoid. Instead, we busied ourselves with topping up our tans and eating cheeseburgers, treating it as a recovery week rather than a party one.

It was on Koh Phi Phi Don that I asked Dave if he thought it was possible to find a Thai island without tourists any more, or whether all the beautiful ones had been developed. I wanted to find somewhere void of tourists wearing hippie pants, baggy beer-branded tops and vacant expressions. I wanted to find an island without an internet connection so I could disconnect for a few weeks. Somewhere with mind-blowing scenery. I wanted to discover an island nobody had heard of. We made it our mission to find that place.

'Stop!' I yelped, digging my fingers in Dave's side. Our scooter came screeching to a halt, flicking sand up into my eyes. 'Ouch,' I squealed as I reached up to shield my eyes.

'What is it?' Dave said impatiently. We'd rented a scooter for the first time in a month and after 2 minutes of riding, I was already shouting for him to stop.

'Did you see that sign back there?' I asked.

'Nope.'

'It was pointing to a beach. Said it was pretty close to here. You want to check it out?' The sign I was talking about was a battered plank of wood, no more than a foot in width. Scrawled across it in black ink were the words 'Beach. 3 kilometres' with an arrow pointing down a shaded dirt track.

I squinted as we pulled up beside it. I could only make out the first few metres of the path before it disappeared around a palm tree.

Dave studied it for a few seconds and shrugged. 'It should be fine on the scooter,' he said. 'It's up to you.'

'I think we should at least see what it's like,' I said. 'It could be amazing.'

'You sure?' He twisted around to study my face.

My smile faded and alarm bells started ringing. 'Why? Do you think we shouldn't go?'

'No,' he laughed. 'It's just the Lauren I met three months ago wouldn't have even considered following this sign. She'd have thought it'd been written by a sex pest in an attempt to lure innocent backpackers into his lair.'

I choked out a laugh and, when he turned his back, ogled the dense jungle. *Was a sex pest lurking behind one of those rubber trees?*

'Right,' he said. 'You ready?'

'Always.'

The engine vibrated dread into my body as we started easing our way down the track. Taking it slow, we veered around a nearby palm tree and a series of narrow curves revealed themselves up ahead. Dave braked for a moment and then we roared towards them, passing straight through the sticky threads of a spider's web.

'Oh no,' I squealed, slapping at my arms. I quickly calculated that to have stretched across the path, the web must have been 5 m in diameter, suggesting its eight-legged creator was almost certainly the subject of my childhood nightmares. *Was this like one of those moments in horror films where everyone screams at the victims not to head into imminent danger?* I had never been able to identify those moments.

Soil transformed to mulch while Dave pretended not to hear my whispered concerns in his ear. I scooted forward in my seat until I was pressed up against his faded grey T-shirt, now misshapen from one too many Southeast Asian laundry experiences.

We shot around a sharp left curve and I winced as we began to wobble from side to side. The trail alternated between steep hills that brought us to a near-standstill and deep ditches where we had to ride at full speed to make it across. Not only that, but Dave also had to battle to keep us on the outskirts of the brown, murky puddles.

Up ahead, I spotted a wooden hut with a blood-red facade. *The sex pest!* I dug my feet into the pedals as we approached. Outside, a mangy-looking dog offered up a languid bark and, once we passed, settled back into its bed of leaves.

'Drive faster,' I whispered to Dave's back, slinking down in case someone fired a shotgun at us.

We turned a corner and entered a small clearing where we came to an abrupt halt. I squinted over Dave's shoulder, worried about what could have caused him to brake so suddenly. In front of us was a long stretch of pristine golden sand.

'No way,' I murmured, my jaw dangling at the sight of what looked like our own private beach. I leapt off the seat and fumbled with my helmet, muttering under my breath as my excited fingers refused to fasten the straps to the handlebars. Leaves crunched beneath my flip-flops as I marched on the spot with glee.

'There's no one else here,' Dave called back to me from the beach.

I threw my helmet on the ground and raced over to join him. Panting by his side, we linked hands and took a look at our island paradise. We were stood in the centre of several kilometres of glistening untouched beach where the only imperfection was our footprints. Behind us was continuous jungle with no signs of development. There wasn't a single hotel or restaurant in sight.

I let go of Dave's hand and tiptoed into the ocean. It was as warm as bathwater and so clear I could see my chipped toenail polish while the water lapped around my waist.

'Why isn't this place overrun with tourists?' I wondered aloud. Out to sea were hundreds of limestone karsts scattered haphazardly across the horizon and beyond that, the outline of Krabi, one of the most popular tourist destinations in Thailand.

'It should be,' Dave said from behind me and I swirled around to face him. My euphoria was reflected in his eyes.

We'd decided to head to Koh Yao Noi in search of a pristine island paradise I wasn't sure existed outside of *The Beach* and it looked like we'd just found it.

Koh Yao Noi ticked every box. Located between the popular trifecta of Phuket, Krabi and Koh Phi Phi Don, you'd fully expect the island to be well on its way to destruction. Instead, a lack of tourist infrastructure and information online had deterred most development. Koh Yao Noi is expensive to get to, has no nightlife and it's tough to find a Wi-Fi connection. All of these factors put off most backpackers in Thailand, but were what had sent me rushing for the nearest ferry. With so little information online, I'd had no idea what to expect.

We'd found a beautiful guesthouse tucked into the hillside where we were staying in a rustic wooden bungalow on stilts and paying just £10 a night. We'd spent our mornings lounging in deckchairs on our balcony, gazing out at the wide ocean vista, and our evenings eating freshly caught red snapper at the restaurant 100 m down the road. Our companionship consisted of the friendly owner, who doubled as the police officer for the island, and his three cats. Unsurprisingly, he never seemed to have much crime to fight. On Koh Yao Noi, locals left their keys in their scooters, offered you a lift on the back of one every couple of minutes if you happened to be walking around and nobody was too busy to offer a friendly hello.

'Dave?' I said, hit by a sudden realisation.

'Yep.'

'Do you think that terrible luck can sometimes be good luck after all?'

He frowned. 'What do you mean?'

'I'm starting to wonder if I'm not as unlucky as I think. I wonder if having all of those awful things happen to me has made being on this beach so much more of a meaningful experience. It feels like all the hard times have been worth it now that I've experienced something like this.'

Koh Yao Noi's small pier jutted out into the ocean with just enough room for the ferry that would take us to Phuket. We were leaving at low tide, which meant, as we stood with our bags at the end of the pier, our ferry was currently bobbing around a metre below our feet. The only way on board was to jump. Dave went first, leaping on to the roof, and I quickly followed, falling to my knees with a crash. Together, we climbed through a hole in the roof to get inside.

After popping a motion-sickness pill and grabbing a life jacket, I wobbled out to the open-air section at the front to bask in the sun.

I lay out on one of the white wooden benches and placed my life jacket underneath my head as a pillow. It would take us 2 hours to reach Phuket, where we'd be heading straight to the airport and onwards to Chiang Mai. I closed my eyes as the boat pulled away, the nauseating vibrations of the engine lulling me to sleep.

A loud bang shocked me awake and I threw myself upwards. The engine shuddered beneath me as I threw on my life jacket and ran to the cabin. I prepared myself for scenes of mayhem, panicking over whether I had all my valuables within easy reach. I swung open the door and rushed inside. Everything was as it should be. Quiet. Calm. Dave was reading his Kindle; the two Thai ladies in front of him were fast asleep on the bench; and an elderly German couple was staring at me with puzzled expressions.

I power-walked up to Dave. 'Please tell me you felt that,' I whispered.

'Felt what?'

'The enormous bang. Our ferry hit something.'

'No, it didn't,' he said with a laugh before turning back to his book.

'It did,' I insisted. 'The jolt woke me up. I was fast asleep and then I heard this bang, and then the boat vibrated and…' I swallowed. 'I think we're sinking.'

'Lauren.' He was giving me that look again.

'But I felt it,' I bleated.

'You were probably dreaming.'

'But—'

'Look.' He put down his Kindle and stared at me. 'The boat is not about to sink. We're not about to die. You need to calm down.'

I pulled my legs up on to the bench and wrapped my arms around them. *How could I have imagined something that felt so real?*

We arrived in Phuket and were swallowed up by a swarm of hungry taxi drivers, desperate for blood.

'You need taxi? Miss! Sir! Miss, you need taxi? Come with me, yes? I take you to the airport. I promise you good rate, Miss.'

'No, no, come with me! I have better rate. I have good car. Air conditioning and music from America, yes? Where you need to go?'

I took a step back and let Dave commence the battle for a decent fare. It hadn't taken long for us to fall into different roles while travelling. I was the planner, thanks to years spent scouring maps and devouring information about as many countries as possible. Dave concentrated on the logistics, making sure we got to our destination without me falling into an open sewer. When it came to bargaining with taxi drivers, he was better suited for the role. In 35°C heat and muggy air, I was always willing to pay £100 for an air-conditioned antidote.

'You feel earthquake?' our driver asked as we walked to the taxi.

'There was an earthquake?' Dave asked, turning to frown at me.

'Yes, a big earthquake,' he said, running his hands through his hair. 'In Indonesia. We felt it here. Strong. Like the big one. The tsunami.'

'Yes,' I announced. 'Dave – that must have been what I felt on the ferry when I thought we'd hit something.'

My brain went into overdrive, remembering the devastation caused in this part of the world by the tsunami in 2004. A quarter of a million people had died and Phuket had been devastated. I remembered the nausea I'd felt watching people being swept to their deaths by an unstoppable wave full of boats, houses, cars and bodies. The destruction had felt so far removed from anything I'd ever experienced – at that point, my anxiety had such a tight grip on me that I wasn't able to step outside my house.

I desperately tried to think of something else. In a few hours, we'd be returning to Chiang Mai for Songkran, the Thai New Year. It's a festival I'd wanted to go to for years, celebrated with an enormous multi-day water fight that has everyone from two to 92 year olds clutching Super Soakers and drenching everyone in sight. I'd spent the months leading up to it fantasising about tipping buckets of water over grannies and researching how to avoid catching conjunctivitis if I happened to fall in the moat.

Twenty minutes later, the glass doors slid open and we were hit by an icy wave of air-conditioning at Phuket International Airport. I fumbled with the straps of my backpack as we lined up to go through a security checkpoint by the entrance. Dave dropped his backpack on the conveyor belt and made his way through the metal detector.

I heard an announcement echoing through the airport – first in Thai and then in English. When it finished, a strange silence descended upon the hall. I glanced up just as the air filled with a harrowing chorus of high-pitched screams.

I jumped back in shock, eyes wide as saucers, as hundreds of people came stampeding towards us, all with an identical look of terror painted on their faces. I reached for Dave but he'd already passed through the body scanner and I grasped at thin air instead.

'Dave? What's happening?' I wailed to him, as a petrified-looking woman sprinted past me as if she was running for her life. Then the crowds came. What felt like the entire airport was now tearing past me as if there was a—

Then it hit me.

There was a bomb.

'Oh God, no,' I wailed, throwing my daypack on the ground and launching myself towards the doors. Material possessions were of no value to me now; I had to leave the airport before the bomb detonated. Outside, I took one look at the ocean of terrified faces and tore down the road.

I was fuelled by adrenaline and fear, running as fast as I could while ignoring the pain in my side until it felt like I was going to rip in two. My legs started to wobble and after an embarrassingly short distance, gave way. I had made it 100 m down the road. I stumbled into the side of a pick-up truck and held on to it as I struggled to catch my breath. I watched a woman leap on the back, pull her children up to join her, and order the driver to find higher ground.

I twisted myself in circles. All around me, people were jumping into cars and tuk-tuks, agreeing to pay extortionate sums of money to get to safety. I searched for a vehicle I could jump into.

'Please,' I pleaded with one family who had a spare seat in the back of their cab. The mum met my eyes through the window. 'Sorry,' she mouthed before they screeched off down the road.

I stood helplessly in the midst of the chaos, breathing in the exhaust fumes and feeling dizzy and disorientated. I spotted an anxious-looking Thai woman wearing airport uniform who was directing people up a hill. I sprinted up to her.

'What's happening?' I panted. 'What's happened?'

She looked me up and down before answering in a shaky voice. 'There is tsunami.'

Her nervous face swam before my eyes and I felt like I was falling. There was a tsunami, caused by the earthquake I'd felt on the ferry. There was a tsunami, just like the one that had killed a quarter of a million people.

Is this how I'm going to die?

I reached for Dave's arm to steady myself but clutched at air instead. I spun around but all I could see were crying children. I'd been so preoccupied with escaping my imaginary bomb that

I hadn't noticed he wasn't with me. I scanned the crowd in the hope I'd see him looking back at me. I knew that everything would be okay if he could wrap me up in his arms and take me to safety.

I stood on my tiptoes but was too short to see over the mass of heaving bodies. An elderly woman slumped at my feet and began to pray, chanting in a language I didn't recognise.

I looked back towards the airport and, a few metres behind it, the glittering turquoise ocean. I wondered if Dave was still inside. It would be just like him to be dawdling around, wondering what all the panic was about. I ignored the voice in my head that was telling me it was a death sentence to go back to the airport, and began to run. As my feet pounded the gravel, I imagined a world where Dave didn't exist. It was then that I knew I had to find him.

I panted up to the shiny glass doors, filled with a heart-wrenching pain when I realised he wasn't there. *Had he been one of the people jumping in a taxi and careering towards the hills? Had he escaped to safety? Had he left me here? Was I about to die alone?*

Shit. What am I doing here?

I thought about my family and imagined their reactions when they found out I'd been killed. I thought about how my mum had been terrified that if I left to travel, I'd never make it home alive. I'd rolled my eyes at her at the time, quoting travel statistics and telling her you only ever heard about the rare cases of backpackers being killed rather than the hundreds of thousands of success stories. I was about to become a statistic.

I spotted our backpacks lying where we'd thrown them, beside the still-moving conveyor belt. Feeling like I was watching a horror movie where even *I* was yelling at the protagonist, I dashed over to them. Unlike riding a scooter past an imagined sex pest, my life was actually on the line.

I dragged a trolley across the floor and hauled everything we owned on to it. The empty airport was dredging up unnerving memories of Chernobyl and what I'd learned during the tour. After the explosion, everyone had been told to leave their belongings and go; told everything was fine and they'd be back before they knew it. I grunted under the weight of Dave's backpack and dropped it on the trolley with a crash. I couldn't seem to stop my brain from recalling everything I'd read about what to do if there's a natural disaster. Rule number one: don't go back for your bags.

I wheeled the trolley around and ran for my life. Joining the mass of terrified faces once more, I charged towards higher ground. Every few seconds, I glanced over my shoulder, expecting to see a colossal black wave consuming the airport before hurtling towards us. I began to berate myself. *Why had I gone back for our backpacks? What does any of this matter now that I'm about to die?*

I heard a loud bang and spun on my heel. This was it. This was the end. I looked for the wave but could only see scenes of panic. Behind me was a middle-aged woman bawling on the ground. The bang had come from her suitcase, which was now lying wide open with her clothes strewn across the road. I hesitated for a second, deliberating whether to help. I shook my head and guilt flooded my stomach. I had to save myself. *She* had to save herself. I broke down in tears, horrified by my callousness. Nobody even glanced at me. When faced by the prospect of our own mortality, we were all fighting for ourselves.

Drowning. I'd always said it was the worst way to die; never once believing it would be my reality. I wondered what it would feel like. Dying. *Was it like going to sleep? Would I flashback over my life? Be consumed by a bright light? Would I be knocked unconscious and have no idea it was happening? Or dragged under by waves as I fought to get to the surface¿ Would I accept my fate and open my mouth, letting the warm water fill my lungs¿*

I didn't believe in an afterlife but in that moment, I wished I could. Wouldn't it be great if there were something more¿ Wouldn't it be great if I believed and was no longer afraid¿ I groaned in frustration. This was the end. This was all there was. The wave was going to wipe me out and that would be it. I'd no longer exist. I'd be gone.

'I'm so frightened,' I whispered to no one and everyone at once. I was struggling under the weight of the trolley, watching as a constant stream of people overtook me. *Were they going to be the survivors¿ Would they reach the evacuation point and then stand and watch me get swept away¿* I cursed myself once more for going back for our bags.

'Excuse me¿' I said, reaching out to touch a hairy arm. The man turned his ample frame to look down at me with piercing blue eyes. 'Could you help me push my trolley¿'

He hesitated, running his hands over his shaved head. I could see him eyeing his family running ahead of him.

'Please,' I pleaded, full of desperation. 'Please. I'm not strong enough.'

'Okay,' he said in a gruff British accent, reaching out an arm and helping me push.

It was strange. In that moment, I was suddenly no longer afraid of talking to strangers. It turned out that all you had to do to get me to open up was convince me I'd be dead within minutes.

'I'm really scared,' I told him.

'We all are, love,' was his grim response.

His words bounced around in my head and we continued to walk in silence. I wondered if my family had heard about the tsunami by now or were blissfully unaware of what was happening. I had forgotten to tell them I was heading to Phuket today, so even if they had heard, they wouldn't have known I was here.

We were halfway up the hill when he stopped pushing. 'We're here.'

I looked up. We were stood next to a small car park lined with bushes. A swarm of people were hovering around and looking frightened. A few others were sunbathing on a patch of grass in front of it. 'This is it?' I asked him. 'This is the evacuation point?'

'Yeah.'

'It doesn't feel high enough,' I said, looking back towards the airport. We couldn't have been more than 10 m above sea level.

He shrugged. 'I'm sure they wouldn't send us here if it wasn't safe.'

I nodded, but I couldn't shake the feeling that we weren't high enough.

'Thank you so much for helping me,' I said, my trembling hands reaching out for his.

'It's okay,' he said as his eyes moved to his family. 'Stay safe.'

I stood and watched him disappear into the throng before turning my thoughts back to Dave. I circled the car park in the hope of finding him, each lap leaving me more defeated. The thought that I might never see him again was too much to bear and I burst into tears.

'Hello?' A timid voice interrupted my thoughts. I wiped my eyes and turned around. Stood in front of me was a girl in her early 20s with short blonde hair and eyes the colour of chocolate. She looked at me with a haunted expression etched across her face. 'I saw you were on your own and I am too,' she said. 'Can I stand with you?'

'Of course,' I said, letting out a wobbly laugh. 'I need some company before I have a complete breakdown.'

Her bottom lip began to tremble. 'I know, me too. I am so frightened.'

'I am, too. I'm so scared we're going to die.'

'I don't want to die.' She pulled at the sleeves of her dress and I watched a single tear slide down her cheek.

'Do you want a hug?' I asked. It was a silly question, but I didn't know how else to comfort her.

She smiled. 'Yes please.'

I'd never felt closer to a complete stranger. We gripped on to each other, united by the acceptance that our lives would soon be over. Her shoulders started shuddering and I squeezed tighter. I felt braver now that I had someone to take care of. Someone else to worry about.

'It's okay,' I whispered. 'It'll be okay.' I rolled my eyes at the futility of my statement. I couldn't stop thinking about how I'd never see my family again. Or Dave.

Dave.

We pulled apart and I saw him jogging towards me across the car park, the sight of his warm blue eyes enough to make me feel safe.

'Dave,' I breathed when he reached me. 'You're here.'

He nodded and pressed my head into his chest. I broke down into great, heaving sobs while he stroked my hair. 'You're here,' I repeated.

'Of course I'm here.'

'I saved our luggage,' I said, taking a step back and motioning towards the trolley. 'I went back inside the airport to find you, but you weren't there. I spotted our backpacks and grabbed them.'

He took my face in his hands and kissed me on the lips. 'You're amazing, you know that?'

I turned to introduce him to the girl I'd been hugging but she'd melted away into the crowd. I felt a pang of sadness knowing I'd never see her again.

'Dave,' I began to cry again. 'I'm frightened. Oh, Dave, I'm so, so frightened.'

As I uttered those words, an unnerving sense of calm settled over the car park. Conversations ceased, birds stopped chirping and a nervous silence filled the air.

Then, a deafening crunch followed by scratching and scraping. The Thai teenagers who had been sunbathing on a patch of grass rose to their feet. To the left of me, I saw parents frantically pushing their children up trees. Some people began scrambling up walls. I stood frozen to the ground as it rippled beneath my feet.

'No,' I whimpered. This was it. The tsunami was here. Sweat poured down my back and filled my fists. I let my emotions pour out of me.

'No! Not now. Oh God, no. Dave!' I screamed, throwing my arms around him. 'I love you so much. Oh my God, I can't do this. Please don't let me die. I don't want to die. Oh God, I can't...'

Dave wrapped his arms around me and said nothing. With my head pressed against his chest, I could hear his heart beating faster than ever.

The sounds grew louder, and I imagined the wave swelling into view and surging towards us. I let go of Dave and searched for something to climb. Behind us was a brick wall. I hoped that the wave would hit us head on, so we'd be thrown into it and knocked unconscious.

Dave's sweaty hand found mine and we stood beside each other, trembling, holding on, waiting for it to happen.

The wave thundered into view from behind the hedges and I fell to my knees in disbelief. It was white and metal and shiny and...

It was a plane charging down the runway.

The crowd, stunned by the turn of events, breathed a sigh of relief. A few people began to laugh. I watched helplessly from the ground as it soared up into the sky and out of danger. The thought of having to go through all this again was too much to bear and I began to retch into the bushes.

I spat my bile on the ground and stood up on trembling legs. I thought back to everything that had gone wrong on this trip. How being scammed had felt like the worst thing to have ever happened to me and how I'd spent the past two weeks panicking about having to have a root canal. It was all so insignificant. I'd happily have every tooth ripped from my mouth if it meant I'd survive this. Even my battles with anxiety felt so trivial when confronted with death.

Towards the other end of the car park, I could hear a man's voice amplified through a megaphone. He was making some kind of announcement. Seconds later, the crowd was buzzing with the news. I strained my ears to overhear.

'He said the wave is ten metres high! It's already destroyed three islands in Indonesia. Killed five thousand people so far.'

'It's okay, honey. It's only two metres. Last time the wave was four metres and didn't reach this area.'

'My friend just told me it's the big one. He thinks we need to leave and find higher ground.'

'Nothing's going to happen! He said the wave has disappeared.'

All I knew was that I couldn't allow myself to believe it would be okay. I knew as soon as I relaxed, I'd exhaust my adrenaline supplies and lose the ability to function. If the tsunami hit, I wouldn't even be able to summon the energy to stand.

I paced back and forth with my head in my hands. Exhausted, weak, spent. I'd lost the will to fight and was ready to give up. This was too hard; too much to deal with. In a moment of madness, I stood and faced the airport, arms outstretched, and challenged the wave to come. *Just get this over with. Just come and kill me.* I stood there for an hour and waited for something to happen. By this point, Dave had taken out his Kindle and was sat on the ground reading.

There was another announcement, this time from our end of the car park. A small Thai man waved his megaphone in the air to attract attention. I searched his face for a sign that it was going to be okay but he was giving nothing away. He looked out into a sea of sober faces and lowered the megaphone to his mouth.

It was over.

There was no tsunami.

We were safe.

My legs gave way and I collapsed on the ground in exhaustion. I heard Dave saying something about our bags, but I couldn't take my eyes off the ants that were scurrying around me. I was envious of them and how they were oblivious of how close they'd been to death. I curled up on my side and continued to stare at them. I stared at the tarmac and I stared at the bushes I'd retched into and I stared at people's feet. I felt a bubbling sense of rage when I heard how light-hearted everyone else sounded. *Why were they laughing?*

I lost an hour to staring and suddenly Dave was tugging on my arm and pulling me to my feet. He'd spent the past hour queuing to talk to an AirAsia representative and she'd told him we'd need to spend the night in the airport. She thought we'd be able to get on a flight in the morning so he was taking me there now. I nodded as he spoke, walking in silence as he led me out of the car park.

That night, I existed in a state of post-traumatic shock. I lay broken on the floor while Dave took care of me, stroking my hair, trying to get me to eat and urging me to sleep. He started queuing at 3 a.m. to get us on the standby list while I stared blankly at the walls and said nothing. *I could have died today.* Every sound made my legs twitch and every vibration had me clutching for my backpack.

Dave's queuing led to us being put on the first flight to Chiang Mai and I had yet to find the words to thank him. My body had shut down in a way I'd never experienced before and I was certain I'd still be lying in the car park if I'd had to go through this alone.

When we stepped on the plane, I turned to look at Dave, my eyes bright with unshed tears. I had expected this moment to bring me nothing but relief, but I was numb to the world. Without saying a word, he put his arm around my waist and guided me to our seats.

'I forgot to mention,' he said as we strapped ourselves in, 'I read a few articles about the tsunami this morning. It turns out the wave only ended up being ten centimetres high when it reached Thailand. All that panic for nothing, hey?' He laughed and squeezed my hand.

I gave him a small smile, too exhausted to feel embarrassed. This had been the scariest moment of my life and I couldn't imagine how I'd cope if I had to live in constant fear of a tsunami, like many people around the world do. *All that panic for nothing. Terror and evacuations; over and over and over.*

Our plane rose above the clouds and I turned to watch out of the window. The rising sun was shimmering over the wing, turning drops of condensation into tiny diamonds. Through gaps in the clouds, I gazed in awe at the labyrinth of green islands and dazzling white beaches stretching out into the glittering cyan. The world had never looked so beautiful.

CHAPTER 11

I stood beside the luggage carousel at Chiang Mai Airport and waited for our backpacks to arrive. It was the first day of Songkran and the airport was packed with crowds and suitcases. Everyone was in a hurry, high on anticipation, desperate to start celebrating the Thai New Year. I longed to join in with their excitement, but the commotion kept sending me back to Phuket.

I glanced up at Dave and wished I could find the words to thank him. He looked exhausted and haggard, like he'd aged 20 years overnight. His skin was sallow and dry and he smelt of sweat and airports. I wrapped my arm around his waist and gave him a small smile.

'You know,' I said. 'The last time I was here, I was just about to meet you for the first time. I was so nervous.'

He stared at me with puffy eyes underscored with black. 'Oh, yeah,' he said, forcing a smile. 'I remember seeing you walk through those doors and my first thought was, she looks like every other backpacker in Southeast Asia.'

I let out a laugh that was on the brink of tears and looked down. I was wearing a light pair of jeans, scuffed from a night spent sleeping on the floor, a black strappy top, and my gripless pair of flip-flops. I still hadn't got around to replacing them. With the exception of my shoes, I now dressed as I used to before I travelled. There were no more baggy hippie pants in my backpack and my face was no longer home to a pair of fake fluorescent Ray Bans.

Our bags emerged and we hauled them on to our backs, my arms jangling from the 20 silver bracelets I'd bought for myself in Bali. Despite my best efforts to look less like a traveller, there were some parts of the uniform I couldn't bear to shun.

'You ready?' I asked, brushing my fingers against Dave's.

'Yeah. Let's get this over with.'

We pushed through the swarm of people to pick up a ticket for a taxi and made our way outside. A thick wave of humidity hit me in the face and I felt like my lungs were closing up.

'Songkran!' The taxi driver cheered as we slid our exhausted selves on to his backseat.

'Happy Songkran,' Dave said in the most unenthusiastic tone I'd ever heard him produce.

I wrapped my arms around my body like I was putting myself in a strait jacket and rested my forehead against the window. The city flashed by in blurred streaks of muddled images: a row of restaurants; a glossy shopping mall; golden temples; the moat; tens of thousands of drunken backpackers screaming and laughing and partying. Someone threw a bucket of water at the car and I gasped as it splashed in front of my face.

'We're here,' Dave said, and I focused on the sight of our old apartment block. As I blinked, I noticed the glistening road outside, the piles of coloured buckets, and the dozen Thai children at the entrance, who were rushing to fill them up. They pointed at me as I left the taxi and I shook my head in frustration. I didn't want to be that grumpy traveller but the last thing I needed was to be drenched from head to toe.

'Happy Songkran!' a small boy shouted at us as we paid the driver. I looked over to see his arms juddering as he fought to keep hold of a bucket that was almost as big as him.

My legs quivered as I walked towards him. 'We have our backpacks,' I called out. 'I don't want to get them wet.'

He scampered up to me with a mischievous grin and threw a bucket of cold water in my face. I felt like I was falling; ice cubes shattering at my feet while his friends collapsed in hysterics. They must have been able to sense I was an easy target because they soon followed suit, throwing bucket after bucket over me while I stood frozen to the spot, each wave sending me straight back to Phuket.

Splash!

Dropping my backpack and running for my life.

Splash!

The woman telling me there was a tsunami.

Splash!

Realising I'd lost Dave.

Splash! Splash! Splash!

Pushing our bags up the hill. Trembling with fear. Dry heaving on the ground.

I was on the verge of a panic attack, but I bared my teeth in a feeble attempt at a smile before shuffling inside.

In the lobby, several elderly men and their younger Thai girlfriends broke into applause.

'They got you good,' one of them said, flaring his nostrils in rapid fire as he guffawed.

I grimaced and ran my fingers through my tangled hair, wanting nothing more than to be in our room.

'Welcome back!' The receptionist greeted us with a warm smile. 'And happy Songkran!'

'Happy Songkran,' Dave and I mumbled in unison.

'Here is the key to your room,' she said, dropping it in front of us. 'Same room as before. It is ready now. You can buy your water guns from the 7-Eleven.'

I dragged our bags into the lift while Dave went in search of weaponry.

Home.

It didn't feel like home any more, though. Our room smelled like disinfectant; was too empty and too silent. I dropped our soggy bags by the door and looked around, numb to our surroundings. I could remember none of the happy times we'd had here; only the tsunami. I threw myself backwards on to the bed and bounced up and down a few times, soaking the fresh sheets.

I tried to cry because that felt like the right thing to do. Clenching a fistful of sheets in my fingers, I opened my mouth and let out empty, shuddering howls but my eyes remained dry. I'd somehow managed to shut myself down and I wasn't sure how to wake myself up again.

I sat up and rested my head on my knees, staring at the white wall in front of me. I stayed sat there in a trance for several minutes, wondering why everything felt wrong. As I stared, I felt tiny pinpricks dancing across the surface of my palms, then jumping into overdrive when I wriggled my fingers. I was dehydrated, but couldn't work up the energy to care.

I flashed back to when I'd been standing in the car park and waiting to die. I'd told myself then that if I somehow managed to survive this, I'd do everything I could to better my life. I'd never have another panic attack again. I'd try every new food I could get my hands on. I'd talk to strangers and I'd get a root canal, and I'd say yes to everything but a normal life. Instead, I felt like I was floating in a bubble, detached from the outside world.

I wandered on to the balcony and watched the chaos unfold. Just below me, a Thai guy about the same age as me had filled a barrel with a human-sized block of ice and was flinging cups of water over shrieking passers-by. I tried to laugh, but it got caught in my throat, coming out as a painful cough instead.

'Hey, baby,' Dave called out, making me jump. 'Check this out.'

I turned around and looked him up and down. He was dripping wet and laden with water pistols, a gleeful smile stretching from ear to ear. 'You're going to love it out there,' he told me, holding out his range of weapons. 'Which ones do you want?'

I want to spend the day in my room, I thought, but Dave had gone through all this effort and I was supposed to be living as if I was dying.

I pointed at the bright pink Super Soaker. 'I'll take the girly one. And that backpack one.' I reached for the bright blue container and slipped the straps over my shoulders. From the bottom stretched a piece of tubing with a pistol at the end. I slipped it on and captured Dave in the crosshair, aiming straight for his heart.

'You ready to head outside?' he asked.

'Ready as I'll ever be,' I said, raising my gun to his smiling face. He'd perked up after his walk to the store. Maybe 20,000 splashes of cold water could pull me out of this funk, too.

'Happy Songkran!' a middle-aged woman called out, before hurling a lukewarm bucket of water in our faces.

'Right in the mouth,' I groaned. 'Gross.' I gulped it down before I had a chance to realise it probably wasn't safe to do so. My eyes darted to Dave as he spat a mouthful over the ground and burst out laughing. *He was finding this funny?*

Panic began to rise in my throat as I fought the urge to run back to the safety of our room. Every splash of water and squeal of laughter took me further and further out of my depth. This was quite possibly the worst way to recover from a near-death experience. *Stay calm*, I warned myself. *Remember: this is fun*.

'Come on,' I said, reaching for Dave's hand in an attempt to gain control. 'Let's head to the moat.'

He laced his fingers through mine and we walked towards the sound of screaming children and a thumping bassline. *I can do this.*

We turned a corner and my jaw dropped. In front of us were several thousand people, all taking part in the biggest water fight in the world. As I gaped at the scenes of carnage, a pick-up truck crawled past us with a dozen hot-pant-clad girls dancing wildly in the back. One of them spotted me watching and threw an icy bucket of water in my direction. Before I had time to blink, a tuk-tuk careered past crammed with Thai teenagers shooting at me with tiny water pistols.

'Dave,' I marvelled, suddenly filled with delight. 'This is *insane*.'

'Isn't it?' he said. 'I can't believe this lasts for five days.'

I could detect the joy in his voice and when I turned to look at him, he looked the happiest I'd ever seen him. Even better: his white V-neck was now see-through and clinging to his chest.

I opened my mouth to tell him he looked great, but was distracted by a timid-looking elderly lady who had started flicking water at my forehead from a bowl full of rose petals.

'Happy Songkran,' she said, her eyes meeting mine.

'Happy Songkran,' I sang back at her.

Someone threw a bucket of dirty moat water at the back of my head, and I spun around to see two backpackers laughing and pointing at me.

'Happy Songkran, love,' one of them shouted in a British accent.

I started to giggle, suddenly feeling giddy with excitement over what the rest of the day would bring. Dozens of barrels lined the pavement beside me, filled to the brim with moat water and surrounded by people topping up their guns before being attacked. I pulled my water pistol backpack off and dunked it in the water. As I did so, I felt a trickle of cold water running down the small of my back. I gasped and spun around to see a tiny Thai boy grinning up at me.

'So cold,' I squealed at him, cracking up over his impish smile. I raised my backpack out of the barrel and hovered it over his head, laughing even harder at the sight of him cowering at my knees in mock terror. 'Watch out,' I warned him, as I emptied the contents all over him. His eyes widened and he scurried towards the nearest bucket of ice for a top-up.

'Can you warm me up?' I asked Dave, holding out my arms to him.

He picked up a bucket of water from his feet and tipped it over my head. As the warm moat water cascaded over my body, I exhaled and finally released the last remnants of tension.

'Thanks,' I grinned.

We spent the next 8 hours standing on that street, saturated with moat water, shivering from iced water and unable to wipe the smiles from our faces. *I was alive*, I reminded myself over and over. *I was alive and I was so freaking happy.*

CHAPTER 12

Leaving Chiang Mai was harder than I expected. Some small part of me was convinced that leaving would mean never returning and after spending four months there, it had come to feel like home. I couldn't bear the thought of never making it back.

In Chiang Mai, I'd had the perfect mix of constants and freedom. When you travel, routines quickly fall to the wayside because no two days are the same. Fridays no longer bring euphoria and Mondays dread. Instead, Monday might be the perfect day to sleep until noon and laze beside the rooftop pool and Friday the day you set aside for blog work, spending 16 hours writing about that time you fell in a rice paddy. It was a life I'd longed for when I'd left the UK, but I hadn't realised how disorientating it could be. It was the freedom that was now driving me towards travel – the freedom to escape routines, but the freedom to chase them, too.

I had my constants, too: the night market where I'd rubbed a chilli in my eye, now a place I visited several times a week;

the breakfast place we'd ride to every Tuesday for pancakes and smoothies; the small cafe where the owner knew our names and orders; and the supermarket stocked with imported foods where we'd spend £10 a week on Cheddar cheese. And there was my freedom: being able to drop everything on a Wednesday morning to spend a romantic two nights in the Thai countryside; waking up every day when I was rested rather than with an alarm; and taking afternoon naps beside our rooftop pool more often than not. Assimilating myself in expat life in Chiang Mai had been one of the highlights of my travels but it was time to move on.

I knew I was making the right decision but that didn't make it any less heartbreaking. The tsunami scare had shown me just how fragile life was and awakened in me an urge to make every moment count. I wanted to explore more of Southeast Asia beyond my Chiang Mai comfort zone.

'I'm going to miss you,' I said, standing in our glossy apartment lobby with my arms wrapped tightly around Dave. I'd spent close to every second of the past four months with this man and the prospect of another stint of solo travel was exhilarating and nerve-wracking.

'I'll miss you too,' I heard him say with a chuckle. 'But it's only for a month. You'll be fine.'

I nodded into his chest, running over my travel plans in my head: ten days in Laos, four in Cambodia and two weeks at home. Dave would be leaving Chiang Mai that evening and heading to Australia for a month to see his family. I inhaled his minty scent one last time in an attempt to memorise every part of him before saying goodbye.

'Come on,' he said suddenly, patting me on the head.

I pulled away to watch the silver minivan park outside and sound its horn. I'd booked myself on a three-day overland journey to the Laos city of Luang Prabang: a day in the minivan to take me to the Laos border, followed by two days on the appropriately named slow boat, drifting along the Mekong River.

I stuffed my backpack into the back of the van and climbed inside, offering a wave at the people already sat down. After taking a seat by the window, I pulled my sunglasses over my eyes to hide the tear that was sliding down my cheek. My heart pounded in my chest as I watched Dave get smaller and smaller until we were driving alongside the moat and I was on my own again.

I'm scared, I realised. I thought of Dave, back in our room, probably heading out for a coffee and planning out his month in Australia. Kiwi men aren't known for being sentimental or emotional and Dave fitted the stereotype. He never fussed over goodbyes, was perplexed by the ease at which I could cry and was disturbingly rational about every aspect of our relationship.

When we reached the Thai border town of Chiang Khong, it was 5.30 p.m. and the sun was starting to set. We turned into the driveway of a grey concrete building and parked. Given that my ticket for the three-day trip cost around £30 – including the first night's accommodation – the shabby building met my expectations.

We piled out of the van and loitered beneath the final shimmering rays of light, watching our driver unload our luggage. A tiny Thai woman rushed out of the building and began talking to him in rapid fire. She looked angry.

'Where are you from?' asked the tall guy I'd been sitting next to. He looked like a basketball player: tall and muscular with tousled black hair.

'The UK,' I said. I spotted my backpack and walked to get it while he followed behind. 'You?'

'Canada.' He pointed towards a guy and a girl dragging two enormous backpacks out of the pile. 'I'm travelling with these guys at the moment. Come on, I'll introduce you to them. What's your name?'

'Lauren.'

'Robin?'

'No, Lauren.'

'Love-ren?'

'*Laur*-en.'

'Maureen?'

I burst out laughing. 'North Americans always have problems understanding my name. I think it's my accent. Here, I'll try it in an American one: *Lauren*,' I drawled.

'Oh,' he groaned. 'Lauren. Got it. I'm Peter,' he held out his hand for me to shake and then motioned for me to follow him across the driveway. We stopped beside his friends, who now were arguing in another language. 'Jason! Steph!' he called, clicking his fingers to get their attention. 'This is Lauren.' They paused their bickering for a second to wave at me. 'They're both from the Netherlands,' Peter told me.

'Hey,' I said with a grin, waving back. 'Nice to meet you.'

'How long have you been travelling?' Steph asked. She had bright-red curly hair and when she smiled, I noticed a gap between her two front teeth.

'Seven months,' I said, realising this was the first time I'd been asked that question since meeting Dave. Travelling as a couple hadn't been conducive to meeting new people.

'Whoa,' she exclaimed, squinting at me from beneath her forest of curls. 'And here I was, thinking travelling for three months is a big deal.'

'For reals,' Peter said, gazing at me in wide-eyed wonder. 'You're my new idol.'

I wasn't sure how to reply so smiled at Steph instead. 'It is a big deal,' I insisted. 'Three months is a huge amount of time. Where have you been so far?'

'Southeast Asia. I met Jason and Peter in Koh Pha Ngan and we've all been travelling together for a month. I have two weeks left and then I'm heading home.' She suddenly looked like she was on the verge of tears.

'Same as me,' Peter told me, adjusting the tattered straps of his vest top. It was black and misshapen, with 'Full Moon Party' written across it in fluorescent lettering. It was hanging so low that I could see his nipples.

'You four,' the driver interrupted, pushing his way into our circle. 'This guesthouse full. Go different guesthouse. Walk.' He marched on to the road outside and pointed to a red house about a hundred metres away.

'No,' Steph blurted out and I stared at her in bewilderment. 'Look at the size of my bag,' she moaned. 'I can't carry it all that way.'

Her backpack was a 90-litre monstrosity and, while I tried to refrain from judging backpackers on the size of their bags, it was excessive if she couldn't even carry it.

'We won't do it,' Jason snapped at the driver. 'You need to carry them for us. This is what we paid for.'

What they'd paid was roughly £30 for three days' worth of transport, a night's accommodation and several free meals. *Why would they expect anything more?* I was gobsmacked, not to mention embarrassed to be associated with them. I wrenched my waist straps tight and left the three of them to argue with the driver, disappointed in their behaviour.

'Lauren, wait!' Steph shouted as I reached the road. 'Someone's going to drive us to the guesthouse on their scooter.'

'I'm okay,' I called back. 'I'm happy to walk.'

'Come on,' she insisted. 'Take the scooter.'

'I can walk a hundred metres with my backpack,' I muttered and turned away. A few seconds later, Steph overtook me, whooping from the back of the bike.

My room was typical for a cheap Southeast Asian guesthouse: a basic room, with a sheet on the bed, a hole-ridden mosquito net hanging from the ceiling, a cold-water shower and a small wooden stool in the corner. I switched on the fan and perched on the edge of bed in front of it, sinking into the mattress.

I was relieved to have made friends so soon but did I really want to spend time with people who had treated our driver so poorly? I shrugged to myself and let the warm air blow my hair out of my face.

'Hey, Lauren!' I recognised Steph's voice as she hammered on my door.

'It's open!' I called to her before running into the bathroom. I stood in front of the scratched mirror on the wall and scrutinised my appearance. My hair looked like it was home to a furry woodland creature and my face was glistening with sweat. I splashed some water over me and forced my fingers through my tangled hair.

'We're going to get some beers on the balcony while we wait for dinner,' Steph said from the doorway. 'I just wanted to see if you'd like to join us.'

'Yeah, sure,' I said, flashing her a small smile as I left the bathroom. I grabbed my key from where I'd tossed it on the bed and followed her into the restaurant. Spending my evening with them was better than spending it alone.

This time around, solo travel felt different to the first few months of my trip. I felt less fragile and incompetent and more like someone who understood how the world worked. As I took a seat beside Steph, I decided to let the backpack incident slide. I wanted to like my new friends. I wanted to see what it was like to be a fearless solo traveller and my first step was getting to know new people.

The guesthouse's balcony overlooked the Mekong and, beyond that, Laos. It looked no different to the Thai side but I couldn't help but feel a tingle of anticipation at the thought of visiting a new country.

We ordered a round of beers, and they came served Southeast Asian style – lukewarm and accompanied with a glass of ice cubes; a wad of toilet paper wrapped around the rim to keep the bottle clean.

'So, what do you guys do back home?' I asked, pulling the soggy tissue from the top of my bottle and discarding it on the table. I tipped the golden liquid into the glass and watched as the bubbles rose to meet the 10 cm-high head. One day I'd remember to tilt as I poured.

Peter went first. 'Not much,' he said. 'I'm starting college when I get back.'

'How old are you?' I asked, taken aback by his answer. He looked to be the same age as me.

'Nineteen,' laughed Steph. 'Still a baby.'

'Awww,' Jason crooned, reaching over to tousle Peter's hair. I watched as Peter shrugged him off, before standing up and reaching inside the pocket of his basketball shorts. I wasn't sure what I was expecting him to pull out but it wasn't a small silver harmonica. He sat back down and raised it to his mouth, blowing out a bluesy melody while he tapped his foot on the wooden floor.

'He always does that,' Jason told me as he rolled his eyes. 'It's how he gets the *lay-dees*!'

'And as for what *we* do back home,' Steph said, pointing at herself and Jason. 'The easiest answer is nothing.'

I could sense her unease so didn't press for details. Taking another sip of my beer, I leaned back in my chair and relaxed. Beside me, the Mekong's dark surface reflected the orange glow of the guesthouses lining its banks. I watched the lights dance along the water for a while until I was hit by a reckless urge to go for a swim. I turned back to face the table.

'So, where have you been so far?' Steph asked me.

I outlined my route for her, talking about how I'd had no idea what I was doing in Eastern Europe, attracted nothing but disaster in Eastern Asia and was still kind of figuring my life out after four months in Thailand.

'You must really love it here then?' she asked, tracing the rim of her glass with her finger.

'It's pretty great,' I said. 'And cheap. I doubt I spent more than around five hundred pounds a month while I was in Chiang Mai. So, while I wish I'd seen more of Southeast Asia, it was good for building up my savings.'

'What do you do?' Peter interjected, placing his harmonica on the table and giving me a quizzical look.

'I'm a travel blogger,' I said nervously, feeling like a fraud. I was still waiting to wake up from the dream where I was actually making a living from my blog. 'I can do it all online so I can technically work from anywhere.'

'How long are you going to do it for?' he asked. 'Are you going to travel forever?' He was giving me that look again, the one he'd shot me when he'd said I was his idol.

'No,' I laughed, because I felt like saying anything else was being unrealistic. *Who spends their life travelling the world?* I refused to even consider it as a possibility, convinced I'd be setting myself up for failure. 'Probably for a year or two,' I said eventually.

'Do you smoke weed?' Jason said suddenly, staring at me through narrowed eyes. Or, at least, I thought that was what he said.

'I—uh, what?'

'Weed. Do you smoke?'

'Oh!' I said, and I felt myself getting flustered. 'No. I don't.'

Nobody said anything and I felt like they were waiting for an explanation. 'I have a few mental health issues,' I said. 'Anxiety and stuff. So I don't want do anything that might exacerbate them. I've spent years getting myself better.'

'Ah,' Jason sighed, looking disappointed. 'Oh well.'

'Yeah,' I said, wondering if I should apologise.

The guesthouse owner took the pressure off by bringing out dinner. I inspected it for a few seconds while everyone else started shovelling it into their mouths. From its smell, I could tell it was some kind of creamy coconut curry and rice concoction. I spooned a small amount into my mouth and relaxed. It was bland, just how I liked my Thai curries.

'So what do you guys feel like doing after dinner?' Jason asked through a mouthful of food. 'Want to see if there's any nightlife in this crappy town?'

'Damn straight,' Peter said, holding out a fist for us all to bump.

I gently knocked my knuckles against his, feeling like a rigid robot version of myself. *Live a little, Lauren*, I reminded myself, recalling how I had wanted to travel like Ally did when I was in Hong Kong. Now was my chance.

We scraped our plates clean and set off in search of some kind of entertainment. I hoped Chiang Khong didn't have a club because if they thought my fist bumping was awkward, it had nothing on my dancing. It was 7 p.m. and I was relieved to discover the town seemed to be fast asleep. Aside from a dozen or so guesthouses, there was nothing. No restaurants, no bars and definitely no clubs. Only the whirring of crickets that broke our deep silence and occasional whine of a mosquito as it passed by me. If I strained my ears, I could make out the low grumble of distant thunder.

I squealed as my toe nudged something warm and furry.

'What's wrong?' Steph hissed.

'Nothing,' I whispered, glaring at the sleeping dog. This ghost town vibe was spooking me out. 'There isn't anything here, guys,' I said. 'Let's just head back.'

'Nah, look,' Jason said. 'I can see some lights up ahead. I bet it's a bar.'

I squinted in the direction he was pointing and was just able to make out a bright green light dancing across the road.

'Woohoo!' he whooped, rubbing his hands together. 'Party time.'

I may have only been in a handful of bars at this point in my life but even I could tell it was lifeless. Unless by 'party time', Jason had meant 'reading a nice book in the corner while holding a whispered conversation', he was going to be sorely disappointed.

The bar was solemn. There was a collection of bare tables and chairs outside and I could make out a sad-looking expat, nursing a beer at the bar inside. *Lively*, I thought, smiling to myself. A relaxed, low-key night was just what I had been hoping for.

Above the depressed expat's head was a black light, which illuminated my vest top as we wandered inside. There was a Bob

Marley poster fastened to the wall and a large plasma television switched to a Thai news channel. I noted the string of Christmas lights and a glowing pumpkin sat atop the bar, an unusual decoration choice given that it was early May.

We ordered a round of beers and sat down at a table outside. Almost immediately, my ankle started to itch and I slapped at it until a cloud of mosquitoes hovered up to my face to greet me. The wind picked up and I watched them drift towards the road.

'I can't believe I only have two weeks left,' Steph burst out. I waited for one of the boys to say something but they were deep in discussion about Peter's harmonica.

I offered Steph a sympathetic smile, altogether uncomfortable having this conversation. I felt guilty over my long-reaching travel plans, as if I should tell Steph I'd go home as well to make her feel better.

'That's got to be tough,' I said. 'Do you have any plans for when you get back? You said you didn't do anything back home?'

She took a gulp of her beer and sighed. 'Nope. I quit my job to travel. It was in marketing, but…' She trailed off and began picking at the label on her beer bottle.

'But what?'

'I hated it. I don't want to go back there but I don't know what else to do. Damn it!' She slammed her fist on the table. 'Nothing excites me back home. Travel's the only thing that makes me happy.' She drummed her fingers on the table in an agitated manner. 'But I can't afford it,' she added quietly.

She buried her face in her hands with a shaky sigh and I whipped a handful of napkins from the dispenser on our table.

'Thanks,' she laughed, fanning her face with them. 'I just get so frustrated. When I travel, I'm the happiest I've ever been. All

I can think about is how I want to do this forever. It's so horrible to know that I can't.'

'I get it,' I said, though she probably thought I was the last person to get it. *What else could I say?* I was doing exactly what she wanted to do. *How could I possibly understand?* I wasn't anywhere near running out of money but it was the one thing that kept me up more nights than not. I didn't want to go home. What would I do? Study for a PhD in particle physics? I couldn't think of anything more soul destroying after experiencing the freedom long-term travel brings. Although I often complained about the 40- to 60-hour workweeks I had to pull as a travel blogger, often for far less than the minimum wage, it was allowing me to be here and do this. I'd never felt more grateful.

I looked over at Peter and Jason, who were now doling out a pack of playing cards.

'You girls fancy a game of Donkey?' Jason asked us, his eyes glinting in the candlelight.

'Maybe,' I said. 'What is it?'

'It's a card game. We take it in turns to put one card down each. When someone puts the same number down – like a ten of hearts followed by ten of clubs or something – you have to put your hand on top of the pile of cards. The last person to do so gets a letter: D-O-N-K-Y. Then the donkey has to do a dare.'

'Do you mean K-E-Y?' I said.

'No,' he sniffed, shuffling the cards. 'That's not how you spell donkey.'

'Oh,' I said, wondering if a donkey was a donky in Dutch.

I hated games that involved dares but couldn't come up with a reason for why I couldn't play. A dare usually involved catapulting myself so far from my comfort zone that I was never quite sure I'd be able to find my way back again. I rubbed away the goosebumps on my arms and, in an attempt to gain some courage, took 20 quick gulps to finish my beer. After two bottles, I was far drunker than anyone at the table and my surroundings were starting to blur.

The knot in my stomach untangled in a matter of minutes when Peter claimed D-O-N-K in quick succession. I kept my breath held as we threw down our cards once more, releasing it only once he'd lost the next round.

'Peter, you're it!' Steph taunted. 'You're the donkey!'

He took a sip of his beer and shrugged. 'Go on then, give me a dare,' he challenged.

Jason, Steph and I congregated to come up with a suitable challenge. Strip naked? Too offensive. Down a pint? Not tough enough. Then Jason came up with the perfect idea.

'Dude,' he said. 'You see those two Thai girls sitting at the next table?' They'd sat down a few minutes after us, and looked to be about 20 years old with long, slender limbs and identical jet-black shiny hair.

'Yeah?'

'Well, how about you go over there and ask if you can serenade them with your harmonica?'

'Sure, whatever.' Peter had more confidence than most 19 year olds I'd met. He strolled over to their table while we watched with bated breath. When he held out his harmonica, the girls started giggling. They nodded and he sat down beside them, closing his eyes and rolling his head back as he played. When he finished, they whispered something to him and he turned to face us.

'They've invited us to drink with them,' he called, waving us over.

The girls generously ordered us all a round of beer, which I accepted, not wanting to offend. *Three beers in one night?* I was going to be suffering tomorrow. I took a small sip and wondered if I'd be able to pour it under the table without anyone noticing.

'My mum is here,' one of the girls said, drawing attention towards the plump lady staggering over to our table. 'Her name is Eve.'

'Hi Eve,' the four of us chorused and she nodded in acknowledgement.

I watched as she staggered over to her daughter, picked up her bottle of beer and examined it. She took a deep breath and downed it in one before slamming it back on the table.

'More beer?' she slurred, staring through us with glassy eyes. She zigzagged up to the bar before anyone could answer.

Within minutes, I had my fourth pint of beer in front of me and several plates of fried food to go with it. I dove into the bowl, desperate for something to line my stomach and help me sober up. It was the perfect accompaniment to my intoxication: cooked in garlic, crunchy on the outside, and soft and juicy on the inside. I licked the salt from my fingers and smacked my lips together.

Eve had ordered three beers for herself and had already drained the first. I picked up an unidentifiable lump of something fried and popped it in my mouth. I was losing sense of my surroundings and the world was spinning around me.

To distract myself, I eavesdropped on Eve and Jason's conversation. During the 1960s, she'd been married to a man from England and he'd taken her travelling around the world. It sounded like she'd been to practically every country in Africa, and over a hundred countries in total. They were divorced now, she told him, before guzzling another bottle of beer in one fell swoop. I dropped another fried lump in my mouth and held on to my chair.

'I love you all,' Eve said to our group, which seemed a little dramatic. 'Please don't leave me. I have no friends here. Stay with me.'

'We have to leave,' Jason chuckled. 'We're going to Laos.'

'Everyone leaves me,' she announced. 'I wish you could stay.'

We exchanged awkward looks as Eve's daughter chattered to her friend. She didn't seem in the least bit phased by her mum's behaviour.

'I can't believe you ate them,' Steph whispered in my ear. 'You're so brave.'

'Can't believe I ate what?' I asked.

'The cockroaches,' she hissed.

I burst out laughing and then frowned. I didn't get the punchline. It must have been some kind of Dutch joke. 'What do you mean by cockroaches?' I asked, my eyes focused on a spot 20 m behind her.

'*Those* cockroaches,' she said, jabbing her finger at the plate in front of me.

'I don't get it,' I said, concentrating all my energy into focusing on the fried lumps. I could make out some small antennae wiggling in the breeze, a crispy wing, some curled up legs and—

'Oh my God!' I squealed, pushing my chair back from the table and spilling my beer in the process. 'I ate a cockroach!'

The entire table erupted with laughter as I tried to scrape the innards from my tongue. That soft and juicy texture I'd thought was a perfectly cooked piece of chicken had been the garlicky insides of a cockroach.

'You Thai now!' Eve roared, suddenly brightening up. 'You eat insect!'

I looked to Jason and Peter for support but they were clutching each other with tears rolling down their faces. 'You ate a cockroach,' Peter crowed.

'I ate a cockroach,' I repeated, trying not to picture it swimming inside me.

~~~

That night, I dreamt I was in Chiang Mai for Songkran, but instead of water being thrown, it was cockroaches. I'd tried to run, but my legs had been frozen to the ground and cockroaches were running up my legs. I'd looked to the moat and spotted Eve swimming in it, gleefully throwing the roaches in the air and beaming as they rained down upon her face. There'd been a loud crash and I'd spotted a tsunami up ahead, surging towards me.

I rose at 3 a.m. and packed my backpack to keep myself busy. I was hungover and sleep deprived, and no matter how hard I brushed my teeth, I could still taste garlic on my tongue. With nothing else to do, I wandered out to the guesthouse's restaurant and worked on my blog while I waited for the sun to rise. Now, more than ever, I was realising how lucky I was to travel and I wanted to do everything possible to stay on the road. When the others came to join me, I pretended I'd been sitting there for 5 minutes.

We crossed the border into Laos and were on the slow boat by nine. I'd half-expected to be greeted with a tiny ferry lined with uncomfortable wooden benches – if it had seats at all – but we lucked out with ours. It was a long, flat, open-air boat, fitted with 20 rows of grey car seats. It was like a floating coach.

I took a seat beside the water and Steph collapsed in the chair next to me. She'd told me she hadn't been able to sleep that night and her hair was in greater disarray than mine. As she blinked against the sunlight, I noticed her eyes were underscored with black, making it look as if she'd been punched in the face.

The engine started with a sputter and our skinny boat throbbed into life. As we waited for the last of the passengers to climb aboard, the hot wooden floor vibrated beneath my feet until I felt like I was sat atop a pneumatic drill.

Diesel fumes filled the air and then we were off, juddering along the caramel-coloured Mekong and kicking off our two-day journey to Luang Prabang. While Steph slunk in her chair almost immediately, I looked to the banks for signs of development; a small village or scattered homes, but could see nothing but untouched jungle. My mind wandered to Dave. He'd be arriving in Australia around now, heading out for breakfast with his sister and chatting away about his travels.

I rested my chin on the wooden side of the boat and watched the whirlpools of current dimpling the surface until it looked like the haggard skin of an old woman. At the foot of the jungle-clad hills, I spotted my first glimpse of life: a topless fisherman wading waist-deep with a net in his hands. He grinned to acknowledge our presence as we drifted past. About a hundred metres on, an elderly woman was squatted on a sand bank, dipping her clothes into the murky water. Steph let out a snore beside me.

There wasn't much to do on the boat besides sit. Peter and Jason, who were sat behind us, had bought a couple of beers for the journey and were discussing which drugs they were going to try in Vang Vieng. In front of me, two girls were playing a card game. All around, people were reading, sleeping, talking or staring out at the riverscape. I was exhausted after my sleepless night but couldn't bear to drift off – I didn't want to miss a second of this journey.

Our stop for the night was Pakbeng and we arrived just before nightfall.

'You wan' guesthouse?' crowed a dozen touts in unison as I stumbled on to the jetty, relieved to be upright after 9 hours of sitting. They waved laminated sheets of paper in my face while I tried to spot Steph in the crowd.

One of the touts prodded me in the side. 'Come with me,' he said. 'I have hot shower, fast Wi Fi. Nine thousand kip.' I performed a quick calculation in my head. Nine thousand kip was around 70p.

'Uh, guys?' I called, spotting our group congregated a few metres away. 'I think we should stay in this guesthouse.'

Within seconds of arriving, I'd learned that touts would say anything to get you inside. Steph and I had decided to share a room and it was filled with insects. Our bathroom shower was a dribble of cold water from a knee-high tap in the wall, and there definitely wasn't any Wi-Fi.

'Can you believe those touts?' I said. 'Hot water showers, internet, modern rooms? I guess we're the idiots for believing we could get that for nine thousand kip a night.'

'Yeah, seriously,' she laughed. 'This is the worst room I've ever stayed in.'

'Still – just think,' I said. 'People are at work right now. We could be sat in an office but we're in Laos instead. Terrible room or not, I think I'd rather be here.' I felt guilty when I remembered that would be Steph's reality in two weeks.

Dinner was a communal affair, set on a tired looking balcony with two large tables set up for guests. Peter and Jason were already sitting down when we arrived, and had ordered us some beers.

'Hello, hello,' said a man who I presumed to be the owner. He rested his hand on the nape of my neck and I stiffened in response.

'Don't forget,' he told Steph and me, leaning forward to whisper in our ears. 'I can make any of these dishes *happy*. Just let me know.' The happy version the owner was referring to is the dish with added marijuana.

'This guy is the best,' Jason announced.

The owner waited for our order, still with his hand on my neck. I studied the laminated menu on the table in front of us.

'I'll have the chicken fried rice, please,' I said. 'Not happy.' I added.

'You are good girl, hey?' The owner said, ruffling my hair with his greasy fingers. 'A very good girl.'

As the evening progressed, more people wandered downstairs until we found ourselves with a dozen people sat around our table. Everyone but me was from the Netherlands, Germany or France, and they slipped in and out of each other's languages with ease. It was unusual for me to be the only one at a table of Europeans who couldn't understand what anyone was saying – the number of travellers I'd met who couldn't speak English was in the single digits – so I entertained myself by staring at my soggy plate of rice. I felt left out but could hardly complain – anyone who doesn't speak English has come across this situation more times than me.

Jason was the first to speak in English. 'Hey, check this out guys!' he said, pulling out a large bag of weed from his pocket and setting it down in front of him. The table erupted in cheers while I chewed on my rice for far longer than necessary. I stared at my hands and wondered whether I should cheer as well.

I started chatting to the two young Dutch guys sat next to me as a distraction – they were 17 years old and travelling in Laos for two weeks. Out of the corner of my eye, I watched Peter rolling a joint. I could sense the tension around the table as everyone breathlessly waited for him to finish.

A few minutes later, Steph tapped my shoulder and I turned to face her. She held out the smouldering joint and exhaled slowly, a grin sliding on to her face. 'Want to try?' she asked, waving it in my face.

'Try it! Try it!' Jason chanted and I hesitated for a moment, wondering if I should. I felt like I was in an anti-drugs commercial. Travel was all about trying new things and I knew it wouldn't hurt to do so. Maybe I'd like it. Or maybe I'd freak out and have a panic attack.

I shook my head. 'I'm okay,' I said and passed it on to the guy sat next to me.

He looked at me like I was his mother and turned away to speak to his friend. I went to talk to Steph but she was deep in conversation with another Dutch girl on the other side of her. I sat and listened as everyone spoke in different languages and I had nobody to talk to. *You are good girl, hey?* I replayed the owner saying, shaking my head in frustration.

After an hour of pushing my food around my plate, I slid back my chair and stood up. Nobody seemed to notice as I walked back to my room, dejected. What a difference 24 hours could make. Yesterday, I was on top of the world, having fun with newfound friends, getting drunk and eating cockroaches. Tonight, I felt like the lamest traveller in the world, ignored and judged by everyone in the guesthouse. I climbed into bed and wondered what Dave was doing right now. As my eyelids began to drop, the world slipped away.

'ARGGGGHHHH!'

I sat bolt upright in bed as Steph screamed at the top of her lungs.

'SOMEONE'S IN OUR ROOM!' she screeched. 'HE'S COMING FOR US!'

I scrabbled beneath the sheets in terror while she flailed in the bed next to me. In a panic, I pulled my Kindle from beneath my pillow and held it up high, ready to smash it over our invader's head.

'Who is it?' I shouted at Steph.

'Oh my God, he's here!' she yelled back at me.

'Who's here?' I screamed. My eyes darted around the room, searching for an intruder. *Was the guesthouse owner coming to attack us? Was he going to pelt me with happy burgers until he transformed me from a 'good girl'?* I couldn't see a thing.

'Oh,' Steph breathed. 'I'm awake now.'

'What?' I gasped, as my heart tried to thump its way out of my chest. 'That was a *dream?*'

She mumbled something in Dutch and then I heard her roll over and start snoring. I sank into my pillow, drenched in sweat, eyes pinned open. I couldn't shake the feeling that someone was in our room.

'FUCKER,' she screamed minutes later, busting into tears. 'NO. Stop it, you fucker,' she wailed.

'Steph!' I snapped. 'Wake up!' This was getting ridiculous.

'I CAN'T DO THIS ANY MORE!' she screeched into the darkness. 'GET OUT OF OUR ROOM! GET OUT OF OUR ROOM!'

I huddled under the covers, more frightened than ever.

'Oh,' she sighed again. 'I'm awake.'

Jason banged on our door in the morning, shouting that the boat was leaving in 5 minutes. Steph and I rushed around the room in a panic, throwing clothes in our bags and ranting at Steph's alarm that hadn't sounded. I pulled my backpack on to my shoulders and waited for her to heave her enormous one on to hers.

'What the hell was wrong with you last night?' I asked as we hurried down to the jetty.

'What do you mean?'

'You were screaming all night. You kept shouting that someone was in our room and mumbling in Dutch.'

'Oh, yeah,' she said dismissively. 'Sometimes I sleep talk.'

'Sleep talk?' I said, turning to stare at her. 'You were sleep *screaming*. I didn't get more than about twenty minutes of sleep.'

'No way? Yeah, I do that sometimes. I'm sorry, I forgot to warn you.'

'It doesn't matter,' I lied, raising a weary hand. 'I'll catch up on sleep now.'

We were late on board, so the only available seats were at the back of the boat, right above the engine. I let Steph have the window seat this time and rested my head on my knees. As the sun shone on my face and arms, I let the tremors of the engine lull me to sleep.

I must have only been out for 5 minutes when I awoke to an urgent prodding in my side from Steph. Snapping open my eyes, I glared at her in a sleep-deprived fury.

'What do you want?' I groaned.

She grabbed my arm and yanked me towards her. 'Lauren,' she whispered in my ear, sounding as if she was on the verge of tears. 'A woman just died.'

'What are you talking about?' I snapped, wondering if it was some kind of joke.

'A woman just died,' she repeated. 'On our boat. There's a dead woman on our boat, Lauren.'

I heard a loud bang towards the front and I raised my eyes for the first time since stepping aboard. The two British girls in front of us were crying and there was an Israeli guy stood with his hands clamped over his mouth.

Then, silence. I craned my neck to try to see what was happening but there were too many heads in the way. When I stood up, I saw a strange bulky object lying in the aisle, wrapped up in blankets like a mummy. I watched as two of the men who worked on the boat sombrely walked towards it and lifted it to waist height. They began carrying it towards me.

I couldn't fully comprehend what was happening as I watched the scene unfold before me. Whatever was wrapped up in those blankets was transported towards us and laid behind my seat. Once the men were satisfied with their work, they peeled the blankets back. Beneath them was a very frail, and *very dead*, woman.

The air filled with whispers while I could think of only one thing: I was sat inches from a corpse.

CHAPTER 13

My first impulse was to run, but I was floating down a river, miles away from civilisation. My legs flinched and I fought the urge to jump overboard.

I couldn't tear my eyes from her. She was an elderly woman; looked like a local. She'd been laid on her back and her left arm was outstretched, like she was reaching for something to hold on to. A gust of wind picked up and blew a few strands of her steel-wool hair over her face. She looked tiny and frail, like a baby bird with leathered skin.

Steph jabbed her elbow in my side and when I turned back to face her, she nodded towards the front of the boat. There, an old man stumbled down the aisle towards us, tears streaming down his face. In his hand, he clutched a filthy dishcloth that looked to be covered in oil. A sea of sober faces watched as he lay down beside the woman – behind us – and moved his arm around her waist. He let out a spine-chilling moan and burst into tears.

I turned back around and focused straight ahead, trying to give him some privacy in one of the least private places for anyone to grieve.

'What happened?' I mouthed to Steph.

'Malaria,' she mouthed back. She moved her face to my ear and whispered, 'She was going to a hospital in Luang Prabang but didn't make it in time.' I didn't ask how she knew.

I stared out at the passing hills in desperation, as if expecting an ambulance to suddenly materialise. I'd never been somewhere so remote; there were no signs of life, no roads and no hospital. We were, for all intents and purposes, in the middle of nowhere. I angled Steph's wrist towards me so I could see her watch. We were 6 hours from Luang Prabang.

I thought back to my easy, mundane childhood. I'd lived a 15-minute drive from a hospital, blissfully unaware that there were people in the world who had to endure multi-day journeys on uncomfortable boats to get to theirs. Malaria had been so far from my frame of reference back when my biggest fear was that I might be allergic to rice. The only time I'd been to a hospital was when my mum had accidentally closed my pushchair with me still sat in it, snapping my arm in two.

My chest tightened as I replayed the past 48 hours in my head. *Had I used insect repellent? Had I covered up? Had I avoided being bitten?* I didn't have to think hard to know the answer to all three questions was no.

A guttural, heart-wrenching wail ripped through the air, increasing in intensity. The husband broke down in great sobs while Steph looked at me as if she was going to be sick. A cold sweat spread through my body and her face started to swim before me. *I can't have a panic attack here. Not now.* I dropped forwards to put my head between my knees and the floor rushed towards my face in slow motion. Slipping a hand inside my daypack, I wiggled it around as explanation for my behaviour, pretending to be searching for something.

My fingers tightened around a warm cardboard box and I wished it were a pack of cigarettes. Now would be a good time to take up smoking. I pulled out the juice box and slurped at the orange drink to try to calm my nerves.

The mood had changed. There was no more laughing, no talking and even the whispers died off eventually. Together, we stared straight ahead and counted down the hours.

The sun was setting when we arrived in Luang Prabang, putting on a mango-coloured welcome display that was streaked with pink blemishes. I felt at peace for a few moments as I watched the technicoloured ripples from our boat shatter the Mekong's surface.

Then it hit me again. Somebody died today, and somebody lost their wife. I felt a heaviness in my chest that permeated through my body, as if my red blood cells had turned into ball bearings.

'Lauren,' Steph whispered.

'What?'

'We need to get our backpacks and they're at the back of the boat.'

'So?'

'So,' she hissed. 'The woman is in the way.'

I turned around and watched a solemn procession snaking towards the storage room, picking their way over her lifeless body in order to reach their backpacks.

'What do we do?' Steph asked.

'What can we do?' was my uncomfortable reply.

She linked her arm through mine and we joined the back of the queue.

Touts swarmed around us on the jetty, clamouring for the opportunity to take us to their guesthouse and we reluctantly agreed; too tired to search for somewhere ourselves. I reasoned that it couldn't possibly be as bad as the previous night's guesthouse.

'Welcome,' the owner of our chosen guesthouse said with a warm smile, extending his arm to us. 'Come in. Put your bags by the door. How many nights will you stay?' He flipped his black hair out of his eyes and looked straight into mine, waiting for an answer.

'Five?' Steph asked me, and I nodded in agreement.

We paid upfront – a risky move considering we hadn't seen our rooms yet – and the owner handed us four sets of keys. Steph, Peter and Jason decided to share a dorm, but I was opting for a private room. It had been 48 hours since I'd had a proper night's sleep and I didn't think I could handle another round of sleep screaming.

I trudged upstairs and slid my key into the lock, thoughts of a steaming hot shower filling my mind. I twisted. Nothing happened. I frowned and wobbled it from side to side, mindful of my key-breaking abilities.

'Come on,' I muttered at the key, but the door wasn't budging. Throwing my hands up in defeat, I padded downstairs to where the owner was sitting and coughed to get his attention.

'Hi,' I said, showing him my key. 'I can't seem to open my door?'

He let out a chortle and nodded. 'The lock broken. I forgot.'

'Oh. Well, okay,' I said. 'Can I change to a different room then? A private room?'

'No. Full.'

'Well, what am I supposed to do then?'

'Follow me,' he said, taking the key from my hand.

I sat on the floor outside my room and watched him work on the lock. He moved slowly and carefully, shifting the door forwards and back as he jangled the key through a range of angles. After an awkward half an hour of failing at this, he began slamming his weight against the door.

'Not working, huh?' I said.

'I can open,' he panted, now ramming his shoulder into the door. 'Just… let… me…'

I leaned my head back against the wall in exhaustion. All I wanted was a hot shower, some clean clothes and to sleep for the next 16 hours.

'I have an idea,' he announced, pocketing the key and jogging down the stairs. I didn't know if I was supposed to follow, but I was too busy using all my energy to pull my eyelids apart.

When the sound of footsteps signalled his return, I blinked at his silhouette and waited for my eyes to focus. In his hand, he held an object with a 6-inch handle and 18 inches of curved blade.

'Is that a machete?' I blurted out, suddenly wide awake.

'Yes,' he said, without further explanation.

He positioned himself in front of my door, pulled back his arm and swung forward, hitting the wood with a dull thump. Over and over, he struck the door, hacking his way around the doorknob.

I heard a noise on the stairs and looked around to see an elderly man shuffling towards us. He paused on the top stair to catch his breath, took in the scene and walked into his room cackling.

With a loud bang, the doorknob flew off and crashed into the wall opposite.

'Open,' the owner announced with a proud smile stretched across his face.

I stood up and examined the splintered wood where there used to be a doorknob. 'So, how do I lock my door tonight?' I asked, prodding the hole. He'd hacked a circular chunk out of the door, exposing the back of the doorknob on the other side.

'You cannot lock. There is no lock.' He shook his head as if to say, 'silly foreigner'.

'But I need to lock my door,' I protested. 'How can I sleep knowing anyone can just walk in?'

'Guesthouse very safe. Nobody will come.'

'But how do you know?' I spluttered. 'You don't know. There could be some kind of murderer or rapist staying here!'

'Tomorrow, new room.'

'No,' I squeaked, my voice shooting up several octaves. 'I can't stay here. I'm going to find another guesthouse.'

'Curfew.'

'What?'

'Luang Prabang has curfew soon. Can't go outside.'

I spotted Steph stood on the stairs, watching us argue. 'Hey, Lauren. We heard banging. What's happening?'

'Oh, just the owner hacking off my door handle,' I said, pointing at the gold doorknob lying in the corridor. 'The lock on my door broke, so he grabbed a machete and cut into the door.'

'Whoa.'

'Yeah.'

'So I guess you don't want to have a drink with us in the lobby?'

'I can't,' I said with a frown. 'I'd love to but I can't lock my door right now and can't just leave my stuff in here.'

'Will you be okay?' she asked, concern etched across her brow. 'Do you want to sleep on our floor?'

I flashed back to last night and shook my head. 'I'm fine. I'll just go to bed and see you in the morning.'

'Well, let me know if you need anything, okay? Try to get some sleep.'

'I will.'

I watched her leave with the guesthouse owner and finally wandered inside my room. It was clean with stark white walls, broken up only by a yellowed painting of a monk that was hanging above one of the two single beds.

I sniffed my clothes and was engulfed in the scent of sweat, petrol and death. *I haven't had a shower in three days*, I realised. After the day I'd had, I wouldn't be surprised if someone ended up walking in on me in the bathroom, so I walked back to the door and yanked on the handle to see how easily it opened. The last thing I needed was to finish my day with someone walking in on me in the shower.

The door didn't move.

'You have *got* to be kidding me,' I cried out before pummelling the door with my fists. I was now locked inside my room.

I sunk to the floor and knocked out a beat with the palm of my hand, falling into a rhythmic trance and bellowing, 'Hello?' every few minutes. It sounded like the sort of song my dance music-loving sister would listen to.

An hour passed.

Then two.

I thought about giving up but the thought of sleeping in a room that anyone could open but me was too risky.

'Hello?' a male voice said from the other side of the door.

'Hello!' I gasped, jumping to my feet.

'Hello?'

'Hello!'

'Can I help you with something?'

'I'm locked inside my room,' I said. 'Can you get the guesthouse owner for me?'

'One moment.'

I listened to his fading footsteps and began to devise a plan of attack. Should I demand a new room even though I knew there wasn't one? Ask him to fix the lock? Ignore the curfew and try to find a new room? Sleep in the guesthouse lobby? I remembered a YouTube video I'd stumbled upon once while looking for confidence tips. I stretched out my arms and legs into a star shape in an attempt to pump myself up into being confrontational. I couldn't let myself back down again.

I heard a rattling outside the room and jumped back. The door swung open, revealing the guesthouse owner, and he looked irritated.

'I can't stay here,' I said.

He cocked an eyebrow in response.

'I mean, I can't. How can I stay in a room that opens from the outside but not the inside? What am I supposed to do? Sleep with the door wide open?'

He thought for a moment and nodded. 'Okay. Come with me.'

I grabbed my bags and trailed after him, down the stairs and into the lobby.

'I have a spare room,' he said, as we stepped outside and across the guesthouse garden. 'You can stay there tonight.' He led me down a gravel path and stopped outside a rusty blue door.

'Thank you so much,' I said, as if he was doing me a favour. 'I really appreciate it.'

I suspected my new room used to be a garage. There was no furniture, no air conditioning and no windows. Just a double bed with a yellow sheet stretched across the top of it. A light bulb dangled from a frayed wire on the ceiling, casting ghoulish shadows across the walls as mosquitoes with a death wish flung themselves into it. I wouldn't have thought it possible but it was far worse than my room in Pakbeng. I walked across the cracked floor tiles and dropped my bags on the floor.

Time for a shower. I pushed on the bathroom door and it creaked open, revealing little but darkness. As I ran my hand along the tiles, I could feel some kind of wet and sticky substance coating the walls.

'Aha!' I brushed against something plastic and a flickering fluorescent light revealed the room to me.

I stood for a moment, convinced I was hallucinating. The bathroom looked like something from a horror film. Its once-white tiles were covered in smears of a tar-like substance and there were several cockroaches scurrying across the floor. I peered into the toilet basin and cringed when I discovered a dozen dead ones floating in the water. In the sink, there were a couple of large beetles. I looked down at my fingers, coated in a black film, and started to whimper.

Slowly, I backed away, closing the door and walking to my daypack to find some hand sanitiser. I struggled to keep my hands steady as I squeezed the warm gel on to my palms, wondering if this day could get any worse.

I froze mid-massage, as if I'd suddenly floated out of my body and was watching myself from above, crouching and hyperventilating in the middle of a bug-infested room. *How did it get to this?* I wondered what my friends and family were doing at this moment, safe in their well-ventilated houses with windows and bathrooms that weren't home to 40,000 bugs. *What on earth am I doing? Is travel really a better alternative? Is this what I want to do with my life?*

I spotted a T-shirt in my daypack and buried my face in it, inhaling the scent of our Chiang Mai apartment. It took a few deep breaths to calm me down. Travel was a better alternative, I reminded myself. Travel had improved my confidence, given me life skills, equipped me for better dealing with panic attacks and led me to Dave. I sniffed defiantly and walked over to the bed. I wasn't going to let this room break me. I'd survived so much already. I could last a night in a dodgy guesthouse.

I pulled the scratchy cotton sheet up to my neck and rested my head on the torn pillowcase. With my heart pounding in my ears, I reached towards the wall and switched off the light. Immediately, the room was shrouded in the kind of darkness that comes from having no windows.

As I huddled beneath the sheet in mute despair, the room buzzed with life, creating a cacophony of surround-sound insect calls, complete with flapping wings, loud humming and the occasional splat as something flew into the wall.

I felt something heavy scuttle across my face and over my ear, landing beside me with a buzz. My eyes snapped open and I stared into the inky night as I felt whatever it was start to tangle itself up in my hair. I clenched my jaw and told myself not to cry.

With a fevered flapping, it worked itself free and I threw myself across the bed in response. Lying like a starfish on my front, I leaned over the edge of the mattress and felt along the tiles for my laptop. I eased open the lid and directed the faint glow at my pillow.

'Oh my God,' I gagged, jumping to my feet. There, on my pillow, was a cockroach the size of my fist.

'Fuck this guesthouse,' I yelled at it before taking off through the door.

I surveyed the garden with wild eyes as I waited for my breathing to normalise. My body trembled with a combination of anger, frustration, fear and sleep deprivation, but I still refused to cry.

With no better idea coming to me, I curled up on my side outside and stared at the splotches of moonlight on the gravel.

'Excuse me?' The tapping on my shoulder stirred me from my sleep and I rolled on to my back. It was still dark. Standing above me were two guys with messy long brown hair and black leather jackets. I estimated I'd been asleep for about an hour.

'Are you okay?' one of them asked.

'Oh, hi,' I mumbled. 'Yeah, I'm fine.'

'Why are you sleeping on the ground?'

'I don't really know.' I sat up and uttered a high-pitched laugh.

The guys exchanged glances that said, *This girl's insane; we should probably leave her for the mosquitoes*.

'I'm not crazy!' I blurted out. 'It's a long story. Let's just say that my room is so terrible that sleeping out here is a better alternative.'

'You can stay in our room if you like,' one of them said, offering me a hand. 'You can sleep on the floor.'

I gripped on to his wrist and he hoisted me to my feet. 'I don't want to trouble you,' I said, waving a wilting arm in their faces. 'I can sleep outside, it's fine.'

'Please,' he said. 'I can't just go to bed and let you sleep outside. I'd feel terrible.'

I weighed up the options in my mind: sleep on the ground, catch malaria and die, or sleep on their floor, feel uncomfortable for a bit and survive. 'Thank you,' I said, trying to muster enough energy to sound grateful. 'I really appreciate it.'

'Where are you from?' he asked as I followed them inside.

'The UK. You?'

'The Netherlands.'

'Oh, that's cool. I'm actually travelling with two people from the—oh!'

We stopped outside a room with a splintered cavity where a doorknob should be.

'You're staying here?' I asked.

They nodded. One of them pushed open the door and they motioned for me to step inside. I hesitated. *Maybe it'll be okay,* I reasoned with myself. *At least I won't have to worry about anyone breaking in and attacking me. I'll have these two guys to look after me.* I smiled and walked inside.

'Hey, thanks again for letting me sleep here,' I said as I settled down on the floor. 'You're both so kind.'

'No problem,' one of them said. They clambered into the single beds and one of them switched off the light. A streetlight shone through the window and bathed the floor in an orange glow.

Thank God this night is over, I thought as I rolled over to face the wall. My eyelids slammed together as if they were made of magnets.

It was still dark when I woke. I lay motionless for a few seconds, listening to my breathing. My face was pressed up against the wall but there seemed to be a second wall against my back as well. In a daze, I retraced my steps from the night before, wondering how I'd managed to end up in a coffin.

The wall behind me shifted and grew a pair of hands. Hands that ran themselves down my back from my neck, slipped around my waist and towards my groin. Hands that pulled my thighs apart. Hands that slid along my stomach and grabbed my breasts.

My eyes shot open and I stared straight ahead as it all came flooding back to me. The horrible guesthouse, the nice Dutch guys who said I could sleep in their room, the nice Dutch guy who was now trying to rape me and the room that was locked from the inside.

Shit.

I kicked backwards and made contact with his knee. I kicked again and his grip on me loosened.

'What are you doing?' I hissed as he started to crawl away from me. I sat up and pushed my back against the wall, keeping my feet aimed in his direction.

He stopped moving and sat opposite me in silence. I wanted to scream, run, kick, punch, throw rocks, do something – anything – but I was rooted to the floor with fear. My attacker stood up with his hands raised, as if I was aiming a gun at him and walked back to his bed.

'What should I do?' I whispered to the room, hoping in my sleep-deprived state that it'd give me an answer. I walked to his friend's bed and shook him awake.

'Huh?' he mumbled.

'Can you let me out of your room please?' I spoke in an even tone. Cold and steady: the opposite of how I was feeling inside.

'What? Why?'

'Just let me out.'

He stared at me for a few seconds while I crossed my fingers behind my back. With a groan, he pulled himself out of bed and grabbed a credit card. I followed him to the door and glanced over my shoulder at my assaulter. He was back in bed and facing away from us. The door clicked open with a pop.

'Thanks,' I mumbled, pushing past him and running down the stairs.

I didn't know where to go. I couldn't leave the guesthouse; I couldn't sleep in my insect infested garage of a room. I wandered out into the garden and beneath the glow of a full moon, I waited for the sun to rise.

It was 6 a.m. when the owner arrived and I was stood at reception, rocking on my heels with balled-up fists.

'I want a refund,' I demanded before he could say a word. He opened his mouth as if to argue but I shot him a cold glare that conveyed everything I'd been through until he closed it again. I hadn't looked in a mirror but I wouldn't be surprised if I had branches interwoven with my hair, splotches of dead ants smeared across my cheeks and eyes so swollen it looked like I was having an allergic reaction.

He walked to his desk and rifled through a drawer for a few moments, eventually handing me four nights' worth of money. I could have argued about how I deserved a refund for my night from hell but I was too tired. I just wanted to sleep.

I left the guesthouse knowing I'd never see Steph, Peter or Jason again. It was too early to wake them and I didn't have a pen and paper to write them a note. I didn't even know their full names. The last thing I wanted was for them to wake up and think I'd abandoned them, but I was too tired to think. I just needed to get out of there.

In the tuk-tuk, I stared vacantly out at the empty streets of Luang Prabang. The morning sun was casting dappled light through the trees on to the pavement, bathing the golden temples in glitter. We passed a whitewashed house with mahogany shutters and a monk in robes of saffron waited to cross the road. I fell into a trance, gazing at the scenes of beauty, until we braked outside my new guesthouse. I'd spent the early hours of the morning on my laptop, browsing for the highest rated guesthouse in the city. I would be blowing a huge chunk of the budget I'd allocated for the next two weeks on this place, but I couldn't bear the thought of staying in another crappy room.

The receptionist greeted me with a warm smile and handed me an iced glass of mango juice. She confirmed they had availability and at £30 a night, it was more expensive than anywhere I'd stayed at so far. When she showed me to my room, I did my best to look like I belonged in a guesthouse this grand.

'Do you need anything?' she asked as I gaped in silent jubilation at the enormous bed with a fluffy looking duvet and a dozen pillows. It was easily the nicest place I'd stayed in on my travels: a gorgeous boutique room with everything I needed to recover.

'No thank you,' I said in a hoarse whisper. 'This is perfect.'

I waited for her to leave, then walked over to the full-length mirror. A pair of bloodshot eyes stared back at me as I studied my sallow complexion. Half of my hair was matted to my face while the other half was pointing straight up at the ceiling. I rubbed at the black smudge on my forehead and peeled a leaf from my neck.

In the mirror, I spotted a vase of flowers beside the bed and wandered over to touch them. They were bright pink and gave off a sweet scent that reminded me of lilies.

'What am I doing?' I wondered aloud. Why was I stood here stroking a flower when I hadn't slept for days? With that realisation, I stepped backwards and took a running jump, diving face first into the crisp white sheets of my four-poster bed.

CHAPTER 14

It's funny how travel can change you. From the big, life-transforming changes, like realising you managed to survive the worst 48 hours of your life and emerge feeling more optimistic than ever, to the smaller, less noticeable changes, that are only realised when you return home after ten months abroad.

'You walk differently,' my mum said through tears, hugging me in the arrivals hall of Gatwick Airport.

I smiled. 'You think so?'

She took a step back and looked at me as if I was a stranger. 'You stand taller,' she said eventually. 'And you look up instead of staring at your feet all the time.'

'I think you look really relaxed,' my sister Victoria told me. 'You walk like you're floating. You used to walk like this.' She hobbled a few steps with her arms wrapped around herself, face pulled into a grimace.

'I guess that's what spending so much time in Southeast Asia will do for you,' I said with a grin.

In the car, I stared out of the window, just as I had done on the morning I was leaving. Everything, from the sheep on the slopes of the reservoir to the graffiti-ridden signs, had stayed the same. I wouldn't have been surprised if someone told me I'd gone to the airport last year, fallen into a coma and just woken up. From my dad's familiar car to the familiar shopping streets to the grey miserable weather, it felt like England was just how I left it.

'Cheese?' My mum held out a sandwich bag full of carefully cubed Cheddar. 'I know you've been missing English cheese so I brought some with me.'

I burst out laughing and popped a cube in my mouth. Now it really felt like I hadn't been away.

Within a few hours of getting home, my mum was cooking a roast dinner, my sister was in her room watching TV and my dad was staring at his laptop. Everything was the same, but I felt different. It was sitting around our table and having a roast dinner when it was really drilled into me how stagnant life had been for my family.

'So what on earth have you all been doing in the last year then?' I asked, eager to hear all the details that had been left out of Skype calls and emails.

'Not much,' my mum said. 'Just working – the usual.'

'Same,' said my dad. 'I've been going to lots of gigs. Work is as stressful as it's ever been. But your mum did finally allow me to buy a jukebox.'

'I saw,' I said. Taking pride of place in the entrance hall was a large jukebox loaded with classic rock and blues 45s, along with the odd novelty record. I'd spotted the *Blue Peter* theme tune while I'd been browsing and rolled my eyes at my dad's often-misguided attempts at humour. It was a Wurlitzer, a blue and green beauty from the 1950s. 'I really like it,' I told him earnestly. I'd inherited my taste in music from him and was certain I'd have had my own sizeable record collection if I hadn't left to travel.

'Don't tell him that,' Victoria said. 'You can't encourage him or he'll play it all night for you.'

'And what's new with you, Vicky?' I asked.

'Nothing, really,' she said. 'Just uni and work.'

'Oh, okay,' I said. 'And how's that going?'

'Alright.'

'Cool.'

I turned back to my dinner, confused. Were they being polite and not wanting to regale me with tales, or could they really summarise an entire year of their lives as 'not much'? I thought back to how my life was pre-travel and it had been the same for me. I went to college, I went to work and I sat at home in a freezing-cold house because turning on the heating would mean having less money for travel. I didn't do anything interesting.

I suddenly felt wracked with guilt, too afraid to speak up about my year away. *How could I possibly summarise the last year of my travels in a sentence or two?* I didn't know where to even begin. A heavy silence hung in the air, interrupted only by knives scraping against plates.

'So, what was your favourite country, then?' my dad asked.

I hummed, running through the list in my head. 'It's really hard to narrow it down,' I told him. 'I kind of feel like the countries I've visited are my children – I couldn't possibly choose a favourite. Apart from China. China's the kid I'd leave on someone's doorstep in the middle of the night.'

He looked startled for a moment while my sister cracked up laughing.

'Oh, Lauren,' my mum tutted.

'What about Cambodia?' he asked. 'That's where you were before here, right?'

'A disaster. I only had four days there and I'd planned to spend them all at Angkor Wat but—'

'What's Angkor Wat?' Victoria interrupted.

'Oh, it's this enormous temple complex in Cambodia,' I told her. 'There are thousands of ruins you can explore there. I think you'd like it, actually. Some of the temples have been taken over by these old, gnarled tree roots and you can climb all over them. It's very *Indiana Jones*.'

'You've been to so many wonderful places,' my mum gushed. 'I don't know how you keep track of them all.'

'Well, sometimes I do wake up in the morning and can't remember where I am,' I said with a giggle. 'I have to look around and try to remember which country I'm in, and then the city, what guesthouse I'm staying at, and what on earth I'm doing there. Sometimes it takes me a good minute to work out where I am. It'll feel weird waking up in my bedroom tomorrow morning.'

'I bet,' she said. 'I can't wait to share a cup of tea with you tomorrow morning.'

'That would be wonderful.' I'd missed my morning routine of tea and gossip with my mum.

'So, Cambodia?' my dad asked.

I began to summarise the past ten days for them. I hadn't expected to be hit by a wave of optimism in Luang Prabang, but once I'd caught up on sleep, I was feeling better than ever. I'd come to the conclusion that the tsunami had been a turning point for me, and being able to capture the blend of fear and fearlessness I'd felt while I was waiting to die was giving me a new outlook on life. I was alive, I kept reminding myself, and everything felt insignificant in comparison.

I'd had food poisoning a few days later, probably from my guesthouse owner in Si Phan Don washing her plates in the Mekong, but not even that could dampen my spirits. From Laos, I'd moved on to Cambodia, with the aim of spending four days at Angkor Wat, but catching glimpses of it in between bursts of sickness hadn't been quite the magical experience I'd hoped for. I shrugged after relaying this to my family. I'd be returning to Cambodia in a couple of weeks and I could make up for it then. *How could I complain when my life contained such freedom?*

My mum had been watching me talk with a terrified expression on her face. 'I'm so happy to have you back,' she said, reaching across the table to squeeze my hand. 'Now if you get sick, you'll have your mum to take care of you.'

I swallowed the pain in my throat and plastered an uncomfortable smile across my face. 'I'm happy to be back,' I told her, chewing on my tongue so I didn't cry.

I leaned back in my chair and listened to my family swap complaints about work: how my dad had too many targets to meet and was more stressed then ever; how my mum had been given more tasks than she felt confident to deal with; how Vicky was struggling to even find a job. All I could think was, *Had they always complained this much? Why does everyone sound so miserable?*

'What's the problem?' I burst out in the middle of my mum's rant. 'That's a great sign, right? That they're giving you more work? It means they think you're good at your job. And anyway, if it *does* turn out to be too much, I'm sure you can talk to your boss and explain that. Don't waste your energy worrying about something that probably won't even happen.'

The silence was broken by the sound of Victoria sniggering.

'Well, aren't you a little ray of sunshine?' my mum said eventually. My parents were looking dumbfounded.

I opened my mouth and closed it again, not sure how to make this better. It hadn't escaped my notice that I was starting to sound an awful lot like Dave. I'd spoken to him before boarding my flight home and knew he was struggling with being back in Australia. He was suffering from reverse culture shock and it was making him depressed.

I'd assumed he just wasn't that close to his family and things would be different for me. Leaving them behind had been the hardest thing I'd ever done and returning was supposed to be one of the happiest days of my life. Instead, I was starting to feel like I no longer slotted into their Lauren-shaped hole. *Had travel changed me so irrevocably that I no longer fitted in with my family?* I tried to change the subject.

'When I was in Bali–'

'*When I was in Bali,*' my dad mimicked while my mum and sister roared with laughter. 'I bet that's how she's going to start every sentence from now on,' he told them while I fought the urge to run to my room.

'Oh, come on, Lauren,' he said, catching a glimpse of my hurt expression. 'You know we're only teasing you. Where's your sense of humour gone?'

I didn't know how to answer, so I shrugged. 'Must just be jetlag.'

That night, I flopped into bed, exhausted and confused. I stared up my ceiling, papered with the bumpy blue design I'd always thought looked like worms. As I traced out the familiar outlines, just as I'd done on the night before leaving, I puzzled over why I was finding this so hard. Travel had built a wall between me and my family. I just wish I knew how to tear it down.

My stomach let out a loud gurgle and I lay my hands on it, frowning as I felt it bubble beneath my fingers. I had a feeling it was struggling to digest British food; this was the first time I'd had something that wasn't Asian in months.

≈≈≈

I knocked on the royal-blue door of the dentist's surgery. The smell of antiseptic floated through an open window and caught me unaware. It took me right back to the height of my anxiety and spending my teenage years having blood test after blood test for every illness that had 'a general sense of malaise' as a symptom.

The door swung open, revealing a feminine figure with fiery red hair. A look of recognition flashed across her face. 'Lauren!' she cooed, pulling down her surgical mask. 'It's so nice to see you!'

'It's great to see you, too, Jane,' I said, smiling at the familiar face of my dentist. I'd been visiting her every six months for over 20 years.

'I can't tell you how surprised I was to see your name on my list this morning.' She pushed her red-rimmed glasses up her nose and blinked at me through the thick lenses.

'Well, I've had a bit of a tooth-related disaster,' I admitted, swallowing a nervous laugh.

She cocked her head to one side so her shiny hair hung behind her like a curtain. 'Come along then,' she clucked, walking briskly down the corridor. I trailed a few steps behind, trying to convince myself I wouldn't need a root canal.

In the surgery, the smell of disinfectant hung over my head like a thunder cloud, causing my eyes to water. I sat down on the chair and my legs adhered to the vinyl surface.

Jane switched on the radio and the latest Top 40 song drowned out the beating in my ears. I'd never put much of an effort into keeping up with current music when I'd lived in the UK but after a year of travel, I was even more out of touch. My sister had collapsed in hysterics the day before when I'd asked her who 'Nicki Minja' was.

I watched as Jane lowered herself on to her chair and wheeled herself across the floor until she was facing me. 'So,' she said, angling her face so she could peer at me over her glasses. 'Tell me about this tooth-related disaster.'

The sun slanted through the window and warmed my face, sending goose pimples crawling across my thighs. I realised I was grinding my teeth. I unclenched my jaw and quickly ran through my list of incidents in my head. 'Well, I went to a dentist in Thailand a couple of months ago,' I started.

'Thailand? Okay.'

She listened intently as I told her about how the dentist had given me two huge fillings.

'Hmmm,' she frowned, twirling around to flick through my file. 'Let… me… see…'

She pulled out an X-ray and pinned it on to a light box for me to see. 'Well,' she said, taking a pen and drawing a circle around my teeth. 'This shows no visible signs of decay. You say this happened two months ago?'

I nodded.

'Strange indeed.' She switched off the light box and spun back to face me.

'Do you think it was a scam?' I asked, desperate for validation. I wanted to be told that the dentist had taken advantage of me; that I knew how to brush my teeth. I loved to challenge stereotypes: I was the Pink Floyd fan who had never taken drugs; the physics student who was a girl; the teetotal university student; the Brit with pearly white teeth. It was almost as though I went through life daring people to make a snap judgment just so I could prove them wrong.

'I couldn't possibly say…'

'A few days after the fillings,' I said, 'one of my teeth started to hurt. I was in so much pain. I couldn't stand having anything hot or cold on them, and even speaking made them hurt.'

I noted the surge of alarm rising in Jane's eyes.

'Right. Let's take a look then.'

I lay back and opened wide, crossing my fingers by my side.

'Well, Lauren,' she said after 10 minutes of X-raying and fiddling with my teeth. 'I'm afraid I have some rather bad news.'

I swallowed hard. *Please don't tell me I need to have a root canal.*

'You need to have a root canal.'

'Oh.'

'The nerve in your tooth is dead,' she said matter-of-factly, making notes in my file as she spoke. She stopped to look at me over the top of her glasses. 'Which is why you no longer feel pain. But we do need to remove it regardless. The good news is that it's unlikely to hurt.'

'And the bad news?'

'You need to have three further fillings.'

I blinked. 'I'm sorry, what?'

'Unfortunately, the fillings you had in Thailand were not performed adequately,' she said in a sympathetic tone. 'I can't say exactly what happened but if I had to hazard a guess, I'd say she drilled very deep, forgot to clean the cavities and then filled the teeth. Bacteria has been growing underneath them ever since.'

My head was spinning.

'That's not all,' she continued, reaching over to touch my left cheek. 'When she performed the filling on this side, she managed to drill into the tooth adjacent to it as well. You now have a hole in that tooth, so I'll have to perform a third filling. And finally, you need to have a root canal, but not in the tooth you suspected.' She moved her hand and touched my right cheek. 'On this side, I believe the filling upset the adjacent tooth and the trauma caused the nerve inside to die.'

I was speechless.

'So, in summary, one root canal and three fillings.'

'So, this dentist destroyed *four* of my teeth?'

'Well, I wouldn't say destroyed,' she said diplomatically. 'But they don't seem to have done a very good job.'

With an aching jaw and four foreign chunks of ceramic in my teeth, I stood anxiously outside an Italian restaurant, working up the courage to go inside. I was about to see my two best friends and I suddenly had last-minute nerves that, just like with my family, I wouldn't be able to connect with them.

I heard a squeal and a pair of arms squeezed me from behind.

'Lauren,' the arms shouted out.

'Hey Maral,' I said, circling around to face her. 'It's so great to see you.' My Afghan friend was barely recognisable from the awkward tomboy who used to dress in fluorescent clothes, matched with spiky silver belts and fingerless gloves. Today, she was wearing a grey pencil skirt with a white silk blouse, open at the neck. Her limbs seemed to have lengthened in the time I'd been away, but it could just be that I wasn't used to her wearing high heels.

'It's great to see you, too,' she exclaimed. 'Hey, where's your tan?' She ran her fingers down the length of my arm. 'Did you even leave England?' One thing that hadn't changed about her was her bluntness. Coming from anyone else, her candour would have taken me aback but it was one of my favourite things about her.

'I like to call it my travel blogger's tan,' I said with a laugh. 'Because I'm always sat inside on my laptop.'

She started to say something but Manlinh came racing out of the restaurant and into my arms.

'Lauren!' she squealed, swinging herself from my neck. 'How have you been, man?'

'I've been good, man,' I said, laughing at her turn of phrase.

I followed them inside and we wandered over to a cosy alcove lit by candlelight and lanterns. A white tablecloth was draped over the table and classical music played softly in the background.

'Manlinh, you look incredible,' I told her. Just like Maral, she seemed older and more sophisticated. I noticed she'd lost a lot of weight and her plain shoulder-length hairstyle she'd had for as long as I'd known her had transformed into long silky waves that reached her waist.

I ran my fingers through my own hair. I hadn't had it cut in over a year and it was threatening to turn into a giant dreadlock.

'You really do,' Maral said. 'You look amazing.'

'I've taken up pole-dancing classes,' Manlinh replied with a shy smile. 'They've been amazing for my figure.' Her phone started ringing and she dove into her bag to answer it. 'Hang on, I've got to take this.'

Only now could I recognise the arrogance in me believing everything would have stayed the same and only I would have changed. Travel had given me so much confidence, life experience and peace, but when I looked at Maral and Manlinh, I saw that not travelling had done the same for them.

'Right,' said Manlinh, hanging up. 'Sorry, guys. It was work and I had to answer.'

'What are you doing for work these days?' I asked. 'I feel so out of touch with everyone back home.'

'I'm working as a personal shopper for some high-end stores,' she told me. 'I love it and the pay's great, but it's so much hard work. Although...' She paused to point at Maral. 'She works even harder than I do.'

'Yep,' Maral nodded. 'I've just passed my exams and I'm a qualified accountant now.'

I nodded along as they discussed work and commuting, and all these other things I had no idea about. I'd only ever worked in retail when I was saving up to travel and had no frame of reference to help me join in with their conversation.

Maral and Manlinh were succeeding in lucrative careers, they looked fantastic and were brimming with confidence. I was grateful for how much of the world I had seen over the past year but, unlike them, I was still only making enough money to survive in Southeast Asia. I was wearing tatty old clothes, my hair was a mess and eating out for every meal had made me the heaviest I'd ever been. Suddenly, unexpectedly, I felt inferior to my best friends.

In Maral's car on the way home, I felt as if I was on the verge of a panic attack as my stomach twisted itself in knots. *Why was my anxiety rearing its ugly head now? Was it being back in the UK? Was it this country that sent me spiralling into a pit of despair? Could I never live here again?* My stomach contracted and I covered my mouth with my hands.

We were 5 minutes from my parents' house when I realised I wasn't going to make it. I was soaked in sweat, my vision was blurred and it felt like the car was rocking me from side to side. I felt my stomach clench.

'Guys?' I choked out, not sure whether to laugh or cry. 'I think I'm going to be sick.'

'What?'

'Are you serious?'

'Stop the car,' I squeaked, mimicking the sound of Maral's brakes. I leapt out before she could come to a stop and fell to my knees on the pavement. Crouching down on all fours, I began to moan as saliva poured into my mouth. My body surged from the powerful heaves until I emptied my dinner over the ground.

'She's being sick, man!' I heard Manlinh shout to Maral from the front of the car.

'What?' Maral shrieked. 'Really?'

'Yeah, look!'

'Oh, *God*.'

I held up my hand and waved as I retched, my throat stinging and eyes streaming. 'I'm okay,' I gagged. When the last of the nausea left me, I stood up and wobbled back to the car, laughing weakly as they stared at me in horror. 'Really, guys, I'm okay. Maybe I was carsick or something.'

The reality was I had no idea what was wrong with me and I was starting to get scared. *Was it a stomach bug? Was it the stress and rush of emotions from being back home? Was it motion sickness?*

The final few moments of the journey were even more nerve-wracking as my stomach twisted and turned with every movement. Our goodbyes were rushed and frantic as I tried to explain how great it had been to see them while wanting to run inside and throw up all over the bathroom.

I grabbed them both in a hug and squeezed them tight, then rushed to the front door and pounded on it with my fists. I heard the car drive away and breathed a sigh of relief. Now they were gone, I could concentrate on how terrible I felt without feeling self-conscious.

'Whatever's the matter?' my mum gasped when she saw me crouched on the doorstep heaving.

'Going… to… sick…' I stood up and rushed past her to the toilet, where I proceeded to violently fill it with pizza.

'Lauren?' She knocked on the door. 'Are you okay?'

'Yeah,' I croaked, wiping my mouth with a piece of tissue. I stumbled out of the bathroom and into her arms. 'I think I might be sick,' I mumbled, feeling like a child again.

'Oh, honey,' she said, as she stroked my hair. 'Come and sit in the lounge with me.' I followed her into the living room and on to the sofa and arranged myself so I was snuggled up against her chest. As we sat together watching mindless reality TV, I found myself wondering why I wanted to travel when this was so comforting.

All it had taken was a few minutes of projectile vomiting for me to lurch from wanting to leave on the next plane out of London to cancelling my ticket.

'I missed you when I was travelling,' I told her in a small voice.

'I missed you more than anything in the world,' she said, squeezing me so tight, I thought I might throw up again.

And just like that, the connection I'd been craving materialised. While I'd had great plans to catch up with friends over the two weeks I had at home, all I wanted now was to spend every moment with my family instead.

My remaining days in London passed in a blur of meals at my favourite restaurants, shopping with my mum to buy a new laptop and to replace the five T-shirts that made up my travel wardrobe and long catch-ups over cups of tea, where I regaled my family with tales of my biggest misadventures.

I pulled the front door shut and turned to face my family. 'So where are we going for our final dinner together?' I asked.

'There's a fish restaurant a ten-minute drive away that we thought we could go to,' my mum said.

'Seeing as you can't stop talking about how much you love fish,' my dad added.

Before I'd left to travel, I'd told everyone I knew that I was allergic to fish, all due to that one time I ate crayfish and threw up. 'Do you mean shellfish?' they'd ask. 'No,' I'd reply. 'All fish. I'm allergic to anything that comes from the ocean.' All it had taken was a tentative mouthful of barracuda on a Thai island to show me I'd been wrong, and seafood was now one of my favourite dishes.

Tears pricked my eyes at their generous gesture and I realised I wasn't ready to leave the UK.

At the restaurant, conversation flowed as much as the wine, as we recounted stories from my childhood.

'Remember that time when she carved her name into the wall and tried to blame it on me?' Victoria burst out. 'Or when she'd call me into her room, saying she had something important to tell me? But then she'd grab my arm and shout that I was in her room and *I'd* end up in trouble?'

'That's nothing,' my dad said. 'What about the time I ended up taking her to hospital because she'd managed to stab her eyeball with that spikey ring she always wore around her thumb? I thought she was going to go blind. It's a wonder she's survived a year around the world.'

'Yeah, yeah,' I smiled, rolling my eyes. 'I'm really going to miss you guys, you know.'

'We'll miss you, too,' my mum said, and silence fell over our table.

'I'm sorry for leaving again,' I said. 'But this is something I have to do. I'm not ready to come home yet.'

'We understand,' my dad said.

'And we can tell it's been wonderful for you,' my mum confessed. 'While part of me wanted you to hate it and come home immediately, I can see it's done wonders for your anxiety.'

'And you're actually nice to me now,' Victoria butted in.

'And you're nice to me,' my dad exclaimed. 'We're so proud of you and all you've achieved.'

My mum reached over and squeezed my hand. 'So proud we could burst.'

CHAPTER 15

It felt like separation anxiety. The second my flight left London, I felt as if I was on the verge of throwing up. I was lost and disorientated, wondering if I even wanted to travel any more. When I touched down in Singapore, I thought about jumping on the next flight home. It didn't make sense. I'd loved visiting my family and had thought that two weeks with them would be more than enough. Now that we'd said goodbye, I was struggling to hold it together.

My idea of home had evolved over the past year. When I first left England, I had an aching desire to make the world my home – travel for the rest of my life, picking up whenever I felt like it and never forming attachments to people or places. After three months in Chiang Mai, I'd felt like I could live there forever. Now, I felt like London was home again and it had taken leaving for nearly a year to show me how much my family meant to me.

I collected my backpack and walked into the shiny arrivals hall at Changi Airport in Singapore. My previous Southeast Asian airport experiences hadn't been quite so glossy.

'Dave!' I squealed when I caught a glimpse of him through the crowd. He looked different, but I wasn't sure if it was because I'd forgotten what he looked like. We'd spoken practically every day over the past month, but it felt like it had been much longer.

Our stint apart had been good for both of us. It had given us a chance to meet other people, be selfish and do what we wanted without having to think of anyone else.

'Hey you,' he said, as I jogged up to him. He held out his arms and wrapped them around me, smelling like mint and comfort zones.

'I missed you so much,' I said, standing on to my tiptoes to give him a kiss.

'We've only been apart for a month,' he said with a chuckle. His accent had changed over the month he'd spent in Melbourne and he now spoke with a slight Australian twang.

Seeing his face smiling down at me was all it took to convince me I was doing the right thing. My separation anxiety melted away and suddenly, I no longer wanted to return to London. I wanted to travel with Dave and start challenging myself again. For me, home was a complicated idea. It was London; it was Chiang Mai; and it was wherever my backpack lay.

We flew from Singapore to Phnom Penh, bought our Cambodian visas and joined the queue at immigration. It was 10 p.m. and, aside from the people on our flight, the airport was empty. I watched Dave pass through without a problem and handed my passport over next. Opening my eyes wide, I smiled at the immigration officer to try to look like someone who wouldn't have 5 kg of cocaine in their backpack.

'Go upstairs,' he said to me.

'Go what?' I asked, my eyes widening for real.

'Upstairs.'

'Why?'

He pointed towards the nearby stairs and said nothing more. I shot Dave a terrified look to try to convey how much I loved him. I was convinced I was about to be thrown in Cambodian jail and this was the last time I'd see him. *Had someone planted drugs on me during the flight? Did I actually have 5 kg of cocaine in my backpack?*

I reached the top floor of the airport and was surprised to find nobody there. My heart pounded in my chest as I tiptoed across the shiny floor, looking for someone who was looking for me.

'Hello?' I called out, shrinking into myself as my voice reverberated around the room.

I walked back to the stairs, puzzled and afraid, flicking through the pages of my passport and looking for a sign that something had gone wrong.

'That's it!' I shouted, stamping my feet with joy. There wasn't a visa in my passport. I had paid $20 for my Cambodian visa and they hadn't given me one. *The guy at the immigration desk must have thought I was meant to take a connecting flight or something.*

I skipped the queue for visas and leaned over the desk, passport in hand.

'Hello?' I called. 'I paid for a visa but nobody put one in my passport?'

The guy behind the desk frowned and took it from my hand. *Was this some sort of scam where I'd end up having to pay double?* I held my breath as he leafed through my passport.

'No,' he said eventually, handing it back to me. 'Your visa is there.'

'Oh,' I said, taking a step back. My face flushed the colour of raw liver, and I kept my head down as I walked back past the queue of sniggering tourists. *What was going on?* I trudged back towards the row of immigration desks and joined a different queue.

The official spent a few seconds flicking through my passport and comparing my photo to my face, then stamped my visa and handed it back to me.

'Thank you,' I stammered, then raced to meet Dave before I was told to go upstairs again.

'What on earth was that?' he asked me.

'I have no idea,' I laughed. 'That guy told me to go upstairs but there was nobody there. So I came back downstairs and this new guy didn't say anything. He stamped my passport and,' I froze, staring at the page. There, stapled to my visa, was the departure card for somebody called Sun Yu Yuan. I held it out for Dave to see. 'I can't believe it; he gave me the wrong one.'

I walked back to the desk, knowing that Dave wouldn't let me leave the airport just to avoid a moment of awkwardness. The official searched half-heartedly around on his desk for my card and shrugged.

'I cannot find,' he said.

'So what am I supposed to do?'

He handed me a blank departure card and waved me away.

'Sorted,' I grinned at Dave. 'Now let's get out of here before anything else goes wrong.' I'd been travelling for less than 24 hours and already come up against my first incident. Unlike my last few misadventures, though, I wasn't going to let it phase me. Chin up, head back, plaster a smile on my face and assume it was all going to be okay.

~~~

'So what are your plans for today?' Dave asked the next morning, as we tucked into our free guesthouse breakfast.

'The Killing Fields,' I said. 'And the Genocide Museum.' My heart filled with a mixture of terror, sadness and intrigue. 'I don't want to go,' I told him. 'It feels weird to go to something like this as a tourist. But I have to, don't I? In order to understand.'

He nodded.

'Do you want to come with me?' I asked. I didn't want to face it alone.

'No,' he said. 'I've been before. And anyway, it's best seen alone.'

His words sent shivers through me and I pushed my plate aside.

I have a feeling Phnom Penh is going to challenge me, I thought to myself. It was the same thought I'd had during our tuk-tuk ride from the airport the previous night. I had been trying not to form a judgement on the city so soon after our arrival, but our driver's swerves around scooters had made me nervous. I'd broken into a coughing fit halfway through the ride, and spent the rest of it covering my face with my scarf and choking on the dust our wheels were kicking up. At one point, the smell of sewage had wafted into my nostrils and, as we'd neared the city, I'd watched child beggars out at midnight, passing from restaurant to restaurant, asking for money, some of them stark naked.

We'd checked into our guesthouse: a slightly upmarket affair for us, but given that we'd both come from Western countries, paying £10 a night instead of £3 felt like no big deal. *Cambodia is like nowhere else I've ever been,* I'd thought to myself before drifting off to sleep.

I was glad I'd held off making judgement because now, as I wandered alongside the river in the bright morning light, I couldn't help but admire its beauty: pagodas glinting in red and gold, the flutter of saffron as a monk turned a corner and giggling teenagers sat gossiping on a bench beneath the shade of a palm tree.

'Tuk-tuk?' someone called to me, and I turned in the direction of the voice.

'Yes, please,' I said.

'The Killing Fields?' he asked.

'Yes, please,' I repeated.

'Genocide Museum?'

'Yes, please.'

'Twenty dollars.'

'Okay.' I should have negotiated for a lower price but given where I was going, I wasn't thinking about saving money.

'What is your name?' the driver asked, as he held out his hand for me to shake.

'Lauren,' I said, wrapping my fingers around his. 'What's yours?'

'Keith,' he said – a name I assumed was a Western one he'd given himself. He beamed as he squeezed my hand. 'It is so nice to meet you, Lauren.'

'You, too, Keith,' I said.

Outside of Phnom Penh, the air filled with dust once more as the potholed roads turned to dirt and I bounced around in the back in silence.

It was the mid-1970s – around the time when Dave was born – when the Khmer Rouge came to power. I'd picked up facts about the genocide that followed here and there, but the one that had always stuck with me was knowing that, in just four years, an estimated 2 million Cambodians – a quarter of the population –

died. Some succumbed to starvation or disease, as the inhabitants of the country's large cities were sent to the countryside to work endless hours in backbreaking conditions. Others were deemed to be impure – teachers, doctors, artists, lawyers, scientists, monks and even those who wore glasses – enough reason for a death sentence. Choeung Ek, one of 20,000 mass graves known as the Killing Fields, was where executions took place. Thousands of bodies had been discovered there, with many graves still left unexcavated.

'Two hours?' Keith asked, as I clambered out the back of the tuk-tuk.

'Yeah,' I said. 'If that's what you think?'

He nodded. 'See you in two hours, Lauren.'

'See you.'

I took a deep breath and stepped forward, walking to pick up a headset for the audio tour, and then through the gates and into the fields. I stopped to take in the scene: the grass was a brilliant shade of green, there was a light breeze in the air and the sky was a cloudless blue. A butterfly fluttered past my face. It was almost peaceful, in a horrifying kind of way.

From the painted wooden signs and the audio guide, I began to collect pieces of a puzzle I didn't know how to put together. There was the room used to store chemicals that were thrown on top of bodies, both to mask the smell and to kill anyone who had been buried alive. There were the bone fragments and scraps of rags poking out through the ground around me – a sobering reminder of what lay beneath my feet. A mass grave of victims found without heads. A mass grave of naked women and children. A beautiful oak tree where babies were grabbed by their heels and swung headfirst against it. The audio guide played the music used by the Khmer Rouge to drown out the screams as these murders took place and I felt like I was going to pass out.

And finally, a Buddhist *stupa* filled with more than five thousand skulls. I glanced at it, swarming with backpackers, and continued on. It made me uncomfortable and I felt like I shouldn't be there. Like I was invading the victims' privacy.

'Very sad?' Keith asked me, when I returned.

'It is,' I said, not sure what else I could possibly say to him. He likely had to drive here day after day after day. 'Very sad.'

'Genocide Museum now?' he asked, waving for me to climb in the back.

'Yes, please.'

As I sat in the back of the tuk-tuk, I chewed on my nails, trying to digest what I'd just seen. It was so far removed from anything I'd had to experience and to think it happened within Dave's lifetime was chilling. More than anything, I was glad I had visited. I wasn't someone who'd say my travels had all been full of rainbows and sunsets and meaningful experiences, but even so, it was important to visit places like this. It was important to remember; to understand why the country was the way it was; and to put my own privileged experiences into perspective. *How could me sitting next to a dead body in a boat or being scammed by a Chinese teenager possibly even compare?*

Tuol Sleng Genocide Museum used to be a high school in the suburbs of Phnom Penh. After the Khmer Rouge took over the city, it was turned into the S-21 prison – the prison that spawned the mass murders out in the Cambodian countryside.

'Two hours?' Keith asked once more, pulling up outside a nondescript building.

'Okay,' I said.

I bought my ticket and walked into a green courtyard lined with palm trees. There were four whitewashed concrete buildings, three storeys high, all facing what used to be the schoolyard. I walked up to a large sign, listing the ten regulations of S-21.

6. While getting lashes of electrification you must not cry at all.

With a thudding in my ears, I walked from building to building, room to room, each more horrifying than the last. Classrooms transformed into torture chambers and cells: a metal bed frame on to which prisoners were shackled, photos of bloated, decomposing bodies chained to it, paintings depicting torture scenes in the prison.

I stepped outside for a moment's escape and gulped at the air before turning around and walking back inside. It was important to remember. Thousands of photographs of the men, women and children who were killed; heavy barbed wire strung up over the balconies. Electrocution, suffocation, drowning, whipping, dismemberment, rape.

I couldn't summon any more energy, so I turned and walked outside, numb from too many emotions clamouring for my attention. I sank on to a bench opposite an exercise bar that had been repurposed as gallows. I recognised it from the horrific paintings inside. Interrogators would string prisoners upside down and question them until they fell unconscious. They would then be plunged headfirst into tubs filled with urine and faeces until they regained consciousness. Then the process would start all over again. The sun shone down on my face as I watched two tiny blue birds chirping from atop the wooden frame. Beside me were the tombs of the last 14 prisoners killed at S-21.

I struggled to reconcile the tragic history of Cambodia with the wonder I felt from being in Phnom Penh. Visiting the Killing Fields and Genocide Museum had shocked me into a sombre state and I didn't want to just forget about it and move on. Staying sombre in Phnom Penh, however, was hard to do. There were too many gorgeous pagodas, too many fun art galleries, bustling markets and buzzing cafes, too many happy, smiling faces.

But then there was the incessant harassment, the fumes of sewage and burning rubbish, the child beggars and prostitutes, and the stories of muggings from others in our guesthouse. I'd only been in Cambodia for a few days and it was already stirring up all kinds of difficult emotions for me.

When Dave asked where I wanted to go next, I opted for the beach instead of a return to Angkor Wat, wanting to discover a side of Cambodia in stark contrast to Phnom Penh. Next stop: Sihanoukville.

We stepped off the bus into a dusty car park, where we were greeted by legions of tuk-tuk drivers and motorcyclists, all clamouring for our fare. I barely batted an eyelid at them, having faced scenes like this a dozen times before in Southeast Asia. We grabbed a tuk-tuk to Serendipity Beach, best known and most hated for its wild party scene.

Before arriving, I knew I'd struggle to like this part of Sihanoukville, but I still wanted to discover its redeeming features. I didn't want to pass it off as a destroyed paradise and not bother visiting. Judging China so harshly had taught me to give everywhere a chance to be something wonderful.

We were greeted by a procession of drunk teenagers wandering the streets shirtless. Sihanoukville looked like a backpacker's paradise – one I suspected I could have loved if I'd travelled straight here from Bangkok, back when I was excited about my short-lived career as a partier. After a year of travel, though, I was struggling to find its appeal. Now, I craved quiet beach towns where I could get some work done, sleep a full 8 hours and not witness tourists behaving disrespectfully in front of locals. Dave and I resolved to stay for one night then go in search of something that was more our style.

'And you know what I really fancy?' Dave said, as we lay out on the beach that afternoon.

'What's that?' I hissed. I was pretending to be asleep so the persistent touts would leave me alone.

'Mexican food.'

An hour later, we were eating the saddest meal of our lives. The nachos we'd excitedly ordered had ended up as a plate with salt and vinegar Pringles, smothered with baked beans and cream cheese. Back before I learned what real food was supposed to taste like, this would have been my ideal meal. Instead, I filled my empty stomach with a margarita and left the restaurant buzzing.

'Dave, guess what,' I slurred, stumbling alongside him. 'I had a drink and I'm not even drunk.'

The ground fell away from my feet and I started to drop. I felt a searing pain in my knee, then my shoulder, my neck and my ankle. I was rolling, rolling, rolling.

The world straightened out just in time for an excruciating pain to travel through my legs. I blinked. I was lying flat on my back in the middle of the road with Dave watching from the pavement with a quizzical look on his face.

'What did you say?' he asked with a glint in his eye. 'You're not drunk?'

'Help,' I grunted, lifting myself up and crab-walking in circles with one leg in the air. I was certain I'd broken my ankle. Dave grabbed my arms and dragged me to the side of the road while I kept my leg pointed out as if I was a pin-up girl. 'I can't stand,' I said through gritted teeth. 'My ankle is broken.'

'You'd know if your ankle was broken.'

'I just said it's broken,' I snapped, tears spilling over my cheeks. 'I know it's broken.'

A tuk-tuk pulled up beside us and the driver ran to my side. As I sat sobbing, he pulled a phone from his pocket and held the screen up to my knee as a light. I was more concerned about my ankle, which I was currently struggling to move.

'Tuk-tuk?' the driver offered. 'Hospital.'

'No thanks,' Dave said firmly, locking his hands beneath my armpits and pulling me to my foot. I stood balancing on one leg as a steady stream of backpackers in fluorescent vest tops milled past. I touched my toe to the ground, but jerked it back up again when a shooting pain travelled all the way up to my spine.

'I can't walk, Dave,' I whispered in a panic, bouncing on one leg. I was now as sober as I had thought I was a few minutes ago.

Dave wrapped his arm around me and I hopped along the pavement, dodging giant holes where entire slabs were missing. After a few minutes, my good leg was starting to burn and when I glanced down, I realised that what had looked like a small graze a few minutes ago was now a gaping wound, 6 cm in diameter.

'Dave,' I whimpered, leaning into his chest.

'Yeah?'

'Look at my leg.' A thick stream of blood was trickling from my knee and pooling in my flip-flop.

'Just keep walking,' he said with a grave expression on his face. 'We'll worry about that when we get back.'

''Kay,' I grunted.

In our room, Dave directed me straight into the bathroom. 'You need to take a shower right now,' he told me. 'Your knee is full of gravel and I can only imagine how dirty the roads in Cambodia are. You really don't want to get an infection.'

'But what about how dirty the water is?' I asked, eyeing the showerhead with suspicion. 'Surely that's worse?'

He groaned. 'Maybe. I don't know. I've got some antiseptic cream, though. We'll cover it with that afterwards. Just get under the water and scrub as hard as you can.'

The next morning, I staggered out of bed and down to the ferry terminal, one knee leaking and one ankle the size of a cricket ball. The violent half-hour speedboat ride had left me close to tears, and the 5-minute walk across the beach to our guesthouse was just as challenging. Trying to hop with two bags hanging from my shoulders was just as ridiculous as it sounds. Though my legs were agony, I was determined not to let them ruin my time in Cambodia. This island seemed like the best possible place to recover.

We were on Koh Rong, an island that perfectly fitted the deserted island paradise stereotype: pristine white sand so soft it felt like talcum powder, vibrant cerulean ocean as warm as the air that surrounded it, electricity for only half the day to keep me offline and a deserted beach a 20-minute walk from the guesthouse.

'This is incredible,' I exclaimed that afternoon, limping in circles. We'd just arrived on the immaculate Long Beach and had the entire 10 km stretch of sand to ourselves. I felt like I'd been shipwrecked.

Getting here hadn't been easy. There were no roads on Koh Rong, so our walk involved clambering over sharp rocks, trampling through dangerous jungle (before leaving our guesthouse owner had cheerfully warned us to look out for King Cobras, the bite of which will leave you with 5 hours to live. Not what I wanted to hear on an island without a hospital) and wading through the sea. At one point, we'd attempted to cross what looked to be a shallow stream, only to find it was about 6 ft deep. I was still apologising for breaking down in hysterics when Dave, walking across with his bag over his head, slowly slipped deeper underwater until all I could see was a pair of hands gliding through the surface.

'Do you think the salt water will help my knee?' I asked, poking his side as he lay on the beach beside me.

'Maybe,' he said grumpily, before standing up and walking into the sea.

'You can't be mad at me,' I demanded, as I followed him in. 'I'm injured, remember. I need sympathy.'

'Like the sympathy you gave when I almost drowned back there?'

I pressed my fist to my lips as I pictured his drifting hands once more. 'Again, very sorry.'

'S'okay,' he said eventually, swimming towards me.

'You know what's a real first-world problem?' I said in an effort to lighten the mood.

'What's that?'

'That the temperature of this water is so warm it's not refreshing. It's not cooling me down.'

'You're a terrible human being,' he said. 'I can't believe you just said that.'

'And not only that,' I continued. 'But the sand is so white that it dazzles me when I look at it. I can't take my sunglasses off.'

'Lauren.'

'I know. My life is so hard.'

'The absolute worst.'

I screamed as he picked me up and dunked me under the water.

Something about being in Cambodia filled me with unwavering optimism, despite being barely able to walk. Just like how the tsunami had taught me not to worry about things I couldn't change, learning about Cambodia's tragic history had put my bad luck into perspective. So what if I couldn't walk? I was still alive. I was seeing the world with the guy I love. Life was good.

That evening, not even an allergic reaction could dampen my spirits. It started with an itch on my left wrist. Over dinner, I scratched at it under the table for hours, drawing blood but still unable to stop. As the night wore on, it started to spread: up my arm, across my chest, down my back and on to my other arm. By the time we went to bed, I was tearing at my irritated skin.

'It's weird,' I said to Dave, pulling on a T-shirt so my blood wouldn't stain the sheets. 'I've never had a reaction to anything like this before.' Our room was one of the more basic bungalows we'd stayed in, with no electricity to power a fan, a holey mosquito net over an uncomfortable bed and an open-air shower that was heated by the sun. At night, we used the torch on Dave's phone to light the room.

'I'm sure it'll be fine in the morning,' he said, arranging the mosquito net around our bed and turning off his phone.

'It definitely will,' I said, snuggling up beside him. 'Everything always is.'

A clanging bell sounded from beneath our bungalow, followed by a loud crash. The resident water buffalo was doing everything he could to keep us awake. Our room, up on a hill on stilts, was just the right height for it to roam around underneath.

'Night.'

'Night.'

I lasted 2 hours.

'Dave,' I whispered, tapping the back of his head with my fingers until he woke.

'What do you want?' he mumbled.

'I'm dying. I'm actually dying.'

'No, you're not. Go back to sleep.'

'I can't stop scratching and I'm covered in blood. Can you take a look? Please. I wouldn't ask unless I was really worried.'

'For God's sake, Lauren,' he grumbled. I heard him climb out of bed and walk to the door to look for the light switch. 'Bugger,' he said after a few seconds. 'I forgot we didn't have power.'

He got back into bed and turned on his phone. I sat up and leaned forward, pulling up my top while he fumbled to find the torch. The room lit up.

'Holy shit.'

'What?' I hissed, trying to stay calm.

'Holy shit,' he repeated. 'It's everywhere. It looks like your back has acne, except there are all these enormous blisters, like an inch in size. They're huge. Oh my God. And there's yellow pus dripping all down your back. I've never seen anything like it.'

I whimpered as I cowered into my thighs, too afraid to move in case I ended up popping the blisters. In my head, I was picturing the Google image results for the dozens of skin diseases I'd thought I'd had over the years. I reached behind me and gingerly ran my fingertips down my spine. It felt so good that I curved my hand around to take big, deep scratches down the length of my back.

In the morning, I limped down to breakfast, feeling like I was in the before stages of a makeover TV show. My ankle was still swollen, my knee was dribbling yellow liquid down my shin and the entire top half of my body was covered in weeping blisters.

I hopped on to the large wooden balcony that acted as a dining area and realised I could smell nothing but eucalyptus. As Dave leaped up to join me, I focused in on another couple sat close by and watched them massage great globs of Tiger Balm on to each other's arms. They had leaking wounds all over their bodies.

I walked up to them. 'Excuse me, guys?'

They looked up.

'What's happening to everyone?' I asked, gesturing to the damp welts on my chest. 'What's causing this?'

'Sand flies,' the guy said in a British accent. 'They're bloody everywhere.'

I examined my arms with curiosity. There was a bubble a centimetre in diameter sticking out of me like a snow dome. Beneath it was an open blister with a dried trail of pus stretching to my wrist. I didn't want to see what my back looked like.

'Are you okay?' I asked Dave, turning to stare at his arms. 'Are you itchy? Do you have any bites?'

'Nothing,' he shrugged.

'How?' I spluttered, sweeping my arms around. 'Look at everyone.' There must have been a dozen depressed backpackers sat on the balcony, all massaging Tiger Balm on each other with the packaging littered across the floor.

'I don't have a single bite.'

'But—'

'Sand flies are really common in Australia and New Zealand,' he said. 'I'd imagine I've got some kind of natural immunity to them. Brits always get devoured by them when they come over to visit.'

'Fantastic,' I muttered, wiping a trail of pus from my forearm.

We had three nights booked on Koh Rong and I wanted to make the most of them. After breakfast, I dragged myself back to the beach, this time soaked in DEET. Not even that seemed able to deter the sand flies from my British skin, as a 5-minute walk from the guesthouse resulted in ten tiny black dots scattered across my thighs.

'I'm going in the sea,' I told Dave, as I slapped at my legs. 'I can't lie out here and get bitten.'

'I'll join you,' he said, holding out an arm to pull me up.

We'd been in the sea for 2 minutes before I felt a prickle on my thigh. *Jellyfish!* I looked down but nothing was there. Shaking my head, I continued to paddle but there it was again: a sharp pinprick on my leg. I broke away from Dave and stood legs akimbo, searching for the culprit. A small fish an inch in length arranged itself so it was facing me and stopped, floating happily in front of me. I smiled at it until it shot forwards and took a bite of my stomach.

'Ouch,' I exclaimed, hopping in circles to try to splash it away from me.

I swam for a few minutes and relaxed, but there it was again. Another bite. In front of me, there were two of those tiny fish, both facing me, both waiting. Within seconds, they were darting forwards, one taking a bite out of my side; the other of my thigh. This was getting weird.

'For God's sake,' I muttered after a few minutes, motioning Dave over. 'Tell me the fishes are biting you.'

'What? I don't see any fishes.'

'Watch,' I said. Five of them lined ahead of me in a V-shaped formation. 'There,' I whispered, pointing at them. In perfect synchronicity, they charged forwards and nipped my stomach.

'Whoa,' Dave exclaimed.

'You saw that, right?' I said. 'They've been doing it for ten minutes. The fish have a vendetta against me!'

'Well, they're not doing it to me.'

'I'm going back to the beach,' I said grumpily. 'The animals on Koh Rong hate me.'

I hobbled across the damp sand to my towel and dove on to my stomach. I couldn't win. If I lay on the beach, I'd be bitten by sand flies. If I swam in the sea, I was bitten by fish.

The wind picked up, causing my bikini bottoms to dance against my skin in the breeze. I forced my eyes closed and reminded myself that I was lucky to be here and I wasn't going to spend the entire day sitting in a dark bedroom with no power.

Another gust of wind blew through, rippling my bikini against me. *That's weird*, I thought. *Why can't I feel the wind anywhere else on my body?* I could have sworn something was flapping against me.

I rolled on to my back and sat up. Something was still moving inside my bikini, but it was doing it towards the front now. I looked around. There were two girls lying a few metres away, deep in conversation.

Sliding my finger around the edge of my bikini bottoms, I pulled at the elastic and peered in. There, staring back at me was the wide, unblinking eye of a fish. It flapped a couple of times in response to being exposed.

'Yeaaarrrrrgggghhhhh!' I shouted, diving in and catching it between my fingers. I threw the fish down on the sand beside me, where it began to flap itself into a panic. 'No,' I squealed, my hands over my mouth.

'What's up?' Dave said, running up the sand to me. 'I could hear you screaming from the water.'

I shook my head and pointed at the flapping fish on the sand.

'Where did that come from?'

'I carried it in my bikini.'

He stared at me as I alternated between crying, trembling and laughing, then picked up the fish and carried it back to the ocean for me. It would live to bite another backpacker.

While I focused on healing my sand fly bites, my knee deteriorated from bad to worse. With climbing all over Angkor Wat now well and truly off the cards, Dave and I returned to Sihanoukville. This time, we were aiming for laid-back Otres Beach, a couple of kilometres from Serendipity. On the way, we stopped off at a pharmacy to buy antibiotics. My wound wasn't healing, and now it was hot and red, swollen and throbbing, and still leaking yellow liquid down my shin.

Otres Beach provided a total contrast to Serendipity. It was calm and peaceful, with roughly 40 guesthouses lining the quiet beach. The vendors were friendly, too. After chatting to one of the child bracelet sellers outside my bungalow and refusing to buy one from her – giving money to child vendors often keeps them out of school and on the streets – she gave me one for free anyway, telling me it was for friendship. We discovered, too, that the owners of the guesthouses had an agreement to turn off their music after 10 p.m., which made for peaceful moonlit walks along the water at night.

Our bungalow was, like all beach guesthouses we'd stayed at in Southeast Asia, basic. It had cockroaches and there was only a fan to keep us cool, but the full-length tinted windows made it all worth it. There was nothing quite like waking up and being able to look across the 10 m stretch of sand into the ocean.

'You coming in?' I asked Dave one afternoon, pointing through the doors at the pouring rain.

'Coming where?'

'Into the sea, of course,' I said, as if it was something I did every day.

'But it's raining.'

'Yes.'

'And there's lightning.'

'It'll be fine,' I said dismissively. 'What are the chances of us being struck?'

It wasn't often I found myself trying to convince Dave to do something.

The sky was an ominous shade of grey when I carefully waded out into the ocean, surprised to find it as warm as bathwater. It was so clear that I could see my toes digging into the sand below, even with the water up to my neck.

I swung my arms around Dave when he came to join me. 'Isn't this so romantic?' I gushed.

A fork of lightning hit the water a couple of miles away, lighting up the sky. I looked around for reassurance that we were safe, but we were the only people left in the water.

'I think we should go back in,' Dave said, untangling himself from my arms. 'This storm's a little too close for comfort for me.'

After my string of bad luck in Cambodia, I paid attention. I limped behind him, still marvelling at how clear the water was. It was so clear, in fact, that I could see the blue salt and pepper grinders floating beside my legs.

I stopped and frowned. *That was weird.* I wondered if the restaurant had lost some. I bent down and reached in to grab them but one of them bounced off my leg and drifted away. When I straightened back up, I noticed I was now surrounded by dozens of blue salt and pepper mills. Then I saw something else: the flash of a tentacle. Was that…⸮

'Jellyfish!' I screamed.

'I know,' Dave said calmly, as if he wasn't in the least bit concerned. He was 5 m ahead of me and surrounded by them, too. 'Just keep walking,' he urged me. A rumble of thunder sounded in the distance.

'I can't do it,' I whimpered, starting to turn back around but there were just as many behind me as there were in front. I was in a swarm of jellyfish that I estimated numbered close to 50.

'Walk!' Dave shouted at me.

I wiggled my leg to try to create a mini tidal wave to push them away. As I splashed, I waited for the stings that would cause my lungs to stop functioning. My tongue felt too big for my mouth and I flopped it outside so I could breathe better.

When I reached ankle-deep water, Dave was there with his hand, pulling me to safety. I immediately looked at his legs, and then mine, searching for red stings and blisters. I began to gasp at the air around me, savouring the sensation of full lungs before they shut down. I shook my right leg and then my left.

'I don't think they were stinging jellyfish,' Dave said, as I hopped on the spot to make sure I wasn't paralysed. Cambodia seemed to be doing everything it could to break me.

That evening, Dave and I sat working at a small wooden table on the beach and watched the sky turn blazing pink. Otres Beach, normally reasonably quiet at this time of night, was packed with hundreds of people, all posing for photos in front of the incredible backdrop. It was a spectacular sight: easily the best sunset of my life, and I was back to feeling deliriously happy.

'Cheers!' I said, holding out my glass for Dave to clink it.

'To a final week in Cambodia without any further incidents,' he said.

I was determined to make it happen. My string of bad luck in the country had been some of the worst I'd experienced but I was starting to react with ambivalence instead of frustration. I was starting to accept that I was the unluckiest traveller in the world, but at least it always made for a good story.

'Touch wood!' I cheered, leaning over my laptop to tap my glass on the wooden table. My eyes met Dave's and I felt a warm glow spreading through my chest. With a cheeky grin, I raised my glass to my lips, moving my hand through a short arc that ended when I knocked it against the screen of my laptop. I watched in horror as my margarita soared through the air and landed on my keyboard with a splash.

'My laptop!' I screamed.

'Bloody hell,' Dave groaned, dropping his head in his hands.

'What do I do?' I shrieked.

'Turn it off,' he shouted. 'Turn it off and turn it upside down.'

'AHHH!' I screamed at it.

'Turn it off, Lauren.'

'Oh no, oh no, oh no,' I muttered, holding down the off button. I swiftly held it upside down and watched as the alcohol dribbled over my thighs. 'My brand new laptop,' I moaned. I'd bought it when I was back in London, spending almost £2,000 on something I'd expected to last me for several years. I had a feeling the warranty wouldn't cover accidental spills.

I stood up from the table and passed turned heads, struggling to keep it together as I hobbled for our bungalow. Once inside, I positioned myself in the middle of the room and raised the laptop above my head, letting its contents drip over the sandy floor.

Dave stormed into the bungalow seconds later with his eyebrows drawn into a line. 'I can't believe you could be so stupid.' He glared at me in an uncomprehending rage. 'That's a brand new laptop, Lauren. A brand new two-thousand-pound laptop. That laptop is how you make money. It's how you travel. How could you be so stupid?'

'You think I don't know that?' I snapped back at him. 'You think I did this on purpose?'

'I think you need to take more care of your belongings, that's what I think. I mean, look at our time in Cambodia. These things only happen to you, Lauren, they never happen to anyone else. You need to stop being such an idiot. Maybe you need to stop thinking of yourself as being unlucky and start thinking of how you can stop doing stupid things.'

My bottom lip started to tremble. There's nothing worse than having the person you love more than anything in the world confess he believes the things you're too scared to admit to yourself. That you're not just unlucky. That it's your fault these things happen.

'You know what would be nice?' I said.

'Oh, I don't know, maybe if you didn't destroy everything you touch?'

'No, that maybe you acted like a supportive boyfriend and gave me some sympathy instead of kicking me when I'm down.'

'You don't think I've been doing that every fucking day in this country while you've seemed to do everything within your power to get yourself killed?'

I broke down in tears.

'Jesus, Lauren,' he said. 'It's not even like it's water. It's a margarita! What's that? Alcohol, lime, salt, sugar? If there's one thing my fifteen years in IT have taught me, it's that those ingredients are the worst things you can pour on a laptop.'

'Get out,' I sobbed. 'Just get out.'

'With pleasure.' He slammed the door behind him.

Everything went black.

I blinked. To my right, the fan slowly whirred to a halt and I could hear the music at the bar had stopped. Silence. Outside the bungalow, Dave was talking to the guy who was staying next door.

'Perfect,' I muttered into the blackness. A power cut. Just what I needed. I was too stubborn to walk outside and face Dave so I continued to stand in the middle of the darkened bungalow.

I tipped my head back to try to see if there was still alcohol inside. I shook the laptop, and a large drop of margarita fell straight into my eye.

CHAPTER 16

'It works,' I gasped, staring at the screen in disbelief. 'I can't believe it – it actually works.'

'I'm astounded,' Dave said, as I began tap-dancing on one leg around the room.

'The power of patience,' I laughed, pumping my fists in the air. I'd been staring at my laptop for the past four days, desperate to find out if it had survived, but Dave had convinced me I had to keep waiting.

'Something like that.'

The wound on my leg opened up and a clear liquid dribbled over the scab and down my leg. I stopped dancing and sat down on the edge of the bed.

'Damn it,' I muttered, holding it out for Dave to see. The course of antibiotics had turned my knee from yellow to red, but almost every time I moved, the scab tore open and I ended up leaking for hours. 'Time for some more antiseptic cream?'

'I think so,' he said, rummaging through his backpack for our first aid kit. He knelt in front of me and began to spread the white cream over my knee. I pulled a face at the stinging.

'Does it hurt?' he asked, concern etched across his brow.

'It's okay.'

'And hey, I'm sorry I snapped over your laptop the other night.'

After the fiery argument of a few nights before, I'd fallen asleep mid-power cut and awakened the following morning to find Dave in bed beside me. It had been our biggest fight to date, but when you spend every second of every day together, they have to be resolved quickly. We hadn't even discussed it. Instead, we'd hugged and kissed and made up without saying a word.

'I'm sorry, too,' I said. 'I know I'm a walking disaster, but damn. Cambodia, man.'

'It's been tough, huh?' he said, pausing to look up at me.

I nodded. 'I can't believe my string of bad luck, and despite all that, I'd say Cambodia is one of my favourite countries. I love it.'

Dave looked just as confused as I felt. There was no doubt about it: from the second I'd touched down in Phnom Penh, it had felt like everything had conspired to bring me down. Unlike my early travels, though, I had been able to look past it and see the country for what it was. And Cambodia was beautiful. The locals were some of the friendliest I'd encountered, with smiles seemingly permanently etched across their faces, the islands and beaches were gorgeous, the sunsets were incredible, I'd barely spent more than £20 a day, the weather was wonderful: it was everything I was looking for in a country.

'Speaking of favourite countries,' I said, 'where do you want to go next?' We only had a couple of days left on our Cambodian visas.

'I'm not sure.'

'Me neither. I mean, part of me wants to hole up on a gorgeous island for a few weeks while my leg heals and then do something crazy, like go on a big scooter trip or something.'

Dave clutched at his chest and feigned distress. 'What's that, you say? Go back to Thailand? Why, I don't think you've ever said that before.'

'Hey, mister. I didn't say anything about Thailand,' I said with a laugh. 'Although…'

'Lauren.'

'Dave.'

'We *always* go back to Thailand.'

'And isn't that the beauty of having a life like this?'

I leapt from the boat into warm, ankle-deep water. Dave handed me my backpack then splashed down to join me. I linked my arm through his and we walked a short distance along the water's edge. Behind us, families lugged oversized suitcases from the long wooden boat and began to drag them over mounds of sand. On Koh Lipe, an island with very few paved paths, they were going to struggle.

'Ready?' Dave asked me, fastening his waist straps.

'Ready.'

We began to make our way along the beach, ogling the row of guesthouses lining the water.

'So how does it feel to be back in Thailand?' Dave asked, examining some upmarket-looking wooden bungalows.

'Like I'm taking the easy way out,' I confessed. 'But I guess I'm okay with that. We have plenty of time to see other places and Thailand makes me happy.'

I'd spent much of the past year torn between feeling like I should be visiting new countries and reasoning that I could go wherever I wanted, even if it meant spending an inordinate amount of time in Thailand. I slipped out of my flip-flops so I could paddle as we walked, enjoying the sensation of soft sand slipping between my toes.

By the time we reached a guesthouse that wasn't too disgusting or too expensive, my skin was slick with sweat. Just like on Otres Beach, our bungalow was basic, but now that we were back in Thailand, prices were noticeably steeper. At £30 a night, Koh Lipe was the most expensive island we'd visited by far. For that, we got a tiny bungalow around 20 metres back from the beach. We had a fan to spin hot air into our faces whenever it was plugged into the only power socket in the room, but if we wanted to power our laptops, we'd be sitting and sweating.

I couldn't have been happier. I was treating our bungalow purely as a place to sweat myself to sleep at night. I didn't need anything fancy when all I was planning on doing was lying out on the beach and recovering from Cambodia.

For dinner that night, we decided on pizza, apparently having not learnt our lesson from the atrocious Mexican food we'd had in Sihanoukville. But I'd had a craving and after all I'd been through recently, Dave didn't object.

I'd found an Italian restaurant with suspiciously good reviews online and we'd traipsed across the island to check it out. When we arrived, they were blasting out Thai love songs, but the second the staff saw us wandering across the empty courtyard, the song was quickly switched to the Spice Girls' 'Mama'. As we sat and chattered, the music selection ranged from Boney M to Boyzone.

'Dave,' I said tentatively, nervous to start a conversation I'd been putting off for a few weeks. 'Can I ask you something?'

'Of course.'

'Did you mean it when you said you think I bring all my bad luck upon myself?'

'Does it matter what I think?'

'Well, I guess not,' I said. 'I half agree with you and I half don't, but your opinion matters to me.'

Dinner arrived: a large pepperoni pizza with a thin crust and extra jalapenos.

'Well, what do you think?' he asked, cutting the pizza into slices. He slid one on to my plate.

When I opened my mouth, I spoke carefully and deliberately. 'I think that sometimes it's bad luck: like the tsunami that wasn't really a tsunami. I couldn't have changed anything about that situation. But other things, like falling for scams, going with the touts in Luang Prabang, spilling my margarita over my laptop: it's a lack of common sense, I guess. I just don't stop and think about what I'm doing before I do it.'

He nodded in agreement. 'I think you don't help yourself, either. You know, things like carrying a phone so you can get hold of me, or know what the time is, or be able to find where you need to go without getting lost. I think it'd make a huge difference.'

'Maybe it's time for me to give in and get one,' I wondered, thinking back over my misadventures and realising just how much easier things could have been if I'd had a phone. Travel had taught me that common sense was unlikely to be something I'd pick up and I was only making it worse for myself by deliberately choosing a difficult path.

By the end of our week in Koh Lipe, I felt brand new. We'd spent seven blissful days lying out on the beach, swimming in the ocean to try to conquer my newfound fear of jellyfish and vaginafish, and eating our way through cafes and restaurants. My knee had finally healed enough that it had stopped dribbling down my leg and the swelling around my ankle had reduced to that of a golf ball.

'I think I'm going to try the ferry journey without motion-sickness pills this time,' I told Dave as we trudged back along the sand with our backpacks. I fancied a challenge after such an easy week on Koh Lipe.

'Yeah?' he asked, stepping over a mooring rope for a nearby boat.

I shrugged in response. Dave had yet to see me truly suffer from motion sickness, as I was cautious to never let it take effect. I took my trusty pills before every journey, whether it was by bus, train, plane or boat. Dave was probably expecting that without the pills, I'd be slightly nauseated but functional. I knew what the reality was like.

Five years ago, I visited Hawaii on holiday with Jeremy. At the time, I'd been obsessed with the idea of whale watching.

We'd been one of the more fortunate groups, our guide had told us afterwards. The whales had been out in full force, playfully waving their tails in our direction, blowing water in great arcs from their spouts and even a few babies came to say hello.

Jeremy had relayed all of this to me once we were back on dry land. When an enormous whale had emerged, 10 m from where I had been sat, I'd felt too sick to even look up. Instead, I'd hung my head in my hands while the hundred-odd passengers clambered on top of me to take photos. I shuddered at the memory, but reminded myself that I was a different person now. I could handle a bit of seasickness.

Our ferry held around 50 people with evenly spaced orange life jackets acting as cushions for the hard, wooden benches. Dave and I left our backpacks piled towards the back of the boat and kept our daypacks hanging from our fronts. Petrol fumes whipped around my face as I led the way down the aisle.

I couldn't explain why, but I'd bought a dry bag on Koh Lipe. I'd kept having a strange feeling of dread every time I'd passed them hanging in the shop window, like I had to buy one or everything I owned was going to be damaged. While we waited for the other passengers to board, I busied myself with filling it with everything important to me: my passport, laptop, money, hard drive, camera. After a year of travelling with just a backpack, I'd learned I didn't need much else to survive. If you threw in a couple of changes of clothes, I could survive for months with just these items.

'How long is this journey again?' I asked Dave, stuffing my dry bag back inside my daypack.

'Two hours or so,' he replied. He reached inside his own bag and pulled out his Kindle, just as the ferry juddered to life. The vibrations increased until we were roaring in the direction of the mainland.

It was just my luck that the day I'd chosen to travel without medicating myself was the first stormy day in weeks. Within minutes I was feeling terrible, with my eyes squeezed shut as we rocked from side to side. I felt like I was on a rollercoaster, digging my nails into the bench as we rose up, riding the wave over a crest to catch some air, and then *slam!* Back into the water we fell with an almighty crash. My stomach lurched with every free fall and my spine felt like it might snap with every landing.

I reached into my pocket and pulled out the motion-sickness tablet, rolling it between my thumb and forefinger for a few seconds. Travel may have cured many of my ailments, but it turned out it had yet to cure my sensitivity to movement. I dropped the pill on my tongue and swallowed.

It started to rain. It was just a few spits at first, but then great, heavy raindrops began to spatter on the top of our heads. I peered out at the ocean, grimacing at its murky grey colour as it swelled beneath us.

The girl in front of me screamed.

I gasped, digging my nails into Dave's arm. 'What's going on?' I whispered.

'Don't know,' he said.

I watched the girl stand up and run to the captain. She looked frantic as she ran her fingers through her hair and gestured in my direction. He turned to where she'd been sat and grimaced.

At that moment, everyone on her row began to throw on their life jackets and run to the other side of the boat. As I rifled through my daypack for my dry bag, a baby started to scream and I thought about doing the same.

Not only were we crashing up and down, but now we were also rocking from side to side and I was certain I was going to vomit.

'What's happening?' I shouted into the wind.

'Don't know,' Dave repeated, brushing the raindrops from the screen of his Kindle. He was the only person on the boat that was still reading.

'Well, can you check?' I snapped. This man would remain calm even if he was swept up by a tornado. *Oh dear*, he'd think as he floated through the eye of the storm. *How unfortunate. Oh well, I'm sure it'll all be fine.* Then he'd get out his phone and start replying to emails.

Dave stood up and leaned over the bench in front of us, where the girl had been sat moments before, and calmly sat back down again.

'There's a hole on the boat.'

'I'm sorry, what?' I gasped, immediately forgetting all about my seasickness. 'What did you just say?'

'There's a hole on the boat,' he repeated.

I shook my head in horror, trying to process what was happening. *Surely there couldn't be an actual hole in our boat?* I knew Dave had sailed in the past. *Perhaps it was just sailing terminology for coming up against choppy water?*

'It's the row in front of us,' he clarified. 'I guess when the driver was crashing into the waves he somehow managed to wreck the side of the boat and cause a hole. We're taking on water. Look.' He pointed to my feet, which were now in the centre of a tiny puddle. This didn't look good.

I heard a thudding sound and craned my neck towards the back of the boat, where the guy who'd been guarding our backpacks suddenly jumped into action. He dashed down the aisle and dove headfirst towards the hole with a panic stricken expression on his face. This really didn't look good.

We continued to accelerate, slamming into the waves as if the driver was trying to force a second hole into the side. At this point, I wasn't sure whether I'd prefer a slow and careful driver or a fast and reckless one, especially when this boat could be on the seabed within minutes.

'Are you scared?' I asked Dave.

'No.'

'Why not?'

'What can happen? If the boat sinks, we put on our life jackets and someone rescues us. If it doesn't then it's all good.'

'But what if—'

'There's nothing to worry about,' he insisted. 'You've got your dry bag haven't you?'

I fell silent. I had. I had everything I needed to survive in there, and I had Dave and I could swim. *But what if something else happened? What if the engine exploded? What if the boat sank and dragged us down with it? What if my life jacket deflated? What if there were sharks or jellyfish or... I could barely even walk on my sprained ankle. How could I tread water for days?*

An unexpected sense of calm washed over me. I didn't want to die. But if I did, I would do so having lived and seen more than most people do in a lifetime. A year spent exploring the world. A year spent challenging myself to be a better person. A year spent conquering my anxiety. I'd gained so much life experience, from the basics of riding a bus and making conversation to falling in love with a wonderful man. I reached over and laced my fingers between Dave's.

There was a loud bang and the sound of screeching metal filled the air.

'Oh my God,' I whispered, digging my fingernails into Dave's hand and preparing myself to die.

The guy with his head in the hole jumped up and patted down his white T-shirt, leaving black smears streaked across it. I peeked over the bench and saw a large pool of water swishing from side to side.

Everyone on the ferry watched, breathless, as he sidled up to the driver and spoke to him in Thai. After a few minutes, the driver shrugged, and the other guy shrugged and he went back to guarding the backpacks. *Were they... giving up?*

'What about the hole?' I hissed at Dave.

'I guess it's not as bad as we thought.'

'There's water all over the floor,' I whispered.

'It'll be fine. Don't worry.'

'What's the time?'

'We're an hour in,' he said, staring ahead.

'So, an hour to go.'

Far in the distance, I could make out the mainland and, although we were powering at top speed, it didn't seem to be getting any closer.

Despite my conviction that drowning was on the cards for the morning, thanks to the frequent bailing of water and a careful reorganisation of weight distribution, we made it to the ferry terminal with everything but our boat in one piece. I was exhausted.

I hurried along the wobbling slab of wood that was acting as a gangplank and rushed to safety, celebrating by burying my feet into the gravel. There, I made a promise to myself that it would be a very long time before I stepped on a boat again.

I waited for Dave to join me and together we walked through the terminal to the road outside. A tuk-tuk's horn blared out and several drivers gathered around us to offer a ride. I shook my head, and led Dave towards a row of silver minivans. The smell of frying noodles filled the air and my stomach rumbled for a *pad thai*.

We had been planning on deciding where our next destination would be during the ferry ride, but we were now stood at the bus station and faced with the freedom to go anywhere in the region.

'Where do you want to go?' he asked.

I thought about it for a second. 'We could go back to Koh Yao Noi and find our perfect deserted beach again,' I suggested. 'Or maybe we could go to Koh Tao and I could finally try scuba-diving. Railay could be nice and I think it would be hilarious for you to see me try rock climbing for the first time. Or we could go to Malaysia? I don't know, though – none of those feel like the right decision. What do you think?'

'I think,' Dave started, staring at something in the distance. 'I think it's time to go home.'

His words sent chills down my spine and I tried to follow his gaze. As he began to wander in the direction of a nearby food cart, I racked my brain for what he could mean.

'I have a question,' I said, hurrying after him. 'Where's home?'

CHAPTER 17

I walked with a spring in my step, the evening air heavy with moisture. My plastic bag brushed against my calves and the heat of its contents threatened to burn me. At the crossing, I stopped, tapping my feet impatiently. The light turned green and I jogged to cross four lanes of traffic in the 7 seconds I had before it would switch to red.

I was too slow and a teenager on a scooter attempted to barrel me down. I made eye contact with him as he passed, missing my toes by inches. He flashed a cocky grin and beneath the full moon it looked as though his teeth were made of diamonds. It was good to be back in Chiang Mai.

'Phew,' I muttered when I reached the safety of the pavement. Only then did I allow myself to relax. I sidestepped a gaping hole in the street and wrinkled my nose as the unmistakable fragrance of an open sewer swirled around me. This time, I didn't even retch. It smelt like home.

I'm proud of myself, I suddenly realised and the thought halted me in my tracks. I took a moment to breathe, to let the sultry air caress my bare arms and to feel grateful for everything that had led me to this point, the good and bad. My life felt easy now, even with the incidents that often wreaked havoc on it.

Behind me was my local night market, full of delicious food and smiling locals. Every night, I'd head to a new stall, sampling everything that looked scary and increasing my tolerance to spice. To my left was the gym. I'd had a wake-up call over my poor levels of fitness after my pitiful struggle to the tsunami evacuation point and was finally trying to make a change. I never thought I'd be someone who'd find calm through weightlifting but my slow and steady progression from struggling to lift 5 kg was doing wonders for my mental health. To my right, some of my favourite restaurants: the small Thai place with mouthwateringly spicy soups; the Mexican restaurant with incredible lime cheesecake that didn't taste like Cheddar; and the tapas place where Dave and I would go for monthly dates. Up ahead, our apartment, just a block away from here. I sped up instinctively.

'Honey, I'm home,' I announced as I pushed open the door.

'I'll be two minutes,' he called from the bedroom.

I dropped my bag by the door and set about rearranging our living area into a dining room. We'd upgraded our apartment since returning to Chiang Mai, deciding to celebrate one year of travel by renting a place with three rooms instead of two.

'How were your explorations?' Dave asked, emerging to help me drag the heavy furniture across the floor. During the day, our space acted as an office and lounge but at night, we rearranged the table and chairs to create a dining area beside the kitchen. Having so much furniture still felt like a novelty.

'My explorations were good,' I said. 'And I think you'll like the selection of treats I picked up for dinner. I went to the night market just down the road from here again – you know, the one that always used to scare me because nothing's in English?'

'Always a bad sign, I find,' Dave said with a wink. 'What do the locals know about Thai food anyway?'

'Exactly,' I laughed, grabbing the bag of food and setting it down on the table. I brought out the dishes one by one, announcing their names as if we were on a game show. 'Crazy-looking squids on sticks! Weird sausages with rice inside! A carton of spicy *khao soi* soup for you! An even spicier *pad krapow* for me!'

'*Pad krapow*, hey?' he asked, raising an eyebrow.

I nodded and sat down, motioning for Dave to sit opposite. I could feel his eyes on me as I pried opened the Styrofoam container and plucked a chilli pepper from amongst the rice. I held it up to my face for a second as if trying to stare it down and then popped it in my mouth.

'I never thought I'd see the day when you'd be happily eating chillies for dinner,' he told me, sounding as if he was about to burst with pride. 'Remember, it was *pad krapow* you were eating when you rubbed one of those in your eye.'

'Hashtag never forget,' I said solemnly, before breaking into a coughing fit when the heat worked its way into my chest. It's a sensation I'd grown to love – once I'd learned it wasn't a symptom of sudden-onset angina, that is. 'Mmm hmmm mmmm,' I garbled, with a mouth full of food. 'Sorry.' I gulped it down. 'I meant to say: speaking of disasters, did you get a chance to look at that guidebook I bought?'

'I did.'

I felt a twinge of anxiety. 'And?'

'I think it sounds amazing.'

I made a noise that sounded like I was laughing, choking and whimpering. It was a sound that could be used to summarise the past year. 'Really?' I asked, trying to ignore the fluttering behind my ribs. 'I'm so pleased to hear you say that. I've planned out something like twenty different routes – all dependent on how long we decide to go for. I think it would be best for us to just turn up with no plans and see how it goes. And I think—'

'I think a minimum of three months would be good,' he interrupted.

'Or six,' I countered. 'Or maybe even a year. There are so many things I want to see.'

'So, you're sure about this? You really want to book flights?'

I hesitated. Now was the time to back out. I didn't have to do this. I could stay in Chiang Mai, where my comfort zone was never far away. 'Yes,' I heard myself say. 'I want to book the flights.'

'I can't believe you're agreeing to this.'

'Me neither.'

'How scared are you?'

'A hundred.'

Dave must have noticed the trepidation on my face, because he reached across the table and rested his hands on my shoulders. 'You're going to love it,' he said. 'The girl I met a year ago was a nervous wreck who was frightened of everything. She had no life experience and didn't know how to function. You're not that person anymore. You're more than capable of doing this.'

I looked up and let a bold smile spread across my face. 'You're right,' I agreed. Over the past 12 months, I'd left a trail of destruction in my wake. I'd been scammed, assaulted and had eaten cockroaches. I'd been caught in a tsunami scare, sat next to a dead woman and been violated during a massage. I'd had panic attacks and near-death experiences; I'd conquered my anxiety and my eating issues; and I'd learned how to function in a world that once terrified me. I'd fallen in love. As my eyes met Dave's, we exchanged ecstatic grins.

'Dave?' I said.

'Yes, baby?' he replied with a sparkle in his eye.

'I can't believe we're going to India.'

ACKNOWLEDGEMENTS

My road to publishing has been much like my travels: a rollercoaster ride full of euphoria and fear. I'd like to take this opportunity to express my gratitude to all who have helped me during the writing of this book.

To everyone at Summersdale for having faith in me, especially during the times I was convinced my book was the worst to have ever been written. In particular, I'd like to thank my editor, Debbie Chapman, for her patience, understanding and support as I bumbled my way through the writing process. I'd like to also thank my literary agent, Adriann Ranta, for taking a chance on me, and for helping me navigate the overwhelming world of publishing.

To my parents, Karen and Mike, and my sister, Victoria, for reluctantly encouraging me to follow my dreams, even if it meant having to hear about me side-stepping near-death experiences on a seemingly daily basis. I appreciate your love and support as I chase this unconventional lifestyle. Thank you for your incredible enthusiasm; for sending me flowers to brighten my writing space (otherwise known as Slob Corner); and for patiently sitting through multi-hour Skype calls as I attempted to piece together the parts of my story.

Thanks also go out to Torre DeRoche for taking the time to send encouragement, advice and many swift kicks to the butt – if it wasn't for you, I'd probably still be trembling beneath my bed in a guesthouse in Belize. To Sanbula Zaidi for helping me find my voice during the first few weeks of writing – your suggestions gave me the confidence to own my lack of life experience and bare it all for the world to see. To Matt Kepnes: I need to thank you first for your insistence that I write this book several years before I was able to work up the courage to do so, and second, for your helpful critiques and reassurance throughout the experience.

Thank you to the readers of Never Ending Footsteps for your patience as I disappeared out of your lives for months at a time to work on this book. Your encouraging emails and unfaltering confidence in my abilities have kept me going during some of my darkest days. If it hadn't have been for you, this book would have never been written.

Finally, the biggest thanks of all go to Dave, who never stopped believing in me. You've been my inspiration, my therapist, my editor and my punching bag, offering unwavering support while I sat in my pajamas for three months straight in order to finish this book. Thank you for building me up through times of self-doubt and exhaustion, and thank you for accompanying me around the world. This trip wouldn't have been the same without you.

Have you enjoyed this book?
If so, why not write a review on your favourite website?

If you're interested in finding out more about our books, find
us on Facebook at **Summersdale Publishers** and follow us on
Twitter at **@Summersdale**.

Thanks very much for buying this Summersdale book.

www.summersdale.com